T0320049

Explaining Civil War

Dedicated to the memory of my late father

Syed Mahbub Murshed (1911–79)

Explaining Civil War

A Rational Choice Approach

Syed Mansoob Murshed

Professor of the Economics of Conflict and Peace, Institute of Social Studies, The Netherlands, and Professor of International Economics, Birmingham Business School, University of Birmingham, UK

Edward Elgar
Cheltenham, UK • Northampton, MA, USA

Published by
Edward Elgar Publishing Limited
The Lypiatts
15 Lansdown Road
Cheltenham
Glos GL50 2JA
UK

Edward Elgar Publishing, Inc.
William Pratt House
9 Dewey Court
Northampton
Massachusetts 01060
USA

A catalogue record for this book
is available from the British Library

Library of Congress Control Number: 2009933400

Mixed Sources
Product group from well-managed
forests and other controlled sources
www.fsc.org Cert no. SA-COC-1565
© 1996 Forest Stewardship Council
FSC

ISBN 978 1 84720 808 8

Printed and bound by MPG Books Group, UK

Contents

Figures

Tables

Acknowledgements

A work such as this by necessity leaves behind a long trail of debts of gratitude. Many individuals and seminar participants have contributed to my understanding of violent conflict. I would like to single out Scott Gates for thanks in this regard. My students and research assistants have contributed immensely to this book: Zulfan Tadjoeddin, Aikaterina Kyrili and Aamer Abdullah Syed, and I thank them profusely. I have received useful feedback from students at the Institute of Social Studies (ISS), the University of Birmingham and elsewhere (York, Amsterdam, Groningen, Eindhoven and UNU-MERIT). I have also drawn inspiration from a variety of public lectures at many places, but mainly in the Netherlands. Felicity Plester at Edward Elgar has cheerfully seen this project through to completion. Support from the Stichting Vredes Wetenschappen (SVW) foundation, with the financial assistance of the ASN Bank is gratefully acknowledged. Hans Opschoor of the ISS through his role in SVW, and more generally, has been a major source of support for me, as have Cobi Schoondergang-Horikx and Piet Terhal of SVW over many years. I thank them very much. I would like to acknowledge the financial support of the European Union funded (Framework 6) MICROCON (Micro Level Analysis of Violent Conflict) research project.

My brother, Syed Marghub Murshed, who has intellectually mentored me from infancy, painstakingly read through the entire manuscript making invaluable suggestions for improvement. Lenneke Warnars has constantly been a patient and understanding source of support, encouragement and love. I thank them both from the bottom of my heart.

1. Introduction

A Dead Statesman
I could not dig: I dared not rob:
Therefore I lied to please the mob.
Now all my lies are proved untrue
And I must face the men I slew.
What tale shall serve me here among
Mine angry and defrauded young?

Rudyard Kipling, from 'Epitaphs of the War'

The preceding poem pithily describes the tragedy and futility of war, as well as the fact that wars are an outcome of human agency or deliberate human action. Leaving aside any primordial human urge to engage in combat, war is, ultimately, irrational in the universal sense of the term. This is because there are less costly ways, in terms of lost human lives and the damage to the economy, of settling disputes. But the logic of limited, bounded or myopic rationality can sometimes make war rational. Misconceptions about the possible gains from warfare, miscalculations about the probability of military victory, discounting the costs of victory, and mistrust in the absence of credible guarantors of negotiated settlements are among a long list of factors and situations that render warfare a rational course of action. In traditional (realist) international relations the failure of collective security or the balance of power that deters war may increase the risk of inter-state war primarily because states interact with each other in an anarchical non-contractual fashion. Within a nation state, choosing the violent option of war usually occurs when the institutions that might peacefully resolve disputes degenerate. According to the realist school in political science, conflict reflects opportunistic behaviour that is rational in the bounded sense of the term. One thing is, however, abundantly clear; the calculus of decision making about war involves the concepts of risk and uncertainty.[1]

The nature of warfare has evolved through human history; a succinct summary may be found in Jacoby (2008). But two points are worth highlighting. The first concerns our 'moral' or ethical stance regarding

---

[1]   Risk involves measurable uncertainty, whereas pure uncertainty cannot be quantified.

warfare. Classical writings during the second half of the first millennium BC, ranging from Sun Tzu in China to Chanakya in India and Thucydides in Greece, record the destructiveness of war and the need to limit this course of events through reason (Jacoby, 2008). We later have the Abrahamic (Jewish, Christian and Islamic) traditions about just wars that are mainly to defend the people or the faith, making them limited in nature (Jacoby, 2008). Jewish traditions included wars ordained by God, and defensive wars of pre-emption. In early Christian thought, St Augustine's view of just war included defence against aggression, repossessing that which is taken dishonestly and punitive war to redress wrongdoing. Islamic values regarded war as a last resort following warnings, with strict injunctions not to molest prisoners and non-combatants, as well as respect for the sanctity of land and physical infrastructure in war zones. Often, these notions of just war were honoured more in the breach than in the keeping, as the example of the Crusades illustrates.

By the 19th century efforts to manage the plight of the wounded and prisoners of war by establishing clear and binding rules about the (civilized, limited and less barbaric) conduct of warfare led to the foundation of the Red Cross and the first Geneva Convention of 1864. The secular influence of the Enlightenment led to liberal pacific ideas about peace between similarly inclined and governed nations, international socialist concepts about worker solidarity and Angell-Lane's (1910) thesis that war could not even benefit a victor. War, therefore, became both reprehensible and ultimately irrational, making its prevention paramount. Sadly, the two great world wars of the 20th century were to follow and warfare still characterizes human interaction.

The second point about the nature of warfare is to do with the technology of warfare, which has evolved from the dominance of massed infantry to the supremacy of cavalry, down to the modern age with the invention of firearms (both small arms and artillery). This rendered fortifications and the supremacy of cavalry gradually obsolete, and also necessitated the maintenance of expensive standing armies, requiring taxation that eventually led to modern European state formation (Tilly, 1992). By the Napoleonic wars, highly motivated national professional standing armies had replaced mercenaries, participating increasingly in wars of peoples (rather than kings). Later, the advent of more rapid firing firearms during the American Civil War and the appearance of airpower during the 20th century rendered traditional land warfare more costly in terms of soldiers' lives, civilian casualties and losses to infrastructure. Further developments heralded the era of weapons of mass destruction, whose ultimate form in the shape of thermonuclear weapons are capable of destroying the planet itself. Perhaps these developments have rendered conventional warfare, particularly between nation states, too costly to contemplate.

In the main what we are left with are: (1) the relatively low intensity civil wars, where the style of warfare is relatively primitive (mainly involving small arms) and combat is intermittent; (2) asymmetric inter-state warfare involving the overwhelming use of technically superior indirect force (principally airpower) by one side only, as in Afghanistan, the Gulf War of 1991, Iraq and Serbia; (3) the use of guerrilla warfare and 'terrorist' violence that chiefly involve hit-and-run tactics, suicide bombing or targeting civilians.

Most wars nowadays are intra-state or civil wars and occur in developing countries. This is the concern of this volume, and the principal focus is on conflict as a source of underdevelopment. A fifth of humanity exists in abject poverty. This is something that should be unacceptable to those living in more affluent circumstances for two inter-connected reasons. First, it affronts our sense of common humanity. Secondly, it undermines international security, as poverty eventually engenders violence and revolt. Enlightened self-interest therefore dictates that poverty should be alleviated. It is difficult to separate the development and security agendas. Development economists have traditionally discussed the design of policy independent of conflict and its occurrence, these being seen as issues for political scientists. But the implications for social conflict of economic decisions cannot be ignored in this way. Similarly, the potential for conflict and civil war in retarding growth and development are equally important. Among donors, those motivated by a genuine commitment to the development per se of the global South are being sidelined by others to whom the security agenda of containing the unpleasant and sometimes violent spillovers of extreme poverty in the third world is paramount (Murshed, 2006). Despite rhetoric to the contrary, the security agenda dominates donor thinking, because bilateral aid and even multilateral aid is often an extension of donor strategic foreign policy. But the important point is that the reduction of absolute poverty yields a double dividend by addressing security considerations and developmental concerns simultaneously. Thus, the achievement of the millennium development goals (MDGs) regarding poverty reduction is twice blessed; it serves both the altruistic and security minded motives of the donor community.

At the very outset, it is worthwhile outlining different forms of civil war, as they are not a homogeneous phenomenon. Their origins, motivations and objectives do vary. A useful guide to the typology of internal conflict can be found in Besançon (2005) and Fearon (2004). I shall confine the typology to four broad types: genocides, revolutions, secessionist wars and internationalized wars, all of which involve the state.[2]

- *Genocides*: these are systematic attempts to physically eliminate a particular ethnic, religious or linguistic group. These episodes, brutal though may be, are relatively short. The state is usually an active participant in these actions. But these events are often one sided, involving an attack that is not resisted by the target group, thus not necessarily making them wars.
- *Revolutions*: these involve attempts to overthrow the state by armed force. Revolutions can be sub-divided into military *coups d'état* and rebellions. The former have a very short duration. Rebellions against the state, for example Maoist insurgencies in Nepal, Peru and the movements in Colombia are much more long drawn out.
- *Secessionist wars*: these tend to take place in areas struggling to sepa-rate from the centre, such as with Tamil separatism in Sri Lanka, and can also be very protracted. The aim is usually the establishment of an independent state, or sometimes an attempt to join some other nation state.
- *Internationalized Internal Conflicts*: these are situations when neigh-bouring countries or other external powers are involved. This is not necessarily a separate category in the typology of war. Often a civil war zone abuts another country. Sometimes rebel groups flee to, or seek succour in, neighbouring countries, as with Maoist insurgents in Nepal or Hutu rebels in Rwanda. Powerful nations adjoining the conflict may interfere in the conflict process, as was the case with Indian involvement in the Sri Lankan civil war. The greater powers may also get involved in active peacekeeping, as with the British in Sierra Leone. The civil war may involve a variety of other states, some neighbouring and others from afar, who take active sides in the civil war, as in the case of the Democratic Republic of the Congo (DRC).

In practice, this typology of civil war can be misleading. Many examples of contemporary conflict do not fit neatly into only one of the boxes described above; rather they may intersect the various categories listed. Rebellion and secessionist motives may sometimes go hand in hand, as can

---

[2] Besançon's (2005) typology involves genocides, revolutions and ethnic wars. Ethnicity or ethnic dimensions can, however, run across all varieties of civil wars. I am, therefore, eschewing this categorization. This definition of pure ethnic conflict is more likely to be appli-cable to 'inter-communal' conflict such as between Hindus and Muslims in India, Christians and Muslims in Indonesia. The state is usually not an explicit participant in these, even if it tacitly takes sides. They are, therefore, not civil wars.

be argued to have been the case in Aceh in Indonesia, or with the Tamils in Sri Lanka's Jaffna province. There are three other forms of violence that deserve mention: inter-state wars are still possible; terrorism, particularly in its transnational form has become important in recent years; and finally violence arising out of 'anomie' and protest can also be significant in an era of globalization and the inequality it produces. The first two are beyond the scope of this book; I shall briefly allude to the last in Chapter 7.

Conflict, like other political-economic phenomena, requires measurement. The quantitatively minded conflict research community has increasingly placed its faith on the Uppsala data set; see Harbom, Melander and Wallensteen (2008) for recent updates.[3] The Uppsala data set defines several types of conflict: inter-state (between nation states), intra-state (civil wars), intra-state internationalized (where foreign powers are involved) and extra-state (wars of national independence, which mostly ended in the 1970s). A conflict is defined as minor if there are at least 25 battle-related deaths per year for every year in the period. It is intermediate when more than 25 battle-related deaths occur per year for every year in the conflict period, and more than 1000 deaths in the entire conflict, but with less than 1000 per annum. War is defined as describing situations with more than 1000 battle-related deaths in each year of the conflict. A conflict can move between these categories as the war escalates and wanes over time.

As far as the duration of the average civil war is concerned, this may be showing an upward trend. Fearon (2004) put the average duration of a civil war at sixteen years in 1999. He also argues that civil wars with sons of the soil dynamics (mainly wars of secession) last longer, as do wars where there is a lootable commodity such as alluvial diamonds or illicit drugs (coca or heroin), or a capturable commodity in terms of rent such as oil. The latter point is also emphasized in Ross (2004b).

Table 1.1 presents some characteristics of all conflict countries since 1960, followed by a summary comparison between conflict affected and peaceful nations. It focuses on the growth of GDP per capita (its annual average percentage growth rate between 1975 and 2005), political institutions based on the Polity scale (which goes from −10 for an extreme autocracy to 10 for a perfect democracy) and its coefficient of variation, which is a measure of the volatility of the country's regime type. Table 1.1 also includes the number of months that conflict countries experienced war (since 1960), the total number of wars, as well as the highest intensity

---

[3] The data are available at http://www.ucdp.uu.se and at http://www.prio.no/cwp/ArmedConflict.

Table 1.1   Basic indicators of civil conflict countries (1960–2005)

Country	Annual average % per capita GDP growth (1970–2005)	Months of conflict	Number of conflicts	Conflict intensity	Polity coefficient of variation	Mean Polity
Sub-Saharan Africa						
Angola	−1.51	392	5	3	0.477	−5.54
Burkina Faso	1.22	1	1	3	0.575	−4.75
Burundi	−0.57	159	2	3	0.533	−5.91
Cameroon	0.30	1	1	1	0.475	−6.42
Central African Republic	−1.45	18	1	1	0.842	−4.02
Chad	0.33	419	2	3	0.776	−6.27
Comoros	−0.46	2	2	–	0.553	−1.14
Congo	0.69	42	3	3	0.893	−4.82
Congo, D.R.	−4.53	156	6	3	0.248	−8.93
Equatorial Guinea	6.32	1	1	–	0.427	−6.11
Eritrea	−2.47	32	2	–	0.134	−6.33
Ethiopia	1.60	915	10	3	0.991	−5.88
Gabon	−0.52	1	1	1	0.755	−7.05
Gambia	−0.13	1	1	1	0.424	4.08
Ghana	−0.04	19	2	1	0.809	−3.21
Guinea	0.57	17	2	3	0.942	−6.56
Guinea-Bissau	−0.53	11	1	3	0.865	−3.83
Ivory Coast	−0.76	28	1	–	1.329	−7.80
Kenya	0.21	1	1	1	0.714	−3.83
Lesotho	2.77	1	1	1	0.932	−1.91
Liberia	−7.18	113	3	3	0.479	−5.11
Madagascar	−1.72	5	1	1	0.595	−0.34
Mali	1.50	19	2	1	0.889	−3.05
Mozambique	1.20	190	1	3	0.881	−2.50
Niger	−1.71	52	3	–	0.909	−4.07
Nigeria	−0.05	36	3	3	0.759	−1.53
Rwanda	−0.06	142	2	3	0.296	−5.91
Senegal	−0.01	163	1	3	0.559	−2.00
Sierra Leone	−1.32	116	1	3	0.778	−2.97
Somalia	−1.79	204	3	3	0.914	−2.94
South Africa	−0.22	364	2	3	0.143	5.33

Table 1.1   (continued)

Country	Annual average % per capita GDP growth (1970–2005)	Months of conflict	Number of conflicts	Conflict intensity	Polity coefficient of variation	Mean Polity
Sudan	0.60	385	5	3	0.971	−4.54
Togo	−1.48	2	2	1	0.482	−5.44
Uganda	0.34	348	4	3	0.718	−3.40
Zimbabwe	−0.71	95	1	3	0.584	−1.71
Middle East and North Africa						
Algeria	0.50	157	1	3	0.958	−6.79
Djibouti	−3.39	50	2	–	0.898	−5.50
Egypt	4.04	70	1	3	0.133	−6.36
Iran	−0.28	359	9	3	1.246	−6.31
Iraq	−1.73	490	8	3	0.698	−7.74
Israel	1.76	540	1	–	0.024	9.29
Lebanon	−1.75	186	1	–	0.113	3.00
Morocco	1.61	179	2	3	0.604	−7.51
Yemen	1.65	120	4	–	0.448	−4.76
Oman	3.65	48	1	1	1.625	−9.62
Saudi Arabia	−1.28	1	1	1	0.000	−10.00
Syria	1.29	34	2	3	0.871	−8.14
Tunisia	2.49	1	1	1	0.783	−6.78
Yemen	1.65	120	4	–	0.448	−4.76
Asia						
Afghanistan	−2.58	320	1	3	0.374	−7.42
Bangladesh	1.61	204	1	2	0.589	0.24
Cambodia (Kampuchea)	0.70	219	2	–	0.827	−4.11
India	3.05	1547	17	3	0.032	8.51
Indonesia	4.11	393	9	3	0.884	−4.89
Laos	2.96	85	2	–	0.337	−6.81
Malaysia	4.05	85	4	1	0.182	4.84
Myanmar (Burma)	2.57	2139	16	3	0.870	−6.33
Nepal	1.78	125	2	2	0.954	−3.64
Pakistan	2.09	74	4	3	0.628	0.24
Papua New Guinea	1.72	85	1	1	0.000	10.00
Philippines	0.63	774	3	3	0.603	1.84

Explaining civil war

Table 1.1   (continued)

Country	Annual average % per capita GDP growth (1970– 2005)	Months of conflict	Number of conflicts	Conflict intensity	Polity coefficient of variation	Mean Polity
Sri Lanka	3.35	141	3	3	0.074	6.11
Thailand	5.02	88	1	3	0.517	1.86
Vietnam	3.11	60	1	–	0.000	−7.00
Latin America and the Caribbean						
Argentina	0.11	59	2	3	0.660	1.20
Bolivia	−0.13	7	1	1	0.593	2.00
Chile	2.88	1	1	1	0.539	2.36
Colombia	1.56	461	1	3	0.038	7.56
Cuba	0.90	1	1		0.000	−7.00
Dominican Republic	2.36	1	1	1	0.332	3.75
El Salvador	0.52	148	2	3	0.342	2.78
Guatemala	0.56	468	1	3	0.467	0.82
Haiti	−1.54	13	3	1	1.349	−5.69
Mexico	1.25	4	2	1	0.583	−1.44
Nicaragua	−2.17	113	2	3	0.814	−1.47
Panama	1.80	1	1	1	0.664	0.73
Paraguay	1.40	1	1	1	1.030	−3.13
Peru	−0.31	213	2	3	0.501	2.02
Surinam	0.42	28	1	–	–	–
Trinidad and Tobago	1.06	1	1	1	0.042	8.67
Uruguay	1.51	12	1	1	0.521	4.53
Venezuela	−0.80	11	2	1	0.072	7.91
Europe and Central Asia						
Azerbaijan	−1.39	33	3	–	0.525	−5.36
Bosnia-Herzegovina	11.01	84	3	–	–	–
Croatia	2.07	48	1	–	0.550	0.23
Cyprus	4.07	–	1	–	0.059	9.40
Georgia	−0.62	49	4	–	0.052	4.86
Macedonia (FYR)	−0.35	8	1	–	0.077	6.64

Table 1.1 (continued)

Country	Annual average % per capita GDP growth (1970–2005)	Months of conflict	Number of conflicts	Conflict intensity	Polity coefficient of variation	Mean Polity
Moldova	−4.98	5	1	–	0.057	7.00
Romania	1.32	1	1	–	0.928	−2.55
Serbia	−3.39	25	3	–	0.550	−7.00
Spain	2.21	60	3	–	0.591	3.83
Tajikistan	−4.83	78	1	–	0.347	−3.43
Turkey	1.99	261	2	3	0.235	6.68
United Kingdom	2.10	253	2	–	0.000	10.00
USSR	−0.78	109	6	–	0.499	−6.44
Russia	–	–	–	–	0.098	5.31
Uzbekistan	−0.12	12	2	–	0.000	−9.00

All-conflict countries

	Annual average GDP growth	Polity coefficient of variation	Mean Polity
Max	11.01	1.62	10
Min	−7.18	0	−10
Median	0.51	0.55	−3.21
Mode	–	0	−7

All non-civil conflict countries

	Annual average GDP growth	Polity coefficient of variation	Mean Polity
Max	7.82	2.01	10
Min	−4.41	0	−10
Median	1.66	0.21	2.81
Mode	–	0	10

Sources: Per capita GDP growth rates: UNDP, Human Development Report.

Months of conflict: own calculations based on UCDP, Armed Conflict data set version4 2006b PRIO/UPPSALA.
Number of conflicts: as above.
Conflict intensity: as above.
Polity coefficient of variation: own calculations from Polity 4 data.
Mean polity: Polity 4 data.

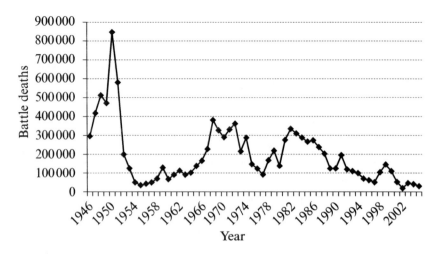

Source: UCDP Data Sets, www.prio.no/cscw/armedconflict.

Figure 1.1 Trends in battle deaths from all types of war: 1946–2005

of war (coded 3, 2 and 1 for high, medium and low intensity warfare respectively). It can be readily discerned from the summary at the end of Table 1.1 that conflict-stricken countries have a lower median growth rate at 0.51% per annum from 1975 to 2005, compared to non-conflict countries whose median growth rate is 1.66% – or more than three times greater – during the same time period. The median Polity score for conflict countries is -3.21, compared to 2.81 for non-conflict countries; the median coefficient of variation for conflict countries (at 0.55) is nearly three times higher than in peaceful countries (0.21). Thus, conflict-affected nations tend to have lower economic growth and are therefore less prosperous. They are also more inclined to be autocratic, as well as having more volatile political regimes. This is somewhat unsurprising, as the rest of the analysis in this book will demonstrate.

Figure 1.1 illustrates that battle-related fatalities from all types of war, worldwide, are on the wane since the mid-1980s. The total estimate is 11.7 million battle deaths between 1946 and 2005. This does not include civilian casualties resulting from war-related epidemics, famines and malnutrition. The peak years were during the Chinese civil war, the Korean, Vietnam and the Iran–Iraq wars.

Is conflict on the decline as well? Gleditsch (2008, fig. 2) presents evidence that wars are diminishing in terms of both the number of conflicts, and the number of nations experiencing war on their territory. The number of conflicts since the Second World War rose steadily, peaking in 1991 when 52 wars were occurring in 38 countries. In 2007, 34 conflicts took place in 25 countries, comparable to the post-1946 low achieved in the mid-1970s. The casualties associated with war seem to have declined, as has conflict intensity. I have already noted that the duration of war may not be declining. Against that are two hopeful signs: no new conflicts began in 2005 or 2006, and the year 2007 was the fourth successive year during which no new inter-state war started. Also, if we control for the fact that the number of countries has increased substantially since 1946, the number of conflicts as a ratio of the number of countries has steadily declined.

Furthermore, there has been a growth in peacekeeping operations and peacekeeping forces since the end of the cold war. Do these developments make our world a much safer place, and is conflict studies obsolete? I would argue not, as the risk factors that promote conflict, including widespread poverty and generalized injustice are very much present in our modern world where there is a risk of new forms of conflict even if civil wars are on the wane in troubled areas such as sub-Saharan Africa. What we may be witnessing is a negative hegemonistic peace based on the triumph of capitalism and one global superpower.

A wide variety of methodologies exist for the study of conflict and civil war. My focus is on work in economics and rational choice political science, both of which see conflict as amenable to analysis using choice-theoretic behaviour. This line of inquiry has been subjected to scathing criticism for being unrealistic (see Cramer, 2002, for a prime example). Granted, not every nuance that, say, an anthropologist might capture in 'thick' description is modelled by rational choice analysts, who confine themselves to irreducible minima. Cramer (2002) is critical of the approaches of pure theorists such as Grossman (1991), Hirshleifer (1995) and Skaperdas (1992). There, conflict between groups is modelled utilizing expected utility approaches, in settings of uncertainty, the absence of property rights and limited prospects of exchange (or trade) between groups. These modelling strategies are extremely relevant for the analysis of civil war in present-day poverty-stricken developing countries.

Cramer (2002) is on firmer ground when he attacks the empirical (econometric) proxies used by analysts such as Collier and Hoeffler (2004b) and others to measure natural resource dependence, and the empirical measurement of social and political indicators. It has to be pointed out that there has been considerable improvement in measuring these phenomena in recent years. These will be discussed in chapters 2 to 5. Furthermore, individual conflict case study analysis, despite all the specificities it is able to address, needs to be buttressed with general propositions emanating from rigorous cross-country analyses. One serious shortcoming, however, of the rational choice approach is that it is ahistorical, ignoring factors such as colonialism, imperialism, the cold war, even the present-day Western led globalization based hegemony. This makes it difficult for rational choice methods always to accurately depict the drivers of change that shape the political and social circumstances within which conflict may erupt.

Be that as it may, the method used in this book is of the rational choice variety, where, however, political and economic decision making are inseparable. Chapters 2 to 7 also contain analytical (mathematical) models in appendices to formalize some of the arguments presented in those chapters.

Chapter 2 focuses on the growth–conflict nexus. It therefore analyses the pre-conditions that enhance or diminish conflict risk; conflict is more likely when there is underdevelopment through insufficient economic growth. The lack of growth prevents poverty reduction in poor countries, and this in turn is a significant contributor to the chances of conflict. In fact several countries, including many in sub-Saharan Africa, are growth failures, and this makes them susceptible to conflict traps as well (as popularized by Collier, 2007). Chapter 2 examines the causes of growth failure, focusing on the important role of institutions in determining long-term growth prospects. Here, an important factor is natural resource abundance, or a heavy economic reliance on natural resource rents. This may retard economic development for several reasons, chief among which are the development of predatory institutions – known as the 'resource curse' in the political economy literature. Institutions, therefore, are key to the conflict–growth nexus, as they contribute to growth as well as conflict. The chapter also examines some causal relations at a cross-country level between conflict, growth, natural resource dependence and institutions; the latter being measured by democracy, which is often also an indicator of good governance.

Having set out the pre-conditions that might breed conflict, Chapter 3 addresses its root causes: greed and grievance. The former reflects elite competition over valuable natural resource rents. The latter argues that relative deprivation and the grievance it produces fuels conflict. Central to grievance are concepts of inter-ethnic or horizontal inequality. Identity formation is also crucial to intra-state conflict, as it overcomes the collective action problem. Measurement issues related to greed (the extent of the capturability and availability of natural resource rents), as well as grievance (indices of relative deprivation, polarization and horizontal inequality) are analysed in detail. The empirical evidence, mainly cross-country, related to the validity of these explanations is then reviewed. Neither the presence of greed or grievance is sufficient for the outbreak of violent conflict, something that requires the breakdown of the institutions of peaceful conflict resolution, which I later describe as the failure of the social contract.

Chapter 4 is concerned with the frequency with which peace treaties ending civil wars break down, resulting in the resumption of war. The success of peace agreements is dependent on the willingness of warring parties to negotiate with their foes, make concessions and adhere to the stipulations (usually involving power and resource sharing) of the peace deal. Since the end of the cold war there has been no shortage of external mediation aiming to end conflict in developing countries. Some parties (or splinter groups) often have little incentive to adhere to the conditions of the peace treaty, resulting in a return to conflict. Chief among these disincentives are an impatience to consume (discounting the future), indivisible stakes and a lack of institutions to guarantee commitment to the peace deal. External intervention can facilitate negotiation, and through involvement in the peace process make parties feel secure, even enforcing the requirements of the treaty. Sustaining the commitment to peace by the erstwhile parties to a conflict requires external intervention that contains both sanctions (including military sanctions) and a peace dividend. But very often these external sanctions-cum-aid packages are inadequate. I also analyse the different types of political, territorial and military pacts that are part of peace agreements and their chances of success.

Chapter 5 is concerned with the longer-term issues in sustaining peace, not just short-term measures to manage greed and grievance and stabilize peace treaties signed a short time ago. It follows up the analysis in chapters 2 to 4 regarding the pre-disposition to conflict, its causes and unstable peace agreements. Long-term peace requires rebuilding and redesigning the social contract that had degenerated before the conflict, allowing violence to surface. The social contract has several dimensions, encompassing political, economic and moral issues. Key to rebuilding the social contract are ideas of fair division from social choice theory, and structures that divide power along multiple majorities. The latter because power sharing may sustain a peace treaty but without further division in decision making processes, the very power sharing arrangements that secure the initial peace may become a source of future conflict. Power dividing institutions may include federal structures, devolving greater power to regions. The chapter also examines the important role of fiscal decentralization in avoiding conflict, particularly secessionist tendencies in natural resource rich regions.

The analysis of post-war economic reconstruction is conducted in Chapter 6. Post-war economic recovery should be broad based (addressing grievances) and poverty reducing. Certain sectors of the economy involving production (especially agriculture) may be more broad based compared to others, say services and construction. But economic recovery or growth is rarely balanced between sectors, and growth that is not broad based may be faster, and this involves trade-offs. Ultimately, the key to economic prosperity lies in the manufactured exportable sector. Contemporary civil war in developing countries is particularly destructive of economic institutions, such as the nation's fiscal and monetary capacities. Thus, simply rebuilding shattered infrastructure is not enough; economic institutions will also need to be reconstructed. Chapter 6 also contains an analysis of the management of possible windfall revenues from aid or natural resources, as well as the role of aid in sustaining recovery, bearing in mind that excessive aid dependence may retard post-war state formation.

The pacific effects of the 'liberal peace' are analysed in Chapter 7. This term refers to the fact that democratic nations that are also economically interdependent do not usually go to war with each other. I review various theories of the liberal peace, some of which stress the ideal of shared values, with others putting more emphasis on economic linkages and international trade. Although this line of reasoning is mainly concerned with the interaction between nation states, it also has important lessons for contemporary civil war. I also examine whether economic globalization is likely to dampen the risk of civil war and other forms of violence in developing countries, bearing in mind earlier arguments that growth serves to lower conflict risk in the long run, and the fact that increased globalization is believed to contribute to growth.

Finally, Chapter 8 presents some conclusions, along with a brief sketch of how transitional justice may assist the peace process. I will end by emphasizing that true peace requires not just the absence of war but the establishment of a wider, more universal form of justice, following the thought of Galtung (1964) and others.

2. Growth and conflict

2.1 BACKGROUND

Despite many reservations, economic growth constitutes the principal avenue via which sustainable poverty reduction can take place in low-income developing countries. Redistributing income without making the cake bigger only serves to make the already poor more equal. Thus, growth is a necessary condition for poverty reduction in low-income countries. Growth can reduce poverty if some of the benefits of growth trickle down to the poor, even if its principal beneficiaries are the wealthy.[1] Such pro-poor growth can also serve to stem the seeds of conflict (poverty and inequality) by fostering human development. Moreover, there are similarities between conflict prevention and the deep determinants of growth in the long run because of factors common to both: institutions, inequality, endowments and so on.

Growth failure, or growth biased against certain groups, can create both greed and grievances, which are prerequisites for the onset of violent internal conflict. Furthermore, in empirical work, the most robust predictor of the danger of conflict breaking out is low per capita income, implying low growth (Ross, 2004b). Thus an important growth–conflict nexus does exist; the purpose of this chapter is to explore that link. This association is, however, complex in that we must first examine the alternative explanations for growth in the long run, then look at the contribution of a rich natural resource endowment to growth and institutional development, before we begin to understand the connection between conflict, growth and institutions, which is then found to be riddled with multidirectional causality.

The rest of this chapter is organized as follows, section 2.2 looks at the pattern of long-term growth, followed by an enumeration of its causes in section 2.3; section 2.4 examines the resource curse associated with natural resource endowments; and finally section 2.5 concludes by examining some relationships between growth and conflict, as well as institutions.

---

[1]   This is where other notions of pro-poor growth, such as those advocated by Kakwani and Pernia (2000), become relevant. According to this view, in order for growth to be truly pro-poor it must disproportionately benefit the poorer segments of society; this requires an improvement in the distribution of income.

Table 2.1   Long-term patterns of growth in the world economy

	Per-capita GDP (1990 PPP)		% annual growth rate 1820–1998
	1820	1998	
Western Europe	1232	17921	1.51
Western offshoots	1201	26146	1.75
Japan	669	20413	1.93
Average-rich	**1130**	**21470**	**1.67**
Latin America	665	5795	1.22
Asia	575	2936	0.92
Africa	418	1368	0.67
Average-poor	**573**	**3102**	**0.95**

Note: Western offshoots implies North America and Australasia.

Source: Maddison (2001).

2.2   LONG-TERM GROWTH: PATTERNS AND CAUSES

One of the precepts of neoclassical growth theory is that poorer regions should grow faster than richer countries because capital yields greater returns where it is scarcer. Eventually, poorer nations should catch up with the higher living standards of affluent nations. The relative gap between rich and poor nations should become narrower over time, a phenomenon known as 'convergence'. In the general sense, this has not occurred, despite the fact that a handful of poor countries have qualified for membership of the club of the affluent. The economic history of the world in the last two centuries is a sorry tale of widening disparities between rich and poor nations (see Maddison, 2001).

As Table 2.1 indicates, the average income gap, measured in 1990 purchasing power parity (PPP) dollars, between rich and poor nations was 1.97: 1 during the early stages of the Industrial Revolution in 1820. In a 178-year period to 1998 this gap widened to 6.92. The increase in average disparity between rich and poor nations was approximately 350% during this period. Table 2.1 illustrates the fact that present-day disparities between rich and poor states are a consequence of the lower growth rates in poor countries.

Turning to more recent experience, Table 2.2 demonstrates that the growth rates for developing countries as a whole were greater in the 1960s and 1970s compared to the more globalized era post-1980. For Africa and

Table 2.2   GDP per capita (1995 constant US$) growth rates

Area/Country	Annual average per capita GDP growth % 1960–70	Annual average per capita GDP growth % 1970–80	Annual average per capita GDP growth % 1980–90	Annual average per capita GDP growth % 1990–2000
All developing countries	3.1	3.3	1.2	1.9
East Asia and Pacific	2.9	4.5	5.9	6.0
South Asia	1.8	0.7	3.5	3.2
Latin America and Caribbean	2.6	3.4	−0.8	1.7
Sub-Saharan Africa	2.6	0.8	−1.1	−0.4
Middle East and North Africa	–	–	0.5	1.7

Source: World Development Indicators (2006), World Bank.

Latin America, the last two decades of the 20th century were lost decades in terms of growth and other human development indicators. Although countries in East and South Asia appear to have sped ahead, the rest of the developing world has lagged behind, and we have ample evidence suggesting divergence in per-capita incomes between rich and poor nations, and growing inequality between nations.[2]

Milanovic (2005) in his detailed study of global inequality points out that we inhabit a downwardly mobile world with a vanishing middle class; most countries by 2000 were either rich or poor, in contrast to 1960 when more nations occupied middle-income groups. Between 1960 and 2000 the Western share of rich countries has been increasing; to be an affluent country has now become an almost exclusively Western prerogative. Sixteen out of nineteen non-Western nations who were rich in 1960 moved downwards to less affluent categories by 2000 (for example, Saudi Arabia, Algeria, Angola and Argentina). Against that is the fact that four Asian non-rich countries moved to the first group.[3] The lack of growth in many parts of the developing world not only serves to perpetuate poverty, but helps to breed greater inequality between countries; something that undermines human security in terms

---

[2]   This does not mean, however, that average incomes in certain affluent groups of countries do not converge to the average for that region (in Europe, say).

[3]   Hong Kong, Singapore, Taiwan and South Korea.

of mankind's freedom from want and fear.[4] More fundamentally, it can promote conflict.

2.3   FACTORS RELATED TO LONG-TERM GROWTH SUCCESS

So what factors underlie growth success or failure? A growth accounting exercise explains a country's relative prosperity as depending on its endowments and application of physical capital (machines) and human capital (skilled workers). Additionally, the technology adopted determines factor productivity. Capital accumulation is related to domestic savings, which can be supplemented from abroad; human capital stocks mainly relate to education expenditure and skill accumulation. Other factors such as the healthiness of the population and the presence of infrastructure and services such as banking are also important to growth. Yet the productivity of factors of production, as well as the profitability of advanced technologies, can be determined by policies and other more long-term considerations. So it is never enough simply to accumulate inputs and factors of production; these must also face the right incentives to ensure their productivity and profitability. For example, even if investment in a new technology is very profitable, entrepreneurs are unlikely to invest if their outlays can be easily appropriated in an uncertain institutional setting.

Clearly, the nature of the economic policies adopted has some bearing on growth. We begin with a discussion on policies towards growth; specifically two problems are considered: coordination failures between sectors that prevent a big push for growth, and the contribution (if any) of more open policies towards international trade. This is followed by an analysis of the deep determinants of growth in the long-term, where we have three contending factors to consider: geography, culture and institutions. The former two are determined by fate and history, whereas the last is amenable, albeit gradually, to deliberate attempts at improvement. The alert reader will have discerned that policies influence economic growth more readily and directly, but their efficacy may depend upon the deeper determinants of growth, such as institutional quality. In many ways, the emphasis on institutional quality has replaced the previously held beliefs about the importance of free market forces in fostering development (monetarism),

---

[4]   The expressions originate in President Franklin Delano Roosevelt's State of the Union address to Congress on 6 January 1941, http://www. Fdrlibrary.marist.edu/od4frees.html, 29 June 2005.

in a way that the newly held view about the saliency of institutions may be described as institutional fundamentalism (see Rodrik, 2006).

2.3.1 Coordination Failure and Openness

Murphy, Shleifer and Vishny (1989) describe a phenomenon known as the big push, which dates back to earlier work done during the closing phases of the Second World War. The idea is that growth requires the adoption of modern as opposed to traditional technologies. The former exhibits increasing returns to scale,[5] whereas the latter does not. What factors drive the adoption of the more profitable new technology? More productive technologies will be adopted by entrepreneurs if they regard it to be profitable, something that will happen only if they expect other businessmen also to accept the new technology, requiring coordination between sectors. This expectation may not materialize except in an environment that enables the right policies and institutions. Otherwise, there is coordination failure. The failure to seize upon profitable new technologies because of pessimistic expectations characterizes the situation in many developing countries, and this, in turn, prevents economic growth.

It has been stressed that more open economies, those with a greater exposure to international trade, grow faster. This argument has traditionally been used to explain the high growth rates of East Asian economies. Trade openness, however, is an outcome and not a policy, often a result of earlier policies aimed at promoting free trade and competitive industrialization. The highly influential Sachs and Warner (1995) paper argued that countries that were more open (based upon a number of openness indicators) grew faster than countries that were not open, hence creating pre-conditions for poverty reduction.[6] Rodriguez and Rodrik (2000) have convincingly demonstrated that the Sachs and Warner (1995) study suffered from sample selection bias and that some openness indicators could be highly correlated to other indicators of good governance or institutional quality. Secondly, another indicator of the lack of openness, a black market premium on the exchange rate, could be highly related to institutional quality (corruption, regulatory capacity). Most damaging to the Sachs and Warner assertion that openness promotes growth is the fact that an Africa dummy variable capturing the special effect of Africa

---

[5] This means if we double inputs, we more than double output.

[6] The indicators are: (1) non-tariff barriers cover less than 40% of trade; (2) average tariff rates are less than 40%; (3) the black market premium is less than 20%; (4) the economy is not socialist; and (5) the government does not control major exports through marketing boards.

on cross-national growth could be substituted for the two crucial openness indicators that contributed significantly to growth. More recently, Rodrik, Subramanian and Trebbi (2004) show that institutional quality, specifically the rule of law, has greater explanatory power than openness in accounting for long-term growth. This, in turn, has been criticized by Glaeser et al. (2004), who argue that another policy-based factor – initial levels of skills in the economy (human capital) – best explains long-term growth, subsequently contributing to superior institutional quality, and eventually leading to demands for democracy. We now turn to the deeper determinants of long-term growth, starting with geographical and cultural factors before moving on to institutions.

2.3.2   Geography and Culture

The relationship between geographical location and development can be traced back to the Baron de Montesquieu in 1748. He argued that tropical locations bred indolence and subservience, while temperate regions produced more industrious and courageous people (see Acemoglu, Johnson and Robinson, 2005, for a quotation). In connection with more modern geographical explanations for economic development, Gallup, Sachs and Mellinger (1998) have argued that a tropical location, particularly a tropical African location, is disadvantageous to long-term growth for the following reasons. Agricultural productivity is lower in sub-Saharan Africa, because of the lack of seasonal variation of the type present in more temperate climates. Secondly, Africa carried a greater disease burden even before the AIDS pandemic; especially virulent types of malaria were found there. Finally, there is a feature of landlockedness; a lot of the population of Africa live at great distances from the sea, making it difficult to transport goods.

Cultural explanations for growth go back to the celebrated study of Weber, who argued that Protestantism instilled values essential to the development of capitalism. Other economic historians have also attempted to explain the Industrial Revolution in Britain as a consequence of the appropriate value systems being prevalent there.

To cite an example of the negative influence of culture, Kuran (2004) points to five harmful historical factors that may have hindered economic progress in the Islamic Middle East, despite the fact that the region was very advanced a millennium ago. First, Islamic contract law only deals with the individual. This may discourage the formation of corporations that can be growth enhancing because of the limited liability of its members. Secondly, uncertainty about the legality of interest, and because lending was between individuals only, meant that institutional lenders such as banks did not develop. Thirdly, the absence of primogeniture (the eldest son inherits the entire estate) can cause difficulties if estates are parcelled into penny packets. Women, however, could automatically inherit under Islamic law from the earliest times, making it more progressive compared to customs among other religions. Fourthly, the *waqf* or *awkaf* system of charitable trusts became a source of nepotism, a device for the private provision of public goods, as well as a way of circumventing laws of inheritance, according to Kuran (2004). Finally, Middle Eastern Muslim empires and kingdoms allowed non-Muslims to live by their own laws. Before the 18th century both Muslim and non-Muslim traders used the Islamic law of individual contracts. After that time, European law was used by non-Muslim traders because they could be enforced by consulates of European powers with extra-territorial jurisdiction. Muslim merchants were left isolated and could not function in a 'corporate' fashion even if they so desired, according to Kuran (2004). Despite the negative points highlighted by Kuran (2004), we have to take into account the positive role of *zakat* and *sad'qa*, acts of charity that tend to lower poverty, and have had an inbuilt redistributive mechanism in them ever since the advent of Islam in the 7th century (something that is also very palpable at present, given the region's low rates of poverty and inequality by developing country standards).

The problem with culturalist explanations, as pointed out by Cuesta (2004), lies in the fact that attitudes change, and a culture judged to be inimical to growth in the past may now be regarded as growth friendly. The best example would be Confucianism, thought to promote atrophy a century ago, but now regarded by culturalists to encourage growth. Few nowadays regard Catholicism to be growth retarding, unlike a century ago. Certain cultures, however, may promote trust among the citizenry that helps to promote growth. But that positive effect may be more at the micro or local level. Furthermore, there is a powerful element of reverse causality between culture and growth, as both affect each other. Culture may have an impact upon economic growth but, equally, economic growth alters cultural characteristics. The problem with both the cultural and geographical explanations for growth is that they are immutable; nothing can be done to change them. I now turn to other explanations for economic growth that are more amenable to choice.

2.3.3 Institutions and their Determinants

Recent empirical studies confirm the independent importance of institutions in determining economic performance as measured by the levels of per capita income. Much of this harks back to the work of Douglass

North, who is credited with the founding of the new institutionalist school: 'The growth of economies has occurred within the institutional framework of well-developed coercive policies, – economic history is overwhelmingly a story of economies that failed to produce a set of economic rules of the game that induce sustained economic growth.' (North, 1990, pp. 14, 98).

Acemoglu, Johnson and Robinson (2001, 2005) have produced the most influential recent theoretical basis for the role of institutions in determining long-term growth. They argue that political and economic institutions need to be differentiated. The latter are mainly related to property rights and contract enforcement, which are associated with the rule of law. Political institutions pertain to both formal rules (the constitution or long-established conventions), as well as the informal exercise of power. In many ways, this corresponds to North's (1990) distinction between formal and informal institutions. Formal political institutions are slow to change, as evidenced by the infrequency with which constitutions are altered. Informal political institutions means the power of the influential, very much related to the distribution of income or wealth.

Political institutions and the distribution of wealth are the two state variables that jointly determine economic institutions, which in turn determine economic performance or growth, and the future distribution of resources and political institutions. Furthermore, economic efficiency and the distribution of power or initial wealth are inseparable. This means that economically optimal policies, from the viewpoint of society at large, cannot always be implemented. Why can't a group of dynamic businessmen, for example, bribe those in power to pursue the right policies that promote investment? The answer is that commitments made by rulers or sovereigns are not completely credible, and can be reneged upon. These promises by rulers are essentially non-contractable, in the absence of credible constitutional anchors of commitment.

According to Acemoglu, Johnson and Robinson (2005) the conditions for the development of good economic institutions consist of the following. The first condition is when there are constraints upon the executive and a balance of power present between different forces in society, implying a degree of democracy, along with a separation of powers. Nowadays, most developing countries are imperfect democracies. Although many hold elections frequently, there are few checks on the elected executive. Consequently, they tend to exercise unbridled power when in office, and frequently adopt economic policies that only enrich narrow support groups. Some actually set about actively dismantling or undermining checks on their executive power, such as the independence of judiciary. The second condition is where the enforcement of property rights (necessary to secure investment) is broad based and is not confined to an elite group's interests. Otherwise predation will be common; violence is the easiest means of protecting the vast estates of the wealthy few. In other words, societies with less inequality and a powerful middle class are more likely to devise superior economic institutions. Finally, when there are few 'rents' that can be appropriated by a small group – implying the absence of rents that can be easily captured – is also a condition for the emergence of more sound economic institutions.

We have currently rich data on governance and government capacity (for example see Kaufmann, Kraay and Mastruzzi, 2006). These correspond most closely to the aforementioned economic institutions. The rankings are for voice and accountability, political stability, government effectiveness, regulatory quality, rule of law and control of corruption. They extend from −2.5 at the lower end of the spectrum, to 2.5 at the upper end. The implication also is that a positive score is good and a negative score is below average. The scores are highly correlated with per capita income.[7] Most developing countries, particularly low-income nations score negatively in these areas. Other examples of sources of data on governance include Freedom House[8] and the International Country Risk Guide (ICRG).[9] As far as political institutions are concerned the most commonly used data set refers to democracy, and is known as the Polity index.[10] This data set gives a democracy score of between 0 and 10 (with Western democracies scoring 10). A truly meaningful democracy is only arrived at with a Polity score of 8. The autocracy data set gives an autocracy score of between −10 and 0. The Polity 2 or 4 score is a combination of both autocracy and democracy, and a reflection of a country's democratic or non-democratic status. Most developing countries occupy an indeterminate zone, and are neither democracies nor autocracies, but with characteristics of both (electoral competition along with weak constraints on the executive), occupying a position on the Polity scale of between, say, −4 to 4. These countries are known as 'anocracies'.

With regard to democracy and growth two relevant sub-questions arise. First, does democracy assist economic growth? Secondly, what economic factors underlie transitions to democracy? With regard to the first question, as Tavares and Wacziarg (2001) point out, it can work in both ways. Democracies could retard growth by:

---

[7] This illustrates the reverse causality or endogeneity problem that exists between institutions and growth. Good institutions may promote growth, but growth also leads to institutional improvement.

[8] See www.freetheworld.com.

[9] See http://www.prsgroup.com/ICRG.aspx.

[10] See www.cidcm.umd.edu/insr/polity.

- Hindering investment in physical capital by favouring labour over capital and by reducing wealth and income inequalities. This is not always true; contemporary third world democracies, and classical 19th-century democracies protected capital (oligarchic interests) against labour.
- Encouraging greater public consumption.
- Not insulating themselves from lobby groups.
- Producing greater market distortions and lower trade openness.

Democracies may promote growth because:

- Inequality is bad for growth.
- Dictatorships are predatory.
- Democracies foster greater access to education – human capital accumulation.
- Unlike autocracies they may not want to expand the public sector like the Soviet Union.
- Democracies may produce fewer market distortions and choose greater trade openness.

Tavares and Wacziarg (2001) find that democracy raises growth by raising human capital accumulation and lowering income inequality, the latter less robustly. They also find that democracy lowers growth by reducing physical capital accumulation, and by expanding the size of government (the latter less robustly). Observe that the channels between democracy and growth are both indirect and numerous. Much depends on which channel we wish to focus on.

With regard to the second question, of which economic factors contribute to transition to democracy, we have two views in the literature. One view, stated in Przeworski and Limongi (1993), may be regarded as the exogenous theory of democratization. According to this approach, most poor low-income countries are dictatorships (at least until recently), and most rich countries are stable democracies. What happens inbetween (typically within the $1001–4000 per capita income range in 1985 PPP dollars) is a random draw: some countries become democracies because democracy is imposed from the outside following defeat in a war, or more typically because they were compelled to embrace democracy following economic crises, as with most developing nations in the post-cold war period.

The alternative to this hypothesis is Lipset's (1960) famous modernization theory, which is an endogenous view of democracy. According to this view, democracy is an inevitable outcome of economic progress. At high levels of income the demand for democracy is unstoppable. Similarly, in prosperous nations the risk of large-scale societal conflict and civil war is less likely, as people have more to lose from violent competition over power or resources. The Lipset view certainly seems to fit the historical experience of Western democracies. Furthermore, according to Glaeser et al. (2004), it may even describe the experience of successful countries in the third world. In the 1960s, all developing countries were dictatorships. Some countries, as in East Asia, pursued enlightened policies and invested more in human capital, unlike in Africa. This raised the income of the Asian countries, they grew faster and most have become democracies, because of pressures from their more affluent and educated populations; not because of external forces as in Africa. Thus, both endogenous and exogenous theories have their applicability in different parts of the world.

The work of Campos and Nugent (1999) represents an early attempt to test more rigorously for the effects of the hitherto amorphous notions of the institutions of good governance. Although their paper lacks a properly specified theory, one can deduce that they are pointing to a 'production function' for good governance. This is composed of: (1) an accountable executive; (2) an efficient civil service; (3) the rule of law; (4) participation by 'civil society' in policy making; and (5) an open and transparent policy making process. The authors construct a data set based on scaling coefficients for the first four characteristics, pertaining to various countries in East Asia and Latin America. These data are then related econometrically to three measures of human development: per capita income, infant mortality and adult (il)literacy. To summarize the results, the rule of law tends to be the most important institutional characteristic in explaining human development, particularly in Latin America. If East Asia is taken alone, the quality of the civil service is the most important factor. Furthermore, in Latin America the quality of the bureaucracy and the rule of law are often substitutes in producing good governance; whereas in East Asia it is strong civil society and the rule of law that are often the substitutable inputs. This study provides us with a hint as to what aspects of governance are crucial to growth; they seem to point in the direction of bureaucratic quality and the rule of law.

Other econometric studies attempt to gauge the relative contribution of economic policies (such as openness examined above) vis-à-vis the role of institutions in explaining differences in per capita income between rich and poor countries. Easterly and Levine (2003) present evidence based on cross-country econometrics that a mineral natural resource endowment, a poor geographical (tropical) location and an excessive mortality rate (disease burden) does retard economic development, but via institutional quality as measured by Kaufmann, Kraay and Mastruzzi (2006). Similarly, bad economic policies and choices also hinder economic development via institutions. Consequently, institutions and institutional functioning are the crucial link between resource endowments, geography and policies on the one hand and economic outcomes on the other hand. Rodrik, Subramanian and Trebbi (2004) also find that institutions dominate policies, as mentioned above, but they have been subjected to criticism by Glaeser et al. (2004), as indicated above.

More generally, and in the more traditional spirit of political economy, Auty and Gelb (2001) construct a typology of states based on whether they are homogeneous or factional (several ethnic groups), as well as benevolent or predatory. A benevolent developmental state, whether homogeneous (Indonesia, North-East Asian countries) or factional (Botswana, Malaysia) tends to maximize social welfare and investment in infrastructure and human capital. Above all a reliance on market forces, and competitive industrialization of a variety not dependent on state subsidies, tends to emerge in the benevolent state. Within the benevolent category is the 'paternalistic' type, applicable to certain oil-rich countries (with a very high oil endowment per capita) such as Saudi Arabia, Brunei and Kuwait. These systems share some of the benevolent characteristics of developmental states that have been just mentioned, usually within the context of a consensual monarchy, but unlike in the developmental state less heed is paid to market forces. A predatory state promotes rent seeking, lobbying and uncompetitive industrialization. The line of reasoning adopted in the Auty–Gelb (2001) typology does, indeed, go a long way to explain the development successes of the last half a century, but we are left wondering what determines the emergence of either of the two models and their associated institutions of governance? The current economic literature points to several sources of institutional determination, some of which relate to natural resource endowment, others to the historical pattern of colonial settlement, and finally we have a role for inequality. I shall consider all three in turn.

As regards endowments, certain varieties of natural resources such as oil and minerals have a tendency to lead to production and revenue patterns that are concentrated, while revenue flows from other types of resources such as agriculture are more diffused throughout the economy. Countries rich in the former category of resource may be called point-sourced economies, while nations abundant in the latter type may be referred to as diffuse; see Auty (1997). Sometimes, agricultural commodities such as coffee or cocoa are also considered point-sourced, because they are produced in plantations or marketed in a manner that makes them akin to the concentrated conditions that prevail with minerals. Murshed (2004) presents evidence that developing countries which export mineral/fuel type natural resources have tended to have lower growth rates in the post-1970 period, compared to resource-poor countries, notwithstanding a handful of success stories such as Botswana.[11] This is known as the resource curse. Natural resource rents can make corruption, predation and rent seeking a more attractive option compared to peaceful production in the presence of poor institutions. Equally, a rich mineral-type natural resource endowment, where ownership and production are concentrated may therefore produce poor institutions. Malfunctioning institutions may then retard growth. Due to the saliency of natural resource rents in determining the greed motivation for conflict, I will leave the detailed discussion of the resource curse to the next section.

Acemoglu, Johnson and Robinson (2001, 2005) relate poor (or good) institutional determination to patterns of colonialization. They distinguish between two types of colonies. The first group corresponds to parts of the new world settled by European migrants, as in North America and Australasia. The second group refers to tropical developing countries, today's third world. The idea is that better institutions, especially property rights and the rule of law, were embedded in the first group.[12] In the second category of colonial countries, an extractive pattern of production was set up. This extractive and exploitative pattern of production is also the legacy of colonialization; malignant colonialization in these cases. Clearly, this pattern was more prevalent in some parts of the world, particularly in Africa and Latin America. As the extractive state is expropriatory and predatory, bad institutions emerge and become entrenched even after independence, and a predatory equilibrium emerges.

The important question that remains is why decolonialization, and the opportunities it provides for policy changes, does not alter the destiny of an extractive economy? It does in some, but not others. Secondly, despite the saliency of the colonial phase in history, many developing nations have had a collective experience prior to, and after, colonialization that must have also shaped institutions. In East Asia, South Asia, the Middle East and North African regions of the developing world, well-functioning institutions of good governance existed well before the advent of colonialization, and European colonial powers merely adapted

---

[11] Note, however, that the historical evidence regarding natural resource abundance suggests that many of these countries such as the United States, Canada, Australia and New Zealand have done well in the past.

[12] The authors argue that the mortality rate amongst Europeans is what determined whether Europeans settled a colony or not.

pre-existing administrative institutions. Indeed, it could be argued that post-independence leaders in these regions whose legitimacy was justified (at least partially) because of their efforts in cold war battles against communism, or more recently the war on terror, have done considerable harm to institutions, especially to democratic constraints on the executive and the separation of powers.

Another strand of the literature builds on the link between the inequality and resource endowment of the point-sourced variety, see the work of Sokoloff and Engerman (2000), who discuss the historical experience of Latin America, and Easterly (2007) for a cross-sectional analysis across nations. Commodity endowments of the point-source variety tend to depress the middle-class share of income in favour of elites, as in Latin America. The idea is that these elites, in turn, use their power, identical with the forces of the state, to coerce and extract rents. When different groups compete with one another for these rents, the rent-seeking contest leads to even more perverse and wasteful outcomes than when elites collude. The important point made by Easterly (2007) is that small elite-based societies do not have a stake in the long-term development of the land, unlike in middle-class dominated societies. Publicly financed human capital formation and infrastructural development falls by the wayside, hence depressing growth prospects.

The other important point of the paper is that inequality does matter for economic growth, but the chain of causation between inequality and growth is unconventional. Here it is the middle-class share of income, and the concomitant middle-class agenda that determines the right policies, particularly in terms of education and infrastructure. Easterly's work is motivated by the theory in Bourguignon and Verdier (2000), whose model introduces the possibility of endogenous redistribution of income by an oligarchic elite leading to democracy. The reason is that mass education promotes growth, although it eventually dissipates the power of the existing elite. Education is costly, but it results in a private benefit for the educated (higher lifetime income), as well as an all-important growth-enhancing public benefit. The benefits from the latter effect also accrue to oligarchies. This may induce the selfish elite to redistribute income as it allows the capital-constrained poor to obtain an education and contribute to rapid national economic development, even though this means the eventual loss of power for the oligarchy through the emergence of democracy. The important point is that a small oligarchy may be more disinclined to redistribute income, and this is more likely in point-sourced mineral and plantation based economies. By the same token, elites in resource-poor countries have a relatively greater incentive to tolerate redistribution.

Not all point-sourced economies go through, or stay with, persistent coercive behaviour by elites. In the point-sourced economies of South-East Asia such as Malaysia, or to an extent in Indonesia, the elites opted for redistribution. The difference here was that the danger of an ideological upheaval in terms of communism was much more real (Communist China was a close neighbour) than in Latin America, and the ruling class wanted to avoid ethnic strife. Botswana, too, avoided ethnic fractionalization, unlike the rest of Africa. In Latin America ethnic minorities have usually been suppressed, and processes of conciliation avoided. In summary, it has to be said that the poor institutions associated with extractive industries or colonial coercive policies are not immutable; they can be altered when enlightened policies are followed.

2.4   THE RESOURCE CURSE

The object of this section is to examine the resource curse thesis. The idea is that countries that rely heavily on natural resource based products do badly in terms of economic performance. More generally, reliance on exports of all primary (non-manufactured agricultural, mineral, fuel and forest based) goods was criticized a long time ago by Prebisch (1950) and Singer (1950). Essentially, this was for two reasons. The first was to do with the fact that in the longer run demand for (unprocessed) primary goods is income inelastic. Primary goods are either food items or inputs for production, and as income rises, the propensity to spend on these (expenditure shares) decline. The second criticism of a development strategy based on the export of natural resource products is to do with the fact that their prices are notoriously volatile. Indeed, a great part of Hans Singer's distinguished career was devoted to demonstrating that there was a secular (long-term) tendency for primary goods prices relative to manufactured goods prices (the terms of trade) to decline. Be that as it may, reliance on natural resource or primary goods exports exposes developing economies to a boom and bust cycle, as revenues from these exports fluctuate over time. Perhaps the problem does not lie with endowments of natural resources per se, but a heavy reliance on unprocessed exports of these in an undiversified economic setting, something that has been described as the 'staple trap' by authors such as Auty (1997). A strategy of development based on manufactures has long been encouraged; Hirschman (1958), for example, advocated the fostering of manufactures on account of the forward and backward linkages that this sector exerted on the rest of the economy.

Table 2.3   Countries with growth failure

Catastrophic		Severe	
1960 or before	During 1960s	During 1970s	During 1980s
Central African	Cote D'Ivoire	Burundi	Kenya
Republic	Mauritania	Cameroon	Republic of Congo
Chad	Togo	Gabon	
Democratic Republic		Malawi	Ecuador
of Congo[c]	Bolivia	Mali	Paraguay
Ghana	Jamaica	Zimbabwe	Trinidad and
Liberia			Tobago
Madagascar		El Salvador	
Niger		Guatemala	Jordan
Nigeria[a]		Guyana	
Rwanda		Honduras	
Senegal		Peru	
Sierra Leone			
Somalia		Algeria[a]	
Zambia		Iran[b]	
		Saudi Arabia	
Haiti			
Nicaragua		Philippines[a]	
Venezuela			

Notes:
[a]   Economy considered large, 1960 population clearly above 25 million.
[b]   Economy considered large, 1960 population clearly above 20 million.
[c]   Economy considered large, 1960 population clearly above 15 million.

Source: Based on a sample of 98 countries for whom data is available, see Perälä (2000). World Development Indicators, World Bank, various issues; UNDP, Human Development Report, 1996.

Table 2.3 presents a list of 42 developing countries[13] that are growth failures with a real per capita income level in 1998 achieved much earlier. Here we are looking at average growth rates over a long period. Catastrophic growth failure is considered to have occurred in economies that attained their contemporary real per capita income level sometime during the 1960s or before. Severe growth failure, in turn, is considered to have occurred in those countries that have had more than a decade of stagnation, achieving

[13]   Former socialist countries in Europe, Asia and Africa are excluded due to incomplete data. Table 2.3 is based on Perälä (2000).

their current real per capita income level during either the 1970s or 1980s. All but six of these countries can be described as having point-sourced or mineral/fuel natural resource endowments, as measured by their principal exports. The diffuse economies are Honduras, Mali, Philippines, Senegal, Somalia and Zimbabwe. Table 2.3 is constructed on the basis of data availability on growth rates extending back to 1960 and earlier, a total of 98 countries. If we look into the picture after 1965, we could add, at least, Angola, Iraq and Ethiopia to the list of growth failures, based on a negative growth.

More importantly, only six (or seven if we include Oman) mineral or fuel exporting, point-sourced economies have real per capita income growth rates that exceed 2.5% per annum on an average in the 1965–99 period; see Murshed (2004). These are Botswana, Chile, the Dominican Republic, Indonesia, Egypt and Tunisia. Of these only two, Botswana and Indonesia, have high growth rates of over 4%. We may wish to consider Malaysia as point-sourced as well. Therefore, in the developing world we have three point-sourced success stories, and we have an empirical prima facie case for a resource curse.

The rest of this section is organized as follows: section 2.4.1 describes the adverse economic effects of resource booms, while section 2.4.2 focuses on the political economy of resource booms and a large resource endowment.

2.4.1   Economic Effects of Resource Booms

2.4.1.1   The Dutch disease

The most common macroeconomic effect associated with natural resource booms is known in the literature as 'Dutch Disease'[14] (see Neary and Wijnbergen, 1986, and Murshed, 1997, chapter 6, for example). A resource boom crowds out the other leading sector of the economy. So in countries that previously exported manufactured goods (UK after North Sea oil, for example), that sector contracts; in developing countries it could be the agricultural sector. In an open economy a substantial current account surplus appears, leading to currency appreciation under a regime of flexible exchange rates. This makes existing (non-resource boom) exports uncompetitive in world markets. Under fixed exchange rates the price of non-traded domestically produced goods and services increases. Either

---

[14]   An expression coined by the *Economist* magazine in 1977. This is because the discovery of gas in the North Sea was said to have contributed to deindustrialization in the Netherlands. Alternatively, we could employ the French term, *syndrome Hollandais*. It is therefore not confined to developing countries.

way, there is real exchange rate appreciation. One of the policy implications of resource booms is to avoid excessive and persistent real exchange rate appreciation.

There is a shift in the composition of domestic output from tradeables towards non-traded goods and services. The resource boom has an expenditure effect as incomes rise, and it has a resource allocation impact, as domestic production switches to non-traded goods and services, such as construction and other forms of public expenditure. In certain cases, severe unemployment may characterize the adjustment path to the new equilibrium following the resource boom because of a huge increase in the demand for financial assets relative to non-traded goods (see Neary and Wijnbergen, 1984). The Dutch disease is not a disease at all if it only shifts the pattern of production towards non-traded goods, as with higher incomes and more foreign exchange certain goods can be more cheaply imported from abroad. Policies of economic diversification need to be pursued to counter these developments. Atkinson and Hamilton (2003) find that resource booms do not hamper long-term growth as long as savings net of resource depletion are robust. This implies increases in public investment relative to consumption. Problems arise if there are distortions and price/wage rigidities within the economy. But commodity prices tend to be unstable, and the resource boom peters out when their prices fall over the long-term business cycle, as with the case of oil. Or it could be that the resource in question (say, oil) is simply exhausted. Is the economy capable of returning to its pre-boom output mix? How will it cope with these medium-term boom–bust cycles? All the evidence, especially for major oil exporters in the developing world, suggests that the adjustment to falling commodity prices is associated with negative growth rates, implying that the boom period is associated with some permanent form of loss of competitiveness; I return to this issue in the next sub-section.

But first, historical experience, particularly with regard to the 1870–1913 period of globalization, informs us that natural resource endowment and/or booms were not always disadvantaging. Findlay and Lundahl (1994) construct an intersectoral model with links between a natural resource sector and manufacturing, where a resource boom can lead to growth expansion. They distinguish between tropical subsistence economies (today's developing world) and the regions of recent settlement[15] such as Australia, Canada and the USA. Both these parts of the world interacted with an industrialized region, Europe. The tropical regions have

---

[15] A term originally coined by the League of Nations.

no manufacturing, unlike the two other regions, but have a subsistence agricultural sector with a fixed wage, as well as the possibility of producing traded primary goods. Manufacturing employs labour and sector specific capital. Production in the resource sector utilizes labour and a sector specific land input. Land utilized in the natural resource based production sector is not just exogenous, but the land frontier (and the output of the resource sector) can be extended by the application of capital input.

Globalization in the 19th century led to a rise in the demand and prices of primary goods produced both in the tropics and the regions of recent settlement. This not only raised the rental rate on land used in primary goods production, but also extended the land frontier. It also increased the demand for labour in the new world and in tropical regions, and led to immigration into the regions of recent settlement (settled by Europeans), and a movement away from subsistence farming to cash crops or mining in tropical regions. Manufacturing, too, expanded in Europe and in the regions of recent settlement. The mechanism underlying the expansion in manufacturing was a decline in the real rate of interest. This raised manufacturing capital intensity, as well as the real wage rate. In tropical areas there was also an increase in the real wage in the primary goods sector, above subsistence sector levels. This wage premium was necessary to finance additional land clearance, allowing the resource sector to expand in the absence of foreign investment. Even with foreign investment, a wage premium may have been necessary, reflecting higher productivity. In plantation-type economies (point-sourced), for example in Latin America, landlords captured the wage premium, whereas in peasant, owner-occupied diffuse type societies, the extra rent accrued to peasant entrepreneurs.

What happened later? The regions of recent settlement would be on their way to a bliss point of high per capita incomes that we nowadays associate them with – because of the backward and forward links to manufacturing – competitive industrialization in contemporary parlance. Many tropical regions did not industrialize, stagnating instead into a staple trap (a fixed reliance on a few commodity exports). This outcome was more likely in point-sourced economies. By contrast, it is the diffuse economies, such as in North-East Asia, where prospects of industrializing were more promising. This is because, as Baldwin (1956) points out, peasant entrepreneurs will generate demand for simple, labour intensive manufactures, which later become exportable. Further on, these economies move up the manufacturing product cycle. Moreover, peasant societies are also more likely to support publicly financed infrastructure and human capital formation, compared to countries dominated by a small elite interested in siphoning off resource rents. Also, when point-sourced or mineral/fuel based economies experiment with industrialization, it is usually capital intensive and dependent on public subsidy. They are often non-traded, as pointed out in Murshed (2001); used for domestic consumption only; also, uncompetitive and unsustainable in the long run. Clearly, the crucial link is between the resource sector and manufacturing. If the nascent manufacturing sector is competitive, resource booms can act as the spur towards future growth and sustainable development.

2.4.1.2 Loss of competitiveness

Sachs and Warner (2001) present empirical evidence suggesting that countries rich in natural resources tend to have higher price levels, and as a result their non-natural resource based goods are uncompetitive and cannot be exported. They, therefore, miss out on the benefits of export-led growth that many other developing countries poorly endowed with natural resources have gained from, say in East Asia. They also argue that a high natural resource endowment adversely affects growth even after previous growth and other factors that militate against economic growth are taken into account such as a tropical location, distance from the sea and a high disease burden.

Why should the loss of competitiveness in non-natural resource based exports be a problem for the future? Surely competitiveness in exports, say labour-intensive manufactures, may be acquired at some future date when natural resource revenues dry up. As the model in Krugman (1987) illustrates, if there are learning by doing effects, a country whose manufacturing base is eroded during a resource boom can irreversibly lose competitiveness, even when the real exchange rate reverts to its initial level after the boom has subsided. Thus, temporary resource booms cause path dependence or *hysteresis*, a permanent loss of competitiveness. For developing countries, this means that their future potential for exporting manufactured goods and diversifying the production base is stunted. If there are positive externalities from human capital accumulation in manufacturing only, as in Matsuyama (1992), and resource booms retard the development of the more dynamic manufacturing sector, the growth path of the economy under free trade is lower than that of more resource-poor countries. The important point is that following a boom–bust cycle associated with natural resource revenues, a country might find itself devoid of these rents, yet not industrialized and unable to catch up with other developing countries that are already moderately industrialized. Also, their wages may be too high to compete with other resource-poor developing nations.

In the paper by Sachs and Warner (1999b) a role for growth-enhancing human capital (or skills in the workforce) is incorporated into a model with a non-traded sector, a traded good and a purely exportable natural resource sector. Human capital accumulation, in the form of an externality, takes place as a result of traded/manufacturing production only. Resource booms, in the Sachs and Warner (1999b) model retard the growth of the economy via the crowding out of production in the traded (manufactured) sector. The stock of human capital is diminished as employment in tradeables declines; this in turn hampers future production of all goods, and hence the growth of the economy. Another Sachs and Warner (1999a) paper on resource booms permits increasing returns to scale in either of the two sectors of the economy (traded or non-traded), but not in both. Increasing returns characterize the production of a range of intermediate inputs that could be employed in final production. The model then addresses whether resource booms can contribute towards 'big-push' type industrialization. A resource boom unambiguously expands the non-tradeable sector, while at the same time shrinking the traded sector. If it is the expanding (non-traded) sector that uses these intermediate inputs, it may contribute to a successful big push. If the opposite is the case, and it is the traded sector that uses the intermediate inputs, big pushes are less likely. Also, unless expectations about the future are optimistic, even the most propitious circumstances may not trigger accelerated industrialization or the big push. Implicitly, these expectations are related to the political system and social capital.

Clarida and Findlay (1992) present a model where absolute and comparative advantage is endogenous and policy induced. The mechanism via which this occurs is a public financed knowledge-based input (non-rivalled and non-excludable) that lowers production costs, similar to the idea in Shell (1966). This input will not be provided by the private sector, and is therefore a pure public good. One can also think of this input as human capital, or infrastructural investment. There are two sectors in the economy, one of which is akin to a resource sector where the benefit from the public financed input in terms of lower production costs is relatively lower. The other sector may be likened to manufacturing, and it derives greater benefit from the publicly provided input.

Capital is a specific factor in manufacturing, whereas land is specific to the resource sector. All sectors require labour input. In these circumstances a resource boom will induce a lower optimal supply of the publicly financed input, as the resource sector obtains a proportionately smaller benefit from this input. Consequently, over the course of time, *both* sectors will be less productive, akin to a loss in absolute advantage in international trade. The expansion of international trade will also make countries with greater capital endowments gain absolute advantage in all sectors, as exports of manufacturing increase, inducing greater provision of the cost-reducing public good. If an additional, non-traded and publicly supported consumption sector is introduced, similar to the functioning of state owned enterprises, resource booms will retard competitiveness in both the other sectors even further in the presence of a strong societal or ruling class preference for this good. The reason is that the reduction of the supply of the publicly financed productive input is greater after a resource boom in the presence of a strong preference for a publicly supported non-traded consumption good. A greater desire for this public good may characterize rentier societies.

Not all, however, is doom and gloom when an economy is blessed with a boom in its natural resource based exports. Several countries, Norway, the Netherlands, Indonesia, Malaysia and Botswana among them, have coped well with these bounties in recent times. Resource booms should not automatically cause the traded sector to contract and the non-traded sector to expand (see Murshed, 2001). This is partially a result of the existence of excess capacity in the economy, and also when the right policies are adopted with regard to the real exchange rate and other manufacturing subsidies.

2.4.1.3   Resource rents and public education expenditure

Before examining whether mineral or energy resource-rich countries spend more on public education than other countries it is worth dwelling on how resource intensity is measured. This can be important, as the ranking among nations with regard to resource dependence might change, depending upon the metric utilized. Furthermore, different units of measurement may cause fluctuating statistical significance in empirical models analysing the effect of resource abundance on other economic phenomena such as growth or education spending. One way of measuring resource dependence would be simply to look at the proportionate contribution of mining (or mining and agriculture) in national income. This is the share of national income method. But a large mining sector does not necessarily imply economic dependence, as the economy might still be quite diversified with a large manufacturing share in national income. The country may be exporting industrially processed natural resource based products, as in Chile.

This brings us to the second method, which could be based on the pattern of exports. We could look at the principal exports of the economy. Alternatively, one could use the share of primary (all unprocessed exports) or mineral exports in GDP as a measure. This would be an export intensity measure. Also, one might want to look at the share of minerals or energy in total exports.

A third type of measurement could look at per capita stocks (for example, of oil reserves) and not flows (of oil exports, say) giving us a measure of national per capita endowment of the value of these stocks. A fourth method may look at ratios of total (not per capita) stocks of different types of capital. We could look at the ratio of natural to physical capital stocks. But, as Stijns (2006) points out, it would be problematic, if not gravely erroneous, to look at natural capital stocks as a proportion of all types of capital stocks (the sum of human, physical and natural capital), as in Gylfason (2001b). So, a country such as Norway, which successfully invested in the past in education and infrastructure, would be classified as resource poor simply because it has a high stock of total capital in the denominator of the ratio! Equally, an oil-rich underdeveloped country (because of low stocks of human and physical capital) would be classified as resource rich simply because of the smallness of the denominator of the ratio relative to the numerator.

A fifth metric is associated with rents. Rent refers to the difference between prices and costs, giving us a measure of 'excess' profit. This in turn can be calculated in per capita terms, or measured as a share of national income. Rents increase when there are booms in commodity prices. Finally, if we wanted to look at agricultural potential we could look at arable land per capita (see Auty, 1997). For most purposes of measuring a country's dependence some sort of export based measure is most appropriate, as it conveys information about what a country is good at and its place in the world economy; something referred to as comparative or competitive advantage by economists. Alternatively as a measure of intensity, perhaps the ratio of natural capital to physical or human capital stocks (but not both) could be used, as it gives us an idea of how resource rents have been used to accumulate other types of capital; a low ratio indicates earlier investment in other forms of capital.

The importance of human capital in fostering economic growth and human development cannot be overemphasized. All of this is related to educational spending, mainly public expenditure on education. Resource rents and oil windfalls should, in principle, provide governments of developing countries with extra resources to invest in education. In contrast, is the idea that in foreign exchange abundant resource-rich countries there is little incentive to invest in basic skills, as there is little need to have a skilled workforce to export processed goods. A good chunk of the educational expenditure will therefore be devoted to elite tertiary education. Again, there are many ways of measuring educational variables (Stijns, 2006) such as the average years of schooling, the net secondary enrolment rate and public spending as a proportion of aggregate spending, or government spending on education as a proportion of total government expenditure.

Birdsall, Pinckney and Sabot (2001) show that resource abundance measured by cropland per capita systematically lowers public investment in education. Similarly, Gylfason (2001b) shows that natural resource-rich countries spend less on education in terms of expected years of schooling for girls, gross secondary enrolment rates and public expenditure on education as a proportion of national income. But his results are flawed because his measure of natural resource abundance is the share of natural capital as a proportion of all types of capital. As indicated above, this biases downwards the resource abundance of high income and successful countries in this category simply because they have high stocks of all types of capital relative to natural capital. In contrast to Birdsall, Pinckney and Sabot (2001) and Gylfason (2001b), Stijns (2006) finds that for developing countries many of the measures of natural resource abundance can cause greater educational attainment and spending, as well as a higher life expectancy at birth. So, natural resource endowments may not be so bad for human development.

There are, however, several exceptions, depending on how we measure natural resource dependence or intensity. Countries with a high share of mineral exports in total exports fare badly, as do countries with a high ratio of natural to physical capital. Similarly, nations with a high ratio of green capital (non-arable forests, pasturelands etc.) to physical capital, high agricultural export intensity and arable land per capita are also poor performers in this regard. These nations may be described as unsuccessful resource-abundant developing countries, and they include some agricultural exporters, as well as pastoralist countries in sub-Saharan Africa. A high primary or mineral export dependence means a country has not diversified or industrialized, otherwise it would have been exporting more processed manufactures as is the case with resource-rich Malaysia. Also, having a high natural or green capital endowment relative to produced capital is another sign of economic stagnation and the failure to develop, as development leads to a higher stock of physical capital via investment. Also, it appears that high proportions of cropland and timber wealth relative to physical capital stocks are worse for education and health indicators than high ratios of oil wealth to physical capital stocks. Furthermore, there are also no signs of countries systematically favouring tertiary over secondary education.

2.4.1.4 Low savings and debt overhang

Metcalfe (2007), interestingly, finds that the resource curse may not be present apart from in the 1970 to 1990 period. This is something I have alluded to above; the curse of natural resources is a recent phenomenon in economic history. Metcalfe's (2007) study is based on a calculation of resource rents, but confined to oil, gas, hard coal, gold, silver, bauxite, copper, iron, lead, nickel, tin and zinc. So many other primary goods are excluded, and no comparisons can be made with nations depending upon them. Also, certain important minerals such as diamonds are also absent from the analysis. Nevertheless, he does find that the resource curse (effect on growth of rents from the resources listed) is very much a post-1970 phenomenon, which may have ended in the 1990s. It is a phenomenon confined to developing countries. It is stronger in Asia, Central America and the Middle East compared to sub-Saharan Africa and Latin America, contrary to prevalent beliefs. Most importantly, he finds that the transmission mechanism causing the resource curse is external indebtedness and poor institutional quality measured by constraints on the executive. It may be that certain resource-rich countries with poorer institutional environments borrowed unsustainably during or shortly after booms in commodity prices. They may have also had lower resource adjusted savings rates, as emphasized in Matsen and Torvik (2005). The debt overhang ensued after commodity prices collapsed in the 1980s, when these countries found it hard to service their debt, and this jeopardized domestic investment and growth. These very same nations had perhaps made unwise domestic investments in less productive areas that did not aid future growth prospects. Once again, there are successful and unsuccessful resource-abundant nations.

In summary, evidence for the purely economically based resource curse is mixed. It may depend upon the time period analysed, as it is a recent phenomenon. Also, it is not a universal malaise; the right policies in a good institutional setting will lead to the avoidance of the curse. We now turn to the political economy of resource rents.

2.4.2 Political Economy of Resource Rents

As noted above, good quality institutions are crucial to fostering growth in the long term. They may be even more important than policies, whose effect is more short term; in any case good or the right policies will be largely ineffective in a poor institutional environment. It has also been suggested that a nation's endowments may have something to do with the determination of its institutions. In this sub-section we examine political economy mechanisms underlying the resource curse.

2.4.2.1 Theory
In a nutshell the negative effects of resource rents from a political economy perspective arise when it leads to rent seeking and corruption, which has a destructive effect on normal productive investment and hence growth. All of this depends upon the incentives that are presented to political leaders, because in certain circumstances they may choose unenlightened rent

seeking policies that suit them and a narrow interest group. In a different environment they could decide to be more benevolent (see Auty and Gelb, 2001). In both instances their behaviour is perfectly rational, except that in the former case it is in conflict with long-term national development. There is also the further possibility that they may deliberately undermine institutions and/or institutional development, so as to further their own ends. We may organize our theoretical discussion along the lines of rent seeking induced by bad institutions, and the impact of resource rents on future institutional development. The former refers to rent seeking in an institutional environment that encourages it and is already quite corrupt; the latter refers to either a deliberate attempt to subvert institutional restraints, such that kleptocracy can flourish, or creating a set of incentives that prevent the development of good institutions. When we come to the empirical examination of these phenomena, the theoretical distinction between the harm caused by malfunctioning institutions already present, and bad institutions created as a result of resource rents almost become observationally equivalent.

With regard to the first type of channel described above, that of rent seeking, in an enabling environment for these activities, mention can be made of a theory of the optimal allocation of talent, as analysed in Murphy, Shleifer and Vishny (1991). The idea is that talent can focus either on production or predation and corruption. This decision is a function of the relative returns to these two activities; predation may be more attractive when there is a wealth of natural resource rents. Capturable resource rents can lead to rent seeking behaviour; revenues and royalties from oil or mineral resources are much more readily appropriable when compared to the income flows from agricultural commodities. Increases in the availability of resource rents following a boom in their world prices can increase the appetite for resource rents among certain individuals or groups within society.

Lane and Tornell (1996) postulate that many societies have powerful interest groups that are coalitions formed in order to extract rents or a tribute from the rest of society. They could exist for historical reasons. Transfers to these groups are effected at the expense of others, and it sometimes even diminishes the general productivity of the economy. Resource booms and windfalls increase the appetite for transfers within these powerful coalitions by a factor that is more than proportionate to the size of the boom. These groups become greedier, and demand an even larger share of national income. This is known as a voracity effect (Lane and Tornell, 1996); a similar mechanism is described as the rentier effect by Ross (2001).

Furthermore, entrepreneurs may choose to become corrupt rent seekers rather than engage in the ordinary business of production, and this constitutes a major diversion of talent away from production (see also Torvik, 2002). Moreover, in some societies rent seeking is more widespread than others, depending on the institutional environment, referred to as grabber friendly institutions by Mehlum, Moene and Torvik (2006), as opposed to producer friendly institutions. In Murshed's (2004) theoretical model, corruption or rent seeking not only detracts from normal production, but can even diminish the availability of productive capital over time, and a lower capital stock is what causes the eventual decline in growth. Unlike recent papers in this genre, it has explicit micro–macro theoretical properties, with an explicit macroeconomic model of growth collapse. Murshed models an explicit rent seeking game where there can be increasing returns to scale in rent seeking, related to institutional quality. The lower the quality of institutions and the poorer the governance the more profitable it is to engage in rent seeking. Thus, not only is rent seeking made explicitly endogenous to institutional quality, but innovatively there can be increasing returns to scale in this activity. The extent of the rent seeking also depends on the available quantity of capturable resource rents, as in Torvik (2002). This encourages more players to enter this game, with more wasteful consequences for the economy, including the macroeconomic growth collapse (details are given in the appendix to this chapter).

Anderson and Aslaksen (2007) find that there is no resource curse for parliamentary democracies, in contrast to presidential systems. Although the result is an empirical finding, it also has theoretical overtones. Essentially, it is related to the fact that presidential systems concentrate more power in one person, and are therefore more factional and rent seeking. The presidential system implies more rent extraction by politicians, a larger public sector, and public spending targeted in favour of powerful groups rather than broad based spending programmes. The problem with this work is that many so-called Westminster-style prime ministerial systems in the developing world are actually quite presidential in practice,[16] as there is a weak separation of powers, combined with clientelism and factionalism.

Robinson and Torvik (2005) also argue that increased resource rents encourage politicians in factional (such as those driven by tribal allegiances) or clientelist (patronage politics) societies to invest in 'white elephant' projects. These are projects that are inherently loss making, but once the sunk cost is incurred, the project is implemented. Despite the fact that they are loss making and actually may be growth retarding in the long term, they are nevertheless adopted because they act as a commitment

---

[16]   Such as Bangladesh between 1991 and 2007, wrongly coded as Prime Ministerial.

device with the faction or support group essential to the politician's political survival. Obviously, it is this client group who benefit from the white elephants that are so costly to the national exchequer.

Caselli and Cunningham (2007) outline a taxonomy of possible situations that shape rulers' incentives. It is based on countries or institutional settings: (1) that are relatively more centralized (ruled by a dictator or small elite) compared to decentralized cases (with wider political participation; and (2) where there is a budget constraint, in contrast to situations where there are no limits to resources to be spent. They also characterize situations where a public good needs to be provided (akin to Findlay and Clarida, 1994) to increase the productivity of the non-resource productive sector; situations where there is effort (creating moral hazard problems) that needs to be exercised by leaders; and also leaders who want to maximize rents accruing to themselves and not national welfare in the context of a limited probability of continuing in power. A sudden natural resource windfall increases the value of staying in power indefinitely as there is more to loot at present and in the future. What happens then depends upon the leader's incentives; consider the types that follow:

- *The busy leader*: this is a constrained leader in a centralized system, who has to allocate effort in the sense of moral hazard into actions that lead to economic development and efforts to stay in power, which could include spending resources on political repression. An increase in natural resource revenues detracts from development effort, and cause a decline in per capita income. If the leader is unconstrained it raises the value of staying in power, and a resource boom will cause him to engage in more repression, although spending resources and effort on development also has a chance of increasing if both activities (repression and development) are complementary. Similarly, political support and aid from the West during the cold war and the more recent war on terror could tip the balance in favour of more repression relative to development effort. Note that political patronage in relatively decentralized and partially democratic systems can be a substitute both for repression and broad based economic development. The question is what cements relationships between the patron and client: a common ethnicity based on religion, language or tribal affinity, or other forms of commitment devices such as inefficient projects, as in Robinson and Torvik (2005).
- *The visionary leader*: this person may spend more resources on development if it increases his chances of survival, as in the case of Suharto in Indonesia, but may do the opposite if it lowers

the perceived probability of his survival, as in the case of Zaire's Mobutu.

- *The resigned leader*: this leader may see that following a resource boom his chances of future survival are low because others will try to overthrow him, so that he becomes resigned. In effect it has raised his discount rate for the future, and he will engage in less productive investment in development in order to survive.

- *The lazy leader*: large windfalls, as in the Gulf, can give leaders enough resources to do everything. They may spend less time governing and more on leisure. Alternatively, in poorer countries they could let the rest of the country languish in poverty as long as they enjoy a lavish lifestyle.

In connection with the second theoretical mechanism, where resource rents explicitly hamper institutional development, authors such as Karl (1999) have described the spending behaviour of oil-rich economies as 'petromania', referring to irresponsible consumption following oil booms. For example, it has been suggested that in Angola more than US$1 billion of oil revenues vanished per year through corruption in the period 1996 to 2001. More generally, a wealth of mineral resources or plantation based production can spawn extractive and non-developmental institutions that eventually become entrenched (Sokoloff and Engerman, 2000). Ross (2001) argues that resource rents, particularly oil revenues, could retard democratic development. A recent empirical study by the International Monetary Fund (IMF, 2005) also suggests that institutional quality could be damaged by the presence of fuel exports.

Acemoglu and Robinson (2006) model underdevelopment as caused by political elites blocking technological and institutional development because such developments may erode their incumbency advantage. This is more likely when rents from maintaining power are high, such as where public income is derived from natural resources. Robinson, Verdier and Torvik (2006) show how politicians have a short time horizon because they discount the future by the probability that they will remain in power, which is damaging from a social perspective. With more resources, the future utility of having political power will increase, and as a result politicians will change policies so that the probability of their remaining in power increases. To do so they create a bloated public sector, rather like the white elephants in Robinson and Torvik (2005).

2.4.2.2 Cross-sectional evidence

Mehlum, Moene and Torvik (2006) find that when they interact natural resource abundance with the quality of institutions in a growth regression, the resultant coefficient is significant. This means that natural resource abundance has adverse effects only in the presence of poor institutions. Their analysis, however, is purely cross-sectional, and they do not take into account the potential reverse causality between institutional quality and growth (both of which have a causal effect on the other). Collier and Goderis (2007) use an error correction panel data regression model, which is both dynamic and addresses reverse causality, to differentiate long- and short-term effects of commodity price booms on economic growth. They find that commodity booms have a positive short-term effect on output, but adverse long-term effects. The long-term effects are confined to 'high-rent', non-agricultural commodities, by differentiating commodity prices between agricultural (diffuse) and non-agricultural (point) goods. Within the latter group, they also find that the resource curse is avoided by countries with sufficiently good institutions, by: (1) including an interaction term between the commodity price index and a dummy for good institutions (with Portugal as the benchmark); and (2) separating the regressions into two groups that differentiate countries with bad and good governance.

Collier and Hoeffler (2007) unpack democracy into electoral competition and checks and balances, and examine their interaction with natural resource rents (as a share of GDP) in determining GDP growth. The blend between resource rents and strong electoral competition is growth reducing, while the mix of resource rents and strong checks and balances yield growth enhancing outcomes. For example, they allude to the fact that in resource-rich regions of Nigeria, strong electoral competition results in the elected executive avoiding taxation so as to circumvent the need for accountability to the electorate. They argue that while the 'neocon' agenda is to promote democracy through electoral competition, in fact what are needed are checks and balances on the executive.[17] Democracy without constraints on the executive could be harmful.

Aoun (2006) studies growth between 1980 and 2000 in a cross-section of countries, including developed and developing countries. A number of oil-rich countries are included in her analysis, but crucially the only oil-rich Middle Eastern country present in the study is Kuwait. She enters the ratio of oil rent (the difference between the price obtained for oil and the cost of extraction times output) over national income, as an explanatory variable for growth. In simple regressions, she finds a negative and statistically significant effect for oil rents, but this significance vanishes when data on institutional quality (corruption, bureaucratic quality, democracy) is

---

[17] The data for democracy is based on Polity, and the data for checks and balances is at http://econ.worldbank.org/view.php?type=18&id=25467.

introduced. This means that oil rents exert a negative influence only where institutional quality is poor. This is an interesting finding despite the fact that her econometric analysis is seriously flawed: she does not control for the endogeneity (or reverse causality) between growth and institutions, as growth impacts on the quality of institutions as well as the other way around; she utilizes only a simple cross-sectional technique and not panel data methods that take the time dimension into account; she does not control for the effects of extreme cases or outliers on the sample.

Ross (2001) finds that countries rich in mineral resources, particularly oil, do not make a smooth transition to democracy, or at least their score on an index of democracy tends to be low. The reasons he identifies are the following. There is a lack of 'modernization' as economic wealth does not translate into social and cultural change. Secondly, there is a repression effect, mineral- and oil-rich states can engage in higher levels of military and internal security expenditure to suppress dissent. Thirdly, public goods may be provided alongside low taxes because resource rents are the main source of revenue for the state. Taxation normally results in eventual pressures from the taxed public to introduce democracy. Finally, and most importantly there is a rentier effect. Revenues from oil and mineral resources create rents that can be utilized to bribe the population into acquiescing to authoritarianism. By contrast, Smith (2004) finds that oil-rich economies exhibit a great deal of political regime durability, arguing that the stability of the political system cannot be accounted for by repression, but that oil economies form stable domestic coalitions implying the absence of strongly negative rentier-type effects.

In their cross-sectional econometric analysis, Isham et al. (2005) find that point-sourced economies identified as exporters of oil, mineral and plantation based crops have lower growth rates compared to diffuse (agricultural) and manufactured exporters in the 1975–97 period because of the poorer governance (based on the Kaufmann indicators mentioned above) engendered by a fuel, mineral or plantation dependent economy. The challenge is to extend the pure cross-sectional econometric analysis so that it has a time dimension, and delve deeper into the role of different types of resource endowment on institutional formation. The Mavrotas, Murshed and Torres (2007) estimation is, however, one of the few panel data analyses in this connection. As with Isham et al. (2005), they instrument for endogeneity problems. Their results suggest that both point-source and diffuse-type natural resource endowments retard the development of democracy (measured by Polity) and good governance (Fraser Institute data), which in turn hampers economic growth. So there is a more widespread resource curse, valid for both endowment types. Point-sourced economies have a more negative impact on governance, and governance is more important for growth compared to democracy. Diffuse economies appear to slow down democratic development fractionally more than point-sourced economies. We should not be tempted into concluding that point-sourced endowments are better for democratic development, because that is patently not the case.

The resource curse of point-sourced endowments definitely looms large, as it is more growth retarding via even poorer governance than are diffuse natural resources. Manufacturing and manufactured goods exports do promote better governance and democracy. This in turn helps to explain the superior growth performance of manufactured-goods exporting nations. Not only is the presence of manufactured exports an indication of a more diversified and growing economy, but this may be so because these countries have better institutions of governance and higher levels of democracy.

Brunnschweiler and Bulte (2008b) challenge the notion of resource curse that relates natural resource endowment with bad economic outcomes in their cross-sectional analysis. Compared with previous empirical studies on resource curse, the paper makes a significant innovation by differentiating between resource dependence (RD) and resource abundance (RA), definitions that were used interchangeably in many previous studies. Their measure of resource dependence is resource exports to GDP and mineral exports to GDP; the per capita value of natural resource and sub-soil asset stocks is their resource abundance variable. They correct for endogeneity in both resource dependence and institutions, using the following instruments: the constitution (presidential versus parliamentarian) and trade openness for resource dependence, and absolute latitude for institutions. They find that resource dependence has no significant effect on growth (although the sign is still negative), contrary to many earlier findings regarding the resource curse. By contrast, they find that resource abundance has significantly positive effects on growth either directly in a growth regression or indirectly through institutional improvements (measured by the rule of law and government effectiveness from the Kaufmann data set). In short, greater resource abundance leads to better quality institutions and more rapid growth, a counter-intuitive finding that is echoed by Smith (2004) in his findings about oil wealth and its negative relation to repression and positive relation to regime survival.

In many ways the Brunnschweiler and Bulte (2008b) results are understandable when one makes a distinction between resource abundance and dependence. As pointed out earlier, a resource abundant nation may not be very resource dependent, if it has wisely chosen to, and has had time to diversify its production structure through economic growth, which also raises the living standards of the citizenry. Indeed, resource dependence may be a reflection of the failure to grow and develop good economic and political institutions, along with the associated poverty, inequality and poor human development outcomes.

2.4.2.3 Country experience

What makes a resource-rich country's economy prosper or falter over the inevitable boom and bust cycle that resource rents imply? The literature reviewed above suggests that the political economy of resource rents, and the (short- to medium-term) economic policies adopted, make up the two main factors underlying success or failure.

With regard to the political economy of development strategies, Dunning (2005) analyses choices by rulers regarding the future growth path of the economy in the context of natural resource abundance. He compares Mobutu's Zaire (1965–97) to Suharto's Indonesia (1965–98) and Botswana during the same period. In Botswana, revenues from Kimberlite (deep mine shaft) diamonds were very stable, due to Botswana's unique relationship with the South African diamond company De Beers and its important position as a major supplier. It did not need to diversify its economy. But it chose a developmental path because of the mature nature of political elites there. In Indonesia and Zaire resource flows were volatile. In one case the dictator (Suharto) chose diversification and growth enhancing strategies, as well as policies aimed at equalization and poverty reduction to contain political opposition. In the other case (Zaire, now DRC), Mobutu did not, because he felt that diversification and investment in infrastructure would loosen his grip on power and strengthen political opposition to him based on ethnicity. The same has been argued for Nkrumah in Ghana. Both Mobutu and Suharto in particular owed their existence, at least initially, to the patronage of the USA and Western powers. Perhaps, in East Asia greater fears of communism strengthened benevolence in dictators (South Korea, Taiwan, Singapore and Indonesia), whereas in Africa a certain type of factionalism dominated policy making and politics, retarding growth enhancing economic diversification and infrastructural development.

When we come to the political economy of resource rents itself, Snyder and Bhavnani (2005) argue that the causal mechanism between rent seeking behaviour and resource rents may lie in a government revenue effect. This implies examining how the state obtains its revenues: whether taxing the mineral sector is important to the state or not. Even if a lootable sector exists it may not be as crucial to the state's coffers if other revenue sources exist side by side. Additionally, the mode of extraction matters: whether it is artisanal or industrial. Only the former makes resources lootable. Consider Sierra Leone. Prior to 1985 its alluvial diamonds were extracted in an industrial fashion rather than by artisans, making it non-lootable.

The country did not collapse into civil war until after that. Finally, and most importantly, how governments spend their revenue matters: if the state spends its revenues on social welfare and growth enhancing investment, conflict is less likely than if it appropriates revenues for factional and kleptocratic purposes.

It should be noted that rent seeking, bribery and corruption are not just about the quality of domestic institutions in resource-rich nations. There are always two sides to the corruption coin, the demand side and the supply side; this principle applies also in the case of resource rents. Large bribes to governing elites, as well as the violent manipulation of governments in the global South by companies and states in the global North in order to gain commercial advantage by their extractive multinationals was very common during the cold war, and have not quite withered away in our unipolar world.[18] Superpower politics during the cold war, and interference by the world's only remaining superpower (the USA) has an important part to play in determining the historical path of institutional development, whose legacy can be more negative in some cases (Zaire), and less negative in others (Indonesia).

This leaves us with policies towards long-term growth, which have a shorter or more medium-term impact. Many of these choices are not as deliberate as we might presume; they are often accidentally adopted or are the outcome of mixed motivations on the part of those deciding on policy. Success may be related to serendipity rather than design. It is, nevertheless, instructive to contrast cases of success such as Botswana and Malaysia after the 1970s on the one hand, against failures such as the Democratic Republic of Congo (Zaire), on the other hand. In the Malaysian case (Mahani, 2001), the government: (1) ended up redistributing income, via government expenditure policies targeting ethnic Malays, who were the poorer community, thus avoiding ethnic conflict at least after 1969; (2) invested in infrastructure and human capital; and (3) pursued policies of competitive industrialization, based initially on foreign direct investment. Botswana avoided factionalism through political consensus. Botswana's economy is, however, considerably less diversified than Malaysia's, providing us with one instance of a high growth, conflict free undiversified economy relying on a capital intensive natural resource (Kimberlite diamonds). Thus, the most important policy goal involves moving away from the nation's dependence on unprocessed natural resource exports, as in the

---

[18] Historically, multinational firms such as the British and Dutch East India Companies literally established empires to further their commercial interests and profitability, even running formidable military establishments (armies and navies) to protect their trading interests.

case of Malaysia and Thailand. These include investment in skills (starting with primary education and universal literacy) that take a longer time to mature, policies to acquire foreign direct investment leading to technology transfer, and above all fostering industrialization that is internationally competitive.

Finland and Norway are two examples of successful European resource-rich countries; the first in its timber resources, and the latter in oil. Finland's current economic success is not built on forestry, but rather revolves around high technology mobile telephony associated with Nokia. By contrast, in Norway oil continues to be the major export, and it does not have high technology manufactured goods sectors comparable to Sweden and Finland. Consequently, a few signs of Dutch disease are discernible. The overall size of the public sector, however, is not significantly different in Norway from in neighbouring Sweden. However, all Nordic countries, which had resource dependent economies at some point, passed through transitions to fully fledged democracies and capitalist industrialization prior to any resource booms. They, therefore, avoided rent seeking surges by special interest groups, which tend to occur in institutionally flawed situations, as pointed out by Torvik (2007).

Another point, and one that is under-researched, is to do with ownership of resource rents. Gylfason (2001a) points out that in Norway the state has not only title to the country's oil wealth, but has had command over 80% of the resource rent since 1980. The revenue is invested in the Norwegian Petroleum Fund, akin to a trust fund for the benefit of current and future generations, but its full use is still impending. Such a policy yields a double dividend; it minimizes macroeconomic problems associated with boom and bust cycles and allows consumption smoothing into the future when resource revenues dry out. A call for setting up similar trust funds is standard policy advice at present.

2.5   CONCLUSIONS: GROWTH AND CONFLICT

Thus, the jury is out on the issue of the negative effects of rich mineral/fuel endowments on institutional determination. After balancing the negative and positive effects, not all societies necessarily experience the disadvantaging political economy effects of resource rents. This will crucially depend upon the past history of institutions, its colonial heritage, and the type of incentives (benevolent or malevolent from a national perspective) faced by its leadership, including the influence of cold war and war on terror geopolitics. Resource rents may have an important part to play in determining political and economic institutions that are important in determining long-term growth and development prospects, although the causal links are far from clear cut. The consensus is that their role has been negative for most developing countries in recent times, although the causal mechanisms (policies and institutions) are the subject of considerable debate. The resource curse was certainly absent when one looks at the economic history of countries such as the USA, Canada and Australia, perhaps because they had better institutions to begin with that helped them transform resource abundance to lower (unprocessed) resource dependence, along with a rising standard of living.

It is also worthwhile reminding ourselves that most indicators of human development and well being are highly correlated with per capita income, which means that for poor countries growth leading to increased per capita income (and poverty reduction) may provide the necessary conditions for improved human development on all counts. As we shall see in the subsequent chapters, greed, grievance and institutional failure (the decline of the social contract) are the main explanatory factors for civil war; if so, they are intimately related to growth. Institutions impact on growth in both directions: good institutions foster growth, growth also improves institutional quality. Similarly, the influence of growth on conflict is also bi-directional, the lack of growth enhances conflict risk, and conflict too may have a negative impact on growth, at least while the conflict lasts (many contemporary civil wars are protracted low intensity wars).

To get an empirical feel for the growth endowments–polity/institutions nexus, and its relation to conflict, a descriptive look at the data may be in order. Table 2.4, based on Murshed (2006), gives us 17 countries with the highest conflict incidence since 1960,[19] along with their average annual long-term growth rates of per capita income accompanied by the typology of the economy and the most frequently occurring regime type. In Table 2.4, we compare growth rates, the combined democracy and autocracy score known as Polity, endowment type and conflict intensity or incidence in selected developing countries during the period 1965–2000. The Polity score is an imperfect proxy for institutional capacity and governance, but we have good time series data on these. This is coded 1 for autocracies (those with an autocracy score below -4), 3 for democracies (for democracy scores above 4) and 2 for anocracies that have both democratic and autocratic characteristics (with scores of between -4 and 4). The endowment typology is based upon a country's principal exports, and is subject to change. Note that countries can have more than one year of civil war

---

[19] I exclude Israel with 49 years, as it is a rich country, as well as Cambodia (36 years) and Yemen (23 years) because of the paucity of economic data.

Table 2.4 Conflict, growth, polity and economic typology in selected countries

Country	Conflict incidence 1960–2000	Most frequent regime type	Annual average per capita income growth rate % 1965–99	Economic typology
Burma (Myanmar)	177	1	1.5	Diffuse, point
India	104	3	2.4	Manufacturing
Ethiopia	81	1	−0.3	Coffee/cocoa
Philippines	59	1;2;3	0.9	Diffuse, manufacturing
Iraq	57	1	−3.5	Point
Angola	43	1	−2.1	Point
Iran	41	1;2	−1.0	Point
Algeria	37	1;2	1.0	Point
Chad	36	1	−0.6	Point
Colombia	35	3	2.1	Coffee/cocoa
Indonesia	32	1	4.8	Point, manufacturing
Guatemala	31	1;2	0.7	Coffee/cocoa
Sudan	31	1;2;3	0.5	Diffuse, point
South Africa	31	2	0.0	Point
Mozambique	27	1	1.3	Diffuse
Uganda	23	1;2	2.5	Coffee/cocoa
Sri Lanka	22	3	3.0	Diffuse, manufacturing

Source: Murshed (2006, Table 4).

in any given calendar year if there are several conflicts taking place within the nation simultaneously, as in Burma or India.[20] This does not imply anything about conflict intensity, which is measured by fatalities.

Only five of these high conflict incidence nations reported in Table 2.4 have a per capita income growth rate in excess of 2% per annum in the long term: Indonesia, India, Sri Lanka, Colombia and Uganda. Generally speaking, poor growth performers have more conflict years in Table 2.4. Only four economies (India, the Philippines, Sri Lanka and Mozambique)

---

[20] Conflict data is taken from the PRIO/Uppsala data set described in Chapter 1.

have not been point-sourced (mineral/fuel exporting) or coffee/cocoa economies (the Burmese conflicts are fuelled by trade in illegal substances, which cannot be reported here, because of data paucity). This lends some support to the arguments about conflict and its association with natural resources across countries. Only three point-sourced countries and four coffee/cocoa economies did not descend into some form of civil war, as noted in Murshed (2006). Diffuse economies also have conflict; examples of the high incidence of civil wars occurring in diffuse economies are in South Asia, the Philippines and Burma, as well as Mozambique and Zimbabwe in Africa. In total, eight out of thirty diffuse economies have avoided civil war, a record that is better than for point-sourced and coffee/cocoa based economies. Notwithstanding the case of India, manufacturing exporters are least likely to experience outright civil war. Perhaps this is because they have the best growth rates and institutional quality. They are also more diversified economies that are able to withstand commodity price and national income fluctuations that make growth failure more likely.

Many of the transitions in regime type from autocracy to anocracy to democracy (during 1960–2000) are described in Murshed (2006). Multiple switches in all directions are possible, and not just from autocracy to democracy. Nevertheless, only five out of the seventeen nations with a high conflict incidence have ever been democracies with a democracy score over 4. Democracy, even stable democracy, does not guarantee the absence of armed conflict, both of the secessionist and rebel varieties, as the examples of India, Colombia, Sri Lanka and the Philippines illustrate. Autocracies also fall into conflict; nevertheless, stable autocracies such as China and Singapore have avoided civil war, as did Taiwan and South Korea, which became democracies recently. Despite outliers such as India, Colombia and Saudi Arabia, most conflict-prone countries are neither stable democracies nor autocracies, lending support to the Hegre et al. (2001) finding that conflict risk is greatest when regime types are in transition, say from autocracy to democracy, rather than in established democracies or autocracies. We have seen that democracy without checks and balances could be harmful to growth prospects in resource-rich countries (Collier and Hoeffler, 2007). Similarly, democracy based solely on electoral competition, without adequate constraints on the executive such as an independent judiciary, could be conflict risk enhancing in all developing countries. I will explore these issues further in Chapter 5.

I now turn to a more systematic cross-country analysis between growth and various conflict and political variables. In Table 2.5, I report OLS regressions where the dependent variable is the annual average growth rate, 1975–2005. I do not claim that the results are robust, due to reverse

Table 2.5   Long run growth rate (OLS)

	Regression 1	Regression 2	Regression 3
Battle deaths	−0.00002*** [0.00001]		
Mean Polity		0.09681*** [0.03033]	
Polity coefficient of variation	−0.94529** [0.44722]		−0.36228 [1.46787]
Exports mode value			0.92398* [0.48239]
Constant	1.64923*** [0.29097]	0.04643 [0.35114]	−0.34244 [0.98131]
Observations	134	135	87
R-squared	0.09	0.08	0.12

Notes: Standard errors in brackets.
* significant at 10%; ** significant at 5%; *** significant at 1%.

causality and potential endogeneity problems between growth, conflict and institutional variables on the right-hand side. Yet, many of the results are indicative of the causal mechanisms in place. The mean Polity indicator is the mean of the combined autocracy and democracy Polity score for each nation. The Polity coefficient of variation for any country is the ratio of the standard deviation to the mean of the Polity score, and is a measure of regime-type volatility, such as switches from autocracy to democracy, vice versa and the emergence of electoral violence, which lower the Polity score. Battle deaths refer to the number of battle-related deaths in civil war, in countries with conflict for 1960–2002, and are drawn from the PRIO/Uppsala data set. The export mode value is derived from the Mavrotas, Murshed and Torres (2007) data set, and is coded 1 for point, 2 for coffee, 3 for diffuse and 4 for manufacturing. Thus, a higher value indicates a more diversified, developed and less resource dependent economy.

The results may be summarized as follows: (1) battle deaths or civil war (regression 1) are growth retarding, although the sign is small; (2) greater democratic values (mean polity) raise growth (regression 2); (3) political regime instability (coefficient of variation) contributes significantly to the lack of growth (regression 1) even in the presence of civil war with a large coefficient on this parameter; and (4) a more manufactured export structure and less reliance on minerals and fuels raises growth significantly

Table 2.6   Probability of conflict (Probit)

	Regression 1	Regression 2	Regression 3
GDP growth rate	−0.05900**	−0.04494*	−0.04603*
	[0.02136]	[0.02020]	[0.02131]
Exports mode value	−0.04248	−0.03680	−0.04690
	[0.04261]	[0.04064]	[0.04326]
Mean Polity		−0.01724*	
		[0.00760]	
Polity coefficient of variation			0.21029+
			[0.12538]
Observations	88	87	87

Notes: Standard errors in brackets.
+ significant at 10%; * significant at 5%; ** significant at 1%.

(regression 3), and when included is more meaningful than regime instabil-ity. The findings corroborate other empirical studies. Collier (1999) finds that during civil wars per capita GDP declines at an annual rate of 2.2% relative to its counterfactual.

Murdoch and Sandler (2004) assess the adverse impact of civil war on a country's growth performance at home as well as in neighbouring coun-tries. They find that a civil war at home can reduce a country's growth by 31% in the long run and by 85% in the short run. This difference in impact highlights how time allows an economy to correct itself. Moreover, each additional nearby civil war can lower growth by approximately 30% of the effect in the host country in the long run and by 24% of the effect in the host country in the short run. Thus, a country in a region with three or more adjacent civil wars may be equally affected as a country experi-encing a civil war itself. Koubi (2005) combines inter-state war and civil war together and finds that the severity of war has a negative effect on growth generally. The severity and the duration of war, however, are positively correlated with post-war medium-term growth, which is termed the Phoenix factor (Organski and Kugler, 1977), and may be due to the spurt in growth that follows the complete cessation of hostilities. Most civil wars nowadays have a protracted duration and are interspersed with many short-lived peace accords, which we will be concerned with in Chapter 4.

Turning to probable causes of civil war, Table 2.6 gives us Probit regres-sions about the probability or risk of civil war as the dependent variable (coded 1 for civil war using the low 25 battle deaths per year definition, and 0 if not), again based on the PRIO/Uppsala data set. Growth significantly and negatively affects civil war risk in all three regressions, as does mean Polity and its coefficient of variation (in regressions 2 and 3). Thus, the lack of growth, less democracy and regime instability all enhance civil war risk. A less diversified export pattern based more on minerals and fuels raises the probability of civil war, but the coefficients are not statistically significant.

The negative effect of growth on conflict always retains its significance, which is consistent with the findings in Miguel, Satyanath and Sergenti (2004). By treating economic growth as endogenous, and by using the rainfall rate as the instrument for growth in 41 African countries during 1980–99, Miguel, Satyanath and Sergenti (2004) find that growth is negatively and strongly related to civil war. A negative growth shock of 5% increases the likelihood of civil war by one-half in the following year. Surprisingly, the impact of growth shocks on conflict is not significantly different in richer, more democratic, or more ethnically diverse countries, which might be because the sample is homogeneously composed of African states that are roughly at a similar level of political and economic development. However, using dynamic panel data methods, Starr (2005) finds that the negative effect of growth on civil war is considerably smaller.

Among the many determinants of civil war, there is a consensus that the level of income (per capita GDP) is the most robust predictor of civil war risk, and is almost always included in any conflict regression; see Ross's (2004b) review of 14 cross-country empirical conflict studies as an example. An exception to this rule can be found in the work of Djankov and Reynal-Querol (2007), who emphasize the role of institutions in determining civil wars. Institutions are proxied by: (1) the protection of property rights; (2) the rule of law; and (3) the efficiency of the legal system. Institutions are endogenized, and colonial origins affect civil wars through their legacy on institutions. The instruments for institutions are colonial origin dummies and the settler mortality rates, similar to Acemoglu, Johnson and Robinson (2001). They find that once institutions are included in their purely cross-sectional conflict regressions, the initial level of per capita income becomes insignificant. This does not, however, invalidate the saliency of (the lack) of growth in determining conflict because institutional quality and growth go hand in hand. In other words, good institutions and per capita income are highly co-linear. And, good institutions contribute to growth (and vice versa), as the discussion in this chapter has demonstrated.

We are now in a position to examine the greed and grievance theories for conflict onset in the next chapter.

APPENDIX: GROWTH COLLAPSE WITH RENT SEEKING

The innovative feature of the model that follows is that the macroeconomic collapse that comes from a reduction of the capital stock has micro-foundations in rent seeking contests. We begin with a competitive game of rent seeking in the spirit of Tullock (1967), although our primary motivation arises from the natural resource revenue induced rentier effect described by Ross (2001). In the Tullock framework, several agents compete for rents in each period that resource revenues are available. The competition to capture this entails a cost, be that bribery, lobbying expenditure and so on.

Let P represent the prize that each rent seeking agent is attempting to seize. This prize corresponds to the contestable or appropriable revenue from resource rents, and for simplicity Tullock-type rent seeking contests assume a winner-take-all situation. This does not preclude collusive group behaviour, as long as groups compete with each other. Each agent's probability of success will depend on their own rent seeking expenditure relative to all others. The expected utility (E) of an agent (i) in a symmetrical setting can take the form:

$$E_i = \pi_i P - c_i \tag{2.1}$$

where π is the probability of winning based upon the contest success function, and c represents lobbying costs or expenditures. The contest success function is given by:

$$\pi_i(c_i, c_j, s) = \frac{c_i^s}{c_1^s + c_2^s}; i = 1, 2; j \neq i \tag{2.2}$$

In this example there are only two agents, $i = 1, 2$. The crucial parameter s represents the 'efficiency or productivity' of lobbying expenditure or bribery, if $s > 1$, there is increasing returns to scale in such expenditure. If that is so, under weak institutions of governance, where the law is honoured more in the breach than in the keeping, lobbying expenditure is even more productive as far as rent seekers are concerned. In many ways, s can be characterized to be negatively related to good governance and institutional quality, with $s > 1$ being a sign of very poor institutional environment. Wick and Bulte (2006) also incorporate increasing returns to scale in connection with resource rents where the agent's choice is between rent seeking and conflict. My set-up is different, the increasing returns to scale emanate from poor institutional quality and not the mere 'pointiness' of resources. My analysis has some similarities to the grabber friendly institutions described in Mehlum, Moene and Torvik (2006), but I incorporate increasing returns to scale to that activity, and the possibility of an attrition game. Other theoretical papers in the natural resource induced rent seeking genre do not model the possibility of a variable institutional environment, which may encourage further rent seeking. Thus, it is not only the total available prize (P) that determines rent seeking, but also that the institutional environment may promote further knavery. This is parameterized by s in my model.

Substituting 2.2 into 2.1 and maximizing with respect to c_i we find:

$$c_i = \frac{sP}{4}; i = 1, 2 \tag{2.3}$$

Equation 2.3 gives us the Cournot–Nash equilibrium level of lobbying spending by each agent. The substitution of 2.3 into 2.1 yields the following expected utility:

$$E_i = \frac{P}{2} - \frac{sP}{4} \tag{2.4}$$

The above expression becomes negative if $s > 2$. If this is so, it will lead to an even more socially wasteful war of attrition game, where the object is to make one's opponents exit the rent seeking contest because an opponent's very presence yields negative expected utility.

Lobbying or rent seeking expenditure is wasteful and detracts from the capital stock. Total lobbying expenditures may cause a decline in the capital stock, as investment in capital declines. At this juncture we introduce two definitions which we intend to utilize in the macro-model of growth collapse:

$$\sum c_i = z_0, \, and \cdots P = z_1 \tag{2.5}$$

We now turn to the macro model, akin to the Ramsey (1928) model, with modifications as to the cost of capital installation along the lines suggested by Tobin (1969). The economy is guided by choices made by a representative agent and all variables are given in per capita values. The growth in population is assumed to be constant. The equilibrium level of the capital stock in the steady state implicitly defines growth rates, and a fall in the equilibrium capital stock implies a decline in the growth rate. Growth collapses are associated with periods of declining capital accumulation. An 'infinitely' lived individual who maximizes utility at each time period (t) according to:

$$\text{Max } U(t) = \int_t^{\infty} u(C(t))\exp(-it) \, dt \tag{2.6}$$

where utility (U or u) depends on consumption, C; exp is the exponential operator; and the real interest rate is i. Maximization is subject to two budget constraints at t:

$$\dot{D}(t) = C(t) + I(t) + iD(t) - f(k(t)) \tag{2.7}$$

$$\dot{k}(t) = I(t) \tag{2.8}$$

We ignore the rate of depreciation. Output subject to constant returns, Y is given by:

$$Y(t) = f(k(t)) \tag{2.9}$$

The stock constraint (2.8) tells us that the rate of capital accumulation at time t is equal to investment (I) at time t. Equation 2.9 is the production function for Y (output) written in per capita fashion, k is the capital–labour ratio. Equation 2.7 is the flow constraint in an open economy. It informs us that the rate of accumulation of international debt is given by the excess of consumption (C) plus investment (I) and debt servicing (iD, where i is the interest rate and D is debt stock), over production or output ($f(k)$). This is the exact counterpart of the current account deficit, the excess of absorption over output. In the closed economy context, or with no debt, investment is equal to output minus consumption.

The current value Hamiltonian (H) is:

$$H(t) = u(C(t)) - \mu(t)\left[C(t) + I(t)\left\{ 1 + g\left(\frac{I(t)}{k(t)}\right)\right\}\right.$$
$$\left. + iD(t) - f(k(t))\right] + \mu(t)p_k I(t) \tag{2.10}$$

Here p_k is the shadow price of capital. The function inside g (.) gives us the cost of installing capital per unit of existing capital, $g' > 0$.[21] In other words, it is the cost of investment per unit of extant capital. The two co-state variables are: $\mu(t)$ and $\mu(t)p_k$.

Maximization yields the following, among other, first order conditions:

$$\frac{\delta H(t)}{\delta C(t)} = u'(C(t)) - \mu(t) = 0 \tag{2.11}$$

---

[21]   Note that p_k is akin to Tobin's (1969) q, which is the market price of capital relative to its replacement cost.

$$\frac{\delta H(t)}{\delta I(t)} = 1 + g(.) + \frac{I(t)}{k(t)} g'(.) = p_k \qquad (2.12)$$

Equation 2.11 tells us that the optimizing agent will equate the marginal utility of consumption, $u'(C(t))$ to the shadow price of consumption, μ. This means that optimal consumption is fixed in every period as it depends on μ, which is a constant (the Ramsey rule). The consumption and investment decisions are separable. We now turn to investment. Equation 2.12 informs us that the ratio of investment to the existing stock of capital is equated to the shadow price of capital (p_k). We may write the ratio of investment to capital as a function of the shadow price of capital (p_k). This will allow us to construct a steady state differential equation in k, with $g(.)$ = 0:

$$\dot{k} = I(t) = k(t) \, \varphi(p_k(t)); \varphi' > 0, \varphi(1) = 0 \qquad (2.13)$$

indicating that investment is an increasing function of the shadow price of capital (p_k). The picture regarding investment is incomplete unless we postulate an equation determining p_k. This is obtained after manipulating the first-order condition of the Hamiltonian 2.10 in connection with the second co-state variable with respect to time $(dH/d\mu(t)p_k)$. Also utilizing the fact that $d\mu(t)/dt = 0$, and $I(t)/k(t) = p_k$ from 2.13:

$$\dot{p}_k = p_k i - f'(k(t)) - \varphi(p_k(t))^2 g'(.)$$

In the steady state equilibrium $p_k = 1$, capital's shadow price is equal to its replacement cost. Given that, in the steady state, we are interested in the deviation of p_k from its steady rate value of unity, and utilizing 2.13 above, the equation above reduces to:

$$\dot{p}_k = p_k i - f'(k(t)) \qquad (2.14)$$

Equations 2.13 and 2.14 can be utilized to describe the dynamics and steady state equilibrium of the system. In order to subject the system to the effects of a resource boom we incorporate an additive and multiplicative effect to the production function in 2.9:

$$Y(t) = (1 - z_0)f(k(t)) + z_1 \qquad (2.15)$$

Here z_0 represents the diversion of a part of the capital stock from ordinary production to rent seeking activities, and z_1 is the revenue component.

They are described by equation 2.5. The revenue component can be either positive or negative. If, as in the case of some countries, resource revenues are mainly transferred abroad via corruption and other forms of leakage, then z_1 is negative in its effect on the macroeconomy. If it generates income in the domestic economy it is positive. The additive component z_1 has no effect on the marginal product of capital, and therefore no effect on investment and the capital stock. When positive, it immediately raises consumption, but not savings, by a proportionate amount. Conversely, consumption declines if revenues are negative. Adjustment in income is immediate and dramatic. In an open economy, however, the country might be able to borrow from abroad to smooth consumption with implications for future indebtedness and debt servicing. Note that the resource rents (z_1) are exogenous in the sense that they are like a pure transfer or manna from heaven. The costs to the economy (the multiplicative term z_0) are, however, an endogenous outcome of rent seeking activities described above in equations 2.1 to 2.4.

I now turn to the effects of extracted resource rents on productivity, investment and the capital stock. This occurs via the multiplicative term.[22] We postulate that rent seeking will reduce the effective marginal product of capital, due to the diversion of productive investment away from normal activities towards rent seeking, analysed in the rent seeking contest above.

In the steady state equilibrium $k = k^*$ and $p_k = 1$. Totally differentiating 2.13 and 2.14 around some steady state values, $k - k^*$ and $p_k - 1$, and utilising 2.15 we obtain the following in matrix notation:

$$\begin{bmatrix} 0 & k^*\varphi' \\ -f''(k^*) & i \end{bmatrix} \begin{bmatrix} k - k^* \\ p_k - 1 \end{bmatrix} = \begin{bmatrix} 0 \\ z_0 - 1 \end{bmatrix} d'f(k^*) \tag{2.16}$$

Note that $f''(k) < 0$. The trace is positive and the determinant is:

$$\Delta = f''(k^*)k^*\varphi' < 0 \text{ implying a saddle-path solution.}$$

$$\frac{d[k - k^*]}{d[f(k^*)]} = \frac{1 - z_0}{f''(k^*)} < 0 \tag{2.17}$$

$$\frac{d[p_k - 1]}{d[f(k^*)]} = 0 \tag{2.18}$$

It can be readily discerned that the slope of $\dot{k} = 0$, and the slope of the $\dot{p}_k = 0$ is negative from 2.16.

---

[22] This effect is similar to a decline in per worker productivity in the Solow model.

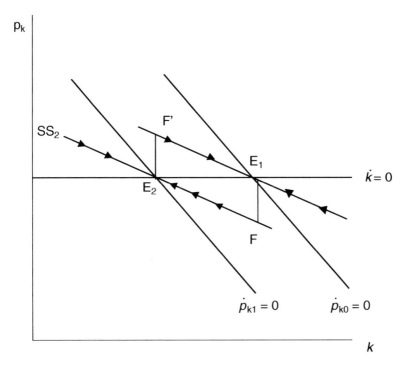

Figure 2.1   Growth collapse

In Figure 2.1 the $\dot{k} = 0$ schedule is a horizontal line. This tells us that the optimal capital stock is related to marginal productivity and not p_k. The $\dot{p}_k = 0$ line is negatively sloped as a rise in p_k increases the rate of investment, which in turn raises the capital stock (k). However, with a fixed interest rate and marginal productivity of capital, the capital stock is given at its optimal level, k^*, such that $p_k = 1$ in the steady state; hence k will decline.

When there is a negative effect on the capital stock, the economy jumps from the initial equilibrium at E_1 to the new saddle-path (SS_2) at point F. The $\dot{p}_k = 0$ schedule will then shift to the left, and the final equilibrium is at E_2. There is an initial, but not steady state, fall in the shadow price of capital. This makes the rate of investment negative between F and E_2 which, in turn, causes the capital stock to decline, prompting negative growth. The economy comes to a rest with a lower steady state capital stock and growth rate at E_2. The growth collapse occurs between F and E_2. Net output declines in the new steady state due to the combined effect of the diversion of output to rent seeking and a lower capital stock. There is also a decline in consumption associated with lower net output. Rent seeking expenditure per se is greater the higher the prize (P) in 2.1 to 2.4 or z_1 in 2.15. This implies a large amount of resource rents. But, more importantly, total rent seeking expenditure for any level of natural resource rents will be greater when the polity is more predatory, oligarchic and poor institutions abound. This means that z_0 is large in 2.5 and $s > 1$. In other situations, where natural resource revenues are more diffuse, the prize (P) in 2.1 to 2.4 could be considerably smaller (say P/n, the population being given by n). Also, in societies where many agents enter the rent seeking contest, the benefit to each of lobbying expenditure is smaller.[23] In either case, z_0 will be smaller, as $s < 1$, and the resultant negative growth effect is also diminished. A developmental state working with superior institutions that is democratic or benevolent would reduce lobbying and rent seeking expenditure. Rent seeking contests would not yield much to corrupt agents, who would be better off in productive entrepreneurial activities. In that case, natural resource revenues would not retard growth ($z_0 = 0$). It would also mean P or z_1 (the resource rents) in 2.15 would become a part of the regular production process in 2.9.

---

[23]   In the n person case, the right hand side of (2.3) is $((n-1)sP)/n^2$, smaller than the expression in (2.3).

3.   Greed and grievance

3.1   INTRODUCTION

Chapter 2 explored the conflict and growth nexus. The failure of economic growth in the long-run is intimately linked to malfunctioning institutions that create problems of their own, including a repressive polity and rampant rent seeking, which may be encouraged by the presence of certain types of resource rents. The foundations for violent conflict are laid in a low-income developing country economy where the failure of growth and economic diversification is characterized by endemic poverty, high asset and income inequality and the failure of the mechanisms for peaceful dispute resolution.[1] It is worth reminding ourselves that according to the rational choice paradigm, conflict is a result of choice. This may be myopic, as negotiated settlements which avoid the losses that ensue from war, are usually Pareto superior. Another way of stating this is that conflict is a special form of non-cooperative behaviour; other forms of less destructive non-cooperative behaviour, and cooperation, are superior to violent and therefore more costly non-cooperative interaction. But circumstances (constraints, poverty, institutional failure), mistrust (coordination failure), impatience and myopia (discounting the future) may rule out cooperation or more peaceful forms of non-cooperative negotiation, making conflict the optimal choice for group leaders who have to take into account at least some of the interests of their followers.

In recent years, two phenomena have been utilized to explain conflict onset among rational choice theorists: greed and grievance. The former is due to the influential work of Paul Collier (see Collier and Hoeffler, 2002, 2004b). According to this view, conflict reflects elite competition over valuable point-sourced natural resource rents, concealed with the figleaf of collective grievance. Additionally, rebellions need to be financially viable: civil wars supported by natural resource based rents like blood diamonds or oil, or when sympathetic diasporas provide a ready source of finance, are more likely to occur. Above all, there was the assertion that inequality played no part in adding to the risk of civil war. More recently, Paul Collier

---

[1]   The fashionable expressions for the most acute cases of these phenomena are 'fragile or failed states'.

and his associates (2003) emphasized the poverty trap: poverty makes soldiering less unattractive, more generally lowering the opportunity cost of war in poor nations. In turn, conflict serves to perpetuate poverty because of war's destructiveness; a vicious cycle of poverty–conflict–poverty ensues. Collier's views are highly influential in donor policy circles (including with ministers in charge of disbursing aid), and have received immense publicity in the Western media (*Financial Times*, *International Herald Tribune* and so on). Fearon and Laitin (2003) assert that ethnic or religious diversity makes little contribution to the risk of civil war, which is mainly caused by diminished state capacity in the context of poverty. This finding, taken together with Collier's work has a simple intuitive appeal; civil wars occur in poverty-stricken, failed states characterized by venal, corrupt and inept regimes, with the dynamics of war sustained by a motivation akin to banditry. It also provides intellectual excuses for direct, colonial style, intervention to prevent failing states from collapsing.

But in many ways, these views go against the grain. There is a long-standing position in political science that relative deprivation (Gurr, 1970) and the grievance that it produces fuels internal violence. Identity is also crucial to intra-state conflict. This is due to the collective action problem, as discussed in Olson (1965). It is difficult to mobilize large groups to undertake collective action, because of mutual mistrust, monitoring difficulties and the free-rider problem. Ethnic identities, whether based on race, language, religion, tribal affiliation or regional differences, may serve as a more effective amalgam for the purposes of group formation, compared to other forms of more transient difference that are traditionally stressed by Marxist writers, such as socioeconomic class.

The formation of enduring identities are therefore central to mobilizing groups, including the machinations of conflict entrepreneurs who organize men to fight each other (see Tilly, 1978 and Gurr, 2000). Conflict cannot proceed without the presence of palpably perceived group differences, or grievances, which may have historical dimensions. More recently, Frances Stewart (2000) has introduced the notion of horizontal inequality, the inequality between groups, rather than the inequality that may exist among an ethnically homogeneous population (vertical inequality). Indeed, it may be the case that vertical inequality in a homogeneous population, despite the class differences it engenders, does not seriously increase the risk of conflict (Collier and Hoeffler, 2004b). But that could still leave a role for group inequality (for which data is scarce), which many authors choose to ignore.

Ultimately, the greed and grievance motivations for conflict may actually be inseparable in the sense that even if one theory is better at explaining the actual onset or start of conflict, the other phenomenon is sure to follow. Furthermore, in most conflicts, once they start and as they evolve, the two phenomena used to explain the beginning of conflict almost inevitably tend to exist simultaneously. Thus, for example, it is not uncommon for a conflict linked to palpable grievances to mutate into a state where the rebels become greedy, and both greed and grievance can be seen to co-exist. This chapter critically reviews the greed and grievance explanations for conflict in sections 3.2 and 3.3 respectively. It then moves on, in section 3.4, to synthesize the arguments; demonstrating how greed and grievance may co-exist, suggesting that they are both necessary, but not sufficient, causes for the outbreak of large-scale violent conflict.

3.2   THE GREED OR RESOURCE RENT EXPLANATION FOR CONFLICT

This section shall proceed as follows: we begin with a discussion on the theory of greed for conflict in sub-section 3.2.1; this is followed by analysis of measurement issues in sub-section 3.2.2; the implications for the cross-country empirical evidence on greed are considered in 3.2.3.

3.2.1   The Theory of Greed

The greed motivation behind civil war has been disseminated and popularized by mainly purely empirical work on the causes of civil war where a cross-section of conflicts in different nations is analysed together econometrically, and greed is proxied by the availability or abundance of capturable natural resource rents. In Collier and Hoeffler (2004b) civil wars stem from the greedy behaviour of a rebel group in organizing an insurgency against the government. Greed is about opportunities faced by the rebel group. The opportunities can be disaggregated into their components: financing, recruitment and geography. The most common sources of rebel finance are the appropriation of natural resources, donations from sympathetic diasporas residing abroad, contributions from foreign states hostile to the government or multinational companies interested in the region. Natural resource wealth is the chief among these in terms of its relative importance. Recruitment is about the opportunity to induct fighting manpower; something made easier when there is a high proportion of young unemployed males in the population, in a setting of endemic poverty and poor education. Geographical situations favourable to rebel groups are mountainous terrain and other safe havens for insurgents. In short, greed simply means the economic returns from fighting, and should be distinguished from sociopolitical grievances.

Collier and Hoeffler's (2004b) empirical findings conclude that the set of variables representing rebel opportunity or greed akin to loot seeking are the main reasons for civil war. By implication, the alternative hypothesis of grievance (justice seeking), focusing on ethnic religious divisions, political repression and horizontal inequality is dismissed, although its invalidity is not formally tested for. Natural resource rents constitute 'booty' and this fact has been used to emphasize the greed or criminal motivation for civil war. Central to the Collier and Hoeffler's empirical testing for the greed hypothesis is the role of primary commodities in the economic structure. They measure the dependence on natural resources by the share of primary commodity exports in GDP, and the validity of this metric as well as the statistical robustness of the relationship between resource rents and the risk of conflict has been called into question.

The econometric models purporting to establish the empirical validity of the greed hypothesis, however, are atheoretical, in the sense of not having a formal economic model based on optimizing behaviour by economic agents to explain why greed may cause conflict. If economic agents (*homo economicus*) are actuated only by self-interest,[2] we must demonstrate why they choose war over other alternatives. Therefore, any theorizing about greed must be based on the economic motivations for violence and criminality. Belligerents in the wars of natural resource-rich countries could be acting in ways close to what Olson (1996) referred to as 'roving bandits' – who have no encompassing interest in preserving the state or its people but are simply intent on loot – than to 'stationary' bandits who take control of the state and seek to maximize their own profit by encouraging stability and growth in their new domain. Civil wars motivated by the desire to control natural resource rents could also mirror 'warlord competition', a term that owes its origins to the violent competition between leaders attempting to control economic resources in the context of medieval Europe (Skaperdas, 2002).

In a nutshell, a proper greed based theory of civil war must relate to the trade-off between production and predation in making a living, where we may view war as theft writ large. Violence is one means of appropriating the resources of others. Note that armed conflict implies the absence of contractual or consensual interaction (Edgeworth, 1881), which is in stark contrast to the alternative method of benefiting from the endowments of others via peaceful and voluntary exchange (trade) between economic agents, groups or nations. This implies that we also need to specify the conditions under which violence becomes a viable or more attractive

---

[2]　This commonly held view is actually a gross over-simplification.

option relative to other alternatives. It is interesting to reflect on the fact that mercantilist wars (such as those between Britain and the Netherlands in the 17th century), as well as colonial wars aimed at capturing rents from monopolized or restricted trade (the British and Dutch East India companies), and the desire to control the sources of natural resources in the 19th-century colonial scramble for Africa, all fit neatly into the greed explanation for war.

A variety of game theoretic models describing the non-cooperative and conflictive interaction between groups exist, where the object is to capture the rival's endowment by force. One such model is Hirshleifer's (1995), where each group has a fixed resource endowment, which can be used to produce either goods for consumption or armaments to fight the other group. Groups exist in a state of non-contractual anarchy vis-à-vis each other; this also implies the absence of enforceable property rights. The object of fighting is to capture some of the rival's endowment. Success in war is uncertain, and the probability of victory is given by a Tullock (1980) contest success function,[3] where the probability of victory for any group is given by their own military expenditure relative to the total fighting outlay made by all sides. Additionally, there is a military effectiveness parameter, akin to what is known as a force multiplier in military establishments; something that raises the effectiveness of each unit of fighting effort. In the absence of increasing returns to scale in military effectiveness, and if a minimum subsistence income is present, there will be a Nash non-cooperative equilibrium associated with some fighting. In other words, in the equilibrium both (or all) parties will be engaged in some fighting with each other, as well as some productive activities, unless one side manages to conquer others due to its military superiority. Hirshleifer (1995) describes this as a state of anarchy – something like primitive tribal warfare. Furthermore, anarchy implies the complete absence of a social contract between different groups; in contrast to the attributes of a functioning modern nation state. Note also, no possibility of inter-group trade is permitted.

Skaperdas (1992) outlines a model that is similar because it has a fixed resource endowment that can be devoted to either production or armament. The probability of success in war also depends on a similar contest success function. Skaperdas (1992), however, allows for a peaceful trading cooperative equilibrium when there is no fighting. The parties simply share the sum of total resources in proportion to the contest success function, or in accordance with what would have been the equilibrium outcome of

---

[3] See equation 2.2 in Chapter 2 for an example of a contest success function related to rent seeking.

war. This is likely when the probability of military success for either side is low, and both parties are similar in their peaceful productive capacities. Secondly, there is a possible outcome where one side only produces, whereas the other party does some fighting and production. This is a more likely outcome when the more pacific side is more productive, and the side that chooses fighting is more efficient at it. Finally, both sides may choose a mix of fighting and production. As with the first possibility, each side must be similar in its economic productivity and fighting effectiveness, but here the technology of war is such that it raises the probability of victory for both sides, hence the presence of fighting. In many ways, Skaperdas's (1992) model puts the trade-off between fighting and predation into sharper perspective, and explicitly mentions the absence of contract or respect for property rights.[4]

Both these models, however, neglect the destructiveness of war (collateral damage), and its capacity to ravage productive capacity, additional to direct military expenditure. These models employ intermediate inputs, and not factors of production, which can be costlessly shifted between fighting and production. Secondly, there is no growth in these models, something that would raise the opportunity costs of war. A similar effect could arise from complementarities in production between groups and/or economies of scale, which would make mergers between groups or cooperation in each faction's self-interest. Thirdly, the possibilities of peaceful exchange need to be limited (absent in Hirshleifer, 1995) in order to rationalize conflict. In traditional economics the gains from trade arise mainly from differences in tastes, technology and endowments, and these gains from trade need to be minimized in order to make conflict an optimal choice. Violent means are attractive when the intention is to extract resources (as in the case of colonial plantations and mines) or accumulate surpluses at the expense of others (mercantilism). Fourthly, these models imply full information. In the presence of asymmetric information, misperceptions about contest success, the opposition's intentions and so on, wars that do not maximize expected utility under full information may break out, akin to problems associated with moral hazard and adverse selection. Fifthly, such theorizing is broadly blind to institutions (despite ruling out the existence of property rights and inter-group contracts), and the presence of transaction costs that breed mutual mistrust. Wars can also reflect the absence of institutions that would facilitate negotiation and peaceful exchange.

Despite these limitations, there is much in these models that can explain the greedy behaviour as analysed by the empirical exponents of the greed

---

[4]   Even in societies with property rights, there still may be violent or non-violent competition over resources that have, as yet, unassigned ownership.

hypothesis. The presence of readily capturable natural resource based rents may make conflict more attractive when compared to peaceful production, as can a shortage of intermediate inputs due to population pressures. These resources are best regarded as a non-produced 'prize' such as oil or diamonds (which apart from extraction costs are like a free gift), whose ownership is violently contested. Secondly, contributions from a sympathetic diaspora (or aid from a superpower in the cold war era) can raise the probability of victory of a potential rebel group against the state. Thirdly, the inability of the state to act as a Stackelberg leader, someone who takes into account the followers' reactions, in a potentially divided nation may raise the chances of war between groups in a manner similar to the weak state capacity mechanism favoured by some political scientists (like James Fearon). For example, in the Hirshleifer (1995) model where different groups are in a state of anarchy vis-à-vis one another, the ability of one group to behave as a Stackelberg leader reduces equilibrium fighting levels and raises each side's per capita income. The leader, however, gains relatively less compared to followers, creating an incentive for each side to be a follower. If one group is strong and militarily more effective it will dominate other groups, and there will be no fighting in the equilibrium. This may lead to state formation, which may or may not lead to the reconfiguration of group identities. If inter-group rivalries persist, state disintegration occurs when the dominant group can no longer control other groups.

Finally, war implies the absence of contract, and warring parties may enter into contracts that make their interactions more peaceful. This will be all the more true if war causes substantial collateral damage. Groups may also decide to merge in order to reap economies of scale in production. If they do not do so when it is clearly in their mutual self-interest, we have to resort to explanations based on misperceptions, mistrust or the lack of institutions that enforce contracts. Alternatively, the institutions that once bound groups together may have disintegrated. I shall return to these issues in Chapter 5. We now go back to the empirical hypotheses that buttress cross-country econometric studies of civil war, which are dominated by various forms of a greed (or modified greed) and state failure hypotheses.

3.2.2 Empirical Issues in Connection with the Greed Mechanism

While Collier and Hoeffler (2002, 2004b) press the greedy rebel hypothesis derived from their findings regarding the strong explanatory power of the share of primary commodity exports to GDP (their proxy for natural resource wealth), others are less sanguine. In short, the empirical controversy over the link between natural resource wealth and greed hypothesis is about the saliency of measurement issues, the problem of reverse causality, and possible mechanisms between natural resource rents and conflict.

On the matter of measurement, two broad sets of issues need to be considered: (1) the measure of natural resource wealth/abundance and resource dependence; and (2) the construction of the relevant conflict dependent variable.

Before we examine the various alternative metrics for natural resource dependence, note that the term primary commodity includes both agricultural commodities and minerals/fuels, but crucially excludes illegal substances (coca and heroin) as well as illicit alluvial diamonds in Collier and Hoeffler (2002, 2004b). Certain varieties of resources are more easily captured: they may be lootable such as alluvial diamonds (in Sierra Leone, Angola) available along riverbeds using artisanal techniques or illicit drugs such as coca in Colombia; obstructable like an oil pipeline (see Ross, 2003, on these issues). Illicit gemstones and drugs are arguably more crucial to financing rogue conflict entrepreneurs in a greed based conflict; their omission is a serious flaw. Collier and Hoeffler (2002, 2004b) do not differentiate different types of natural resources, such as between lootable and non-lootable natural resources (Lujala, Gleditsch and Gilmore 2005), and between point-sourced and diffuse natural resources (Murshed, 2004). Lootable point-sourced natural resources are in particular prone to be illegally exploited and traded. Collier and Hoeffler (2002, 2004b) are only concerned with past production, neglecting future prospects for extraction (Humphreys, 2005). They also only focus on exports, even though production might be a better measure of the availability of these resources, including commodities that were first imported and then re-exported (Humphreys, 2005).

Below is a summary of different proxies to measure resource wealth used in cross-country empirical conflict literature:

- *Primary commodity exports* as percentage of GDP (Collier and Hoeffler, 1998, 2002, 2004b). This is the indicator from where the initial greed hypothesis is derived.
- *Agricultural value added* as percentage of GDP (Humphreys, 2005).
- *Oil dependence*; different ways of measuring this have been employed:
    - *Oil production and reserves* per capita (Humphreys, 2005). This is to distinguish between past and future exploitation of natural resources. Furthermore, Lujala, Rød and Thieme

(2007) differentiate oil-hydrocarbon production and reserves into offshore and onshore types. It is the onshore variety that adds to the risk of conflict onset, because offshore facilities can be more easily protected.

- *Oil rents* per capita, that is further distinguished between offshore and onshore oil (Ross, 2006).
- *Oil exporter dummy*, where oil exceeds one-third of total exports (Fearon and Laitin, 2003).
- *Oil exports* as percentage of total exports; Fearon (2005) adds this measure to the Collier–Hoeffler model specifically to locate the oil effect, finding that the effect of primary commodities on conflict is confined to oil.
- *Diamonds*; different ways of measuring diamond wealth have been employed:
    - *Diamond production* per capita (Humphreys, 2005). Ross (2006) further disaggregates it into primary and secondary production to differentiate the unlootable and lootable nature of this resource.
    - *Diamond dummy* for the presence of diamonds, disaggregated further into primary and secondary types by Lujala, Gleditsch and Gilmore (2005). They find that the lootable secondary diamonds increase the risk of civil war onset and its duration, while the primary variety do not. They create mainly ethnic civil wars rather than other forms of civil wars. This risk has been greater since the end of the cold war. Non-lootable deep mine shaft (primary) diamonds, however, lower the risk of civil war onset.
- *Resource rents* as percentage of gross national income (de Soysa and Neumayer, 2007). They differentiate between energy rents and mineral rents; the former consists of oil, gas and coal, while the latter includes bauxite, copper, iron ore, lead, nickel, phosphate rock, tin, zinc, gold and silver. Various measures of natural resource intensity, and the distinction between natural and physical capital have been reviewed in Chapter 2.
- *Contraband dummy*; conflicts in which a rebel group derives major funds from contraband such as opium, diamonds or coca tend to have longer civil war duration (Fearon, 2004).

However, those measures represent both resource dependence and resource abundance, and are referred to interchangeably by most studies. This confusion is criticized by Brunnschweiler and Bulte (2008a), who clearly differentiate resource dependence and abundance and use them simultaneously in their cross-country conflict regressions. They use the share of primary commodity exports to GDP for their resource dependence measure. For resource abundance, they use the aggregate measure of the net present value of rents (in US$ per capita) of a country's total natural capital stock, and by considering two disaggregated measures: focusing on sub-soil mineral resources and land (crop and pastureland, protected areas and forest resources).

Another related issue is the proper specification of the conflict dependent variable in econometric analyses; it can either be the onset or duration of civil war. With regard to onset, the question is whether natural resource wealth increases or decreases the risk or likelihood of civil war; and with duration, whether or not it prolongs civil war. Collier and Hoeffler (1998, 2002, 2004b) claim that resource dependence measured by primary goods exports to GDP in increasing the likelihood of civil war onset is significant and robust. Others say that it is not significant (Fearon and Laitin, 2003; Fearon, 2005; Montalvo and Reynal-Querol, 2005; Brunnschweiler and Bulte, 2008a) or it is not robust (Ross, 2004b).[5] On duration, the results are again contradictory. Collier, Hoeffler and Söderbom (2004) find that primary commodities have no significant effect on the duration, but decreases in primary commodity prices would shorten conflict since it squeezes rebel finances, when the level of dependence upon primary commodity exports is high. Using contraband dummy measures, Fearon (2004) and Ross (2006) find that natural resources lengthen civil war duration; while, using diamond production per capita, Humphreys (2005) finds that this reduces war duration.

When civil war onset is a dummy (0, 1) variable, an additional complication is regarding the appropriate fatality threshold for coding a case as a civil war/conflict. There are three variants employed: (1) 1000 battle-related deaths annually (Collier and Hoeffler, 2004b), (2) 1000 battle-related deaths during the course of the conflict (Fearon and Laitin, 2003; Fearon, 2005); and (3) 25 battle-related deaths annually (de Soysa, 2002).

Any measure of natural resource dependence may also be endogenous to conflict, which has two implications: (1) reverse causality, in which civil wars might cause resource dependence by reducing the size of a country's non-resource sector (e.g. manufacturing); and (2) spurious correlation, where both civil war and resource dependence might be independently caused by an unmeasured third variable, such as poor property rights or the weak rule of law. On reverse causality, Brunnschweiler and Bulte (2008a) treat resource dependence, together with per capita income as endogenous independent variables in their conflict regression, while previous studies always assumed resource dependence to be truly exogenous.

---

[5]   A robust econometric result withstands changes in data coverage, concerning, say, the number of conflicts, countries, period of analysis and so on.

They use a set of instruments for resource dependence, as well as income, which consist of a measure of resource abundance, trade openness, the constitution (presidential versus parliamentary systems), absolute latitude, percentage of land in the tropics and distance from the nearest coast or navigable river. They find that by treating these two variables as endogenous, resource dependence loses its significance and resource abundance has a negative indirect effect on conflict through income. Based on these findings, they reject the previous arguments for placing natural resource wealth or dependence as the principal culprit for civil war. They go on to speculate that resource dependence (a reliance on primary goods exports) may be a manifestation of the failure to grow and diversify as a consequence of conflict, but does not contribute directly to conflict. In a related paper, Brunnschweiler and Bulte (2008b) argue that resource abundance may actually promote good institutional development.

On the mechanisms in between conflict and resource dependence, Humphreys (2005), for example, argues that other factors may be present. First is the greedy outsider mechanism: the existence of natural resources may be an incentive for third parties – states and corporations – to engage in or indeed foster civil conflict. Secondly, we have the grievance mechanism: natural resource dependence could in fact be associated with grievances rather than greed. There are at least four variants of this mechanism: (1) countries with middling levels of dependence on natural resources may experience transitory inequality as part of their development process; (2) economies that are dependent on natural resources may be more vulnerable to terms of trade shocks; (3) the process of extraction may produce grievances, for example, through forced migration; and (4) natural resources wealth may be seen as more unjustly distributed compared to other forms of wealth. Thirdly, there is the weak state mechanism, as also emphasized by Fearon and Laitin (2003). Natural resource dependent economies may be weaker states, a feature that stems from the nature of state revenue, which is mainly dependent on resource rents. On the one hand, untaxed citizens have less ability or incentive to monitor state activity. On the other hand, governments relying more on natural resource rents rather than taxation have weak incentives to create strong and accountable bureaucratic structures, similar to the logic of no accountability without taxation, as in Ross (2004a).

3.2.3 Summary of the Evidence on Greed and Civil War

On estimation techniques, Fearon (2005) provides the strongest challenge to Collier and Hoeffler's (2002, 2004b) empirical findings about primary commodity exports and civil war. Fearon, who re-estimates Collier and

Hoeffler's model using country year observations, as opposed to country five-year averages employed by Collier and Hoeffler, finds that the significance of statistical associations between primary commodity export and civil war onset vanishes in the country year regression, meaning that the previous claim that such a relationship exists is simply not robust.[6] In other words, this cross-country result will not withstand variation in sample and data coverage. More recently, in their cross-country conflict regression, Brunnschweiler and Bulte (2008a) also find that the primary commodity export loses its significance when treated as an endogenous variable. A similar view is shared by Ross (2004b), who reviews 14 cross-country empirical studies on natural resources and civil war, complemented with many qualitative study reports. Those studies vary in terms of time coverage, estimation procedures, resource measures, dependent variable construction (different conflict databases and thresholds) and sets of independent variables used; therefore they yield varying results. Ross (2004b) concludes that the claim that primary commodities are associated with the onset of civil war does not appear to be robust, oil dependence appears to be linked to the initiation of conflict, but not its duration, and illicit gemstones and drugs seem to lengthen pre-existing wars. Furthermore, Fearon (2005) shows that the effect of primary commodity exports is confined to oil. He demonstrates this by adding the variable (oil exports to total exports) into the country year regression. Humphreys (2005) checks the effect of past oil exploitation (oil production per capita) on civil war onset and finds it positively significant. However, he asserts that such a relationship works through the weak state mechanism. This is evidenced by adding interaction terms between measures of natural resource wealth and state strength that is measured in three ways. The first way is by a political instability dummy (whether a state has undergone a large change in its political institutions over the past three years; such changes may indicate weakness of state structures). The second measurement is by an anocracy dummy (a combination of Fearon and Laitin's instability measure and their 'anocracy' measure; it takes the value of 1 if a state is a robust democracy or a robust dictatorship and a 0 otherwise. The third measurement is of the 'Weberianness' of state structures, also a measure of state strength. In a similar vein to Humphreys, Fearon (2005) interprets the oil effect as a weak state mechanism rather than a greedy rebel hypothesis; this is by

---

[6] The method of multiple imputations does not lead to Collier and Hoeffler's (2004b) list-wide deletion, because in the latter case arbitrary five-year averages result in 27 out of the 79 conflict cases being dropped due to missing data on right-hand side explanatory variables. However, it should be noted that Fearon (2005) used a lower threshold for civil war than did Collier and Hoeffler (2004b).

using the correlation between oil export and state weaknesses, measured by government contract observance.

The Collier and Hoeffler greed hypothesis is basically an interpretation of their empirical finding that natural resource dependence increases the risk of civil war. As Collier and Hoeffler (2004b, p. 588) conclude, 'we have interpreted this as being due to the opportunities such as commodities provide for extortion, making rebellion feasible, and perhaps even attractive.' This lies at the heart of their famous greedy rebel mechanism. However, there is really no empirical evidence showing the validity of such an interpretation. In this respect, Fearon (2005) and Humphreys (2005) go one step further by providing empirical evidence of their weak state mechanism as the intervening mechanism between natural resource endowments and civil war, as opposed to the greedy rebel mechanism; de Soysa and Neumayer (2007) support such an argument. Using resource rents data as the percentage of national income (differentiated into energy and mineral rents), they re-estimate both Collier and Hoeffler (2004b) and Fearon and Laitin (2003) models using different thresholds for civil war. They find that only energy rents matter for civil war onset, and reject the curvilinear relationship between resource dependence and civil war as proposed by Collier and Hoeffler. Also, de Soysa and Neumayer argue that the significant role of energy rents is more relevant with the weak state mechanism than the greedy rebel hypothesis. I have noted above that several studies also show that only onshore oil and secondary diamonds contribute to civil war onset. A related, and yet unexplored, issue could relate to the ownership of natural resource rents, and what revenue sharing mechanisms are present between the state and multinational extractive industries, as some arrangements may further encourage kleptocracy.

Facing these challenges, Collier, Hoeffler and Rohner[7] revisit their previous greed argument by saying that, 'the feasibility hypothesis proposes that where rebellion is feasible it will occur: motivation is indeterminate, being supplied by whatever agenda happens to be adopted by the first social entrepreneur to occupy the viable niche' (2007, p. 21). They differentiate between two theories of civil war: 'feasibility' and 'motivation', which in turn has two variants: either 'greed' or 'grievance'. But the content of their previous 'greed' hypothesis (now part of motivation) is almost identical to what they now rephrase as 'feasibility'. If feasibility is about

---

[7] In 2005, an entire issue of the *Journal of Conflict Resolution*, called 'Paradigm in Distress', 49(4), was devoted to demonstrating the non-robustness of the main conclusions of Collier and Hoeffler's greed hypothesis.

opportunity, greed is also about opportunity. The basic arguments and empirical evidence are much the same as before.

In summary, greed based explanations for conflict require further refinement by utilizing better measures of point-sourced resource abundance or dependence on capturable resource rents. Proper consideration also needs to be given to institutional mechanisms that cause the competition for resource rents to descend into outright warfare. Ultimately, greed theory is unsatisfactory, even in its new guise as a feasibility hypothesis. This is because conflict is rarely a rational, Pareto optimal strategy, except in exceptional circumstances illustrated by the Hirshleifer (1995) and Skaperdas (1992) models discussed above, where property rights are absent and the possibilities of exchange limited. More generally it points to institutional failure that encourages non-contractual behaviour, as well as the existence of asymmetric information. The presence of grievances is necessary for group formation and violent collective action, and this is what we now turn to.

3.3   GRIEVANCES AND HORIZONTAL INEQUALITY

In the context of civil war or rebellion, grievance is sometimes described as a justice-seeking motivation. The discussion in this section on grievances begins with grievance based theories of conflict before moving on to measurement issues, similar to the previous section.

3.3.1   Theories of Grievance

Central to grievances is identity and group formation. An individual's utility may be related to his identity, specifically the relative position of the group he identifies with in the social pecking order; see Akerlof and Kranton (2000). An individual may derive utility from certain normative forms of behaviour appropriate to his identity but considered deviant by other groups, and may even face sanctions from like-minded group members if he deviates from them. This type of behavioural paradigm may be related to solving the collective action problems (Olson, 1965), without which organized large-scale violence is impossible, even if we believe conflict is primarily motivated by greed. As noted above, some appropriate definition of ethnicity may be a superior basis for group formation compared to social class in an ethnically homogeneous society.

We sub-divide theories of grievance into relative deprivation, polarization and horizontal inequality. While it is important to differentiate these, some overlap between the three is inevitable.

3.3.1.1 Relative deprivation

The notion of relative deprivation dates back to the work of Ted Gurr (1970), who defined it as the discrepancy between what people think they deserve, and what they actually believe they can get; in short the disparity between aspirations and achievements. It also needs to be distinguished from a state of absolute deprivation, which occurs in situations characterized by endemic poverty. In these situations, no group may feel relatively deprived, and the forces of rebellion may be more muted. Relative deprivation is more likely to arise when the situation is improving for some, and not for others. It is the difference between what 'ought' to be, and what actually 'is' according to Gurr (1970). Thus, educational achievements may raise the aspirations of young people, but they will become frustrated if unemployed, occasionally venting their feelings in mass political violence. Gurr puts forward the following hypothesis: 'the potential for collective violence varies strongly with the intensity and scope of relative deprivation among members of a collectivity' (1970, p. 24). This lays down the notion of relative deprivation as the micro-foundation for conflict. Relative deprivation is considered to be a major cause of civil war, as well as sectarian and routine violence, since it can stimulate general frustration or be used by conflict entrepreneurs as a unifying tool or as a means of group mobilization for collective action.

The applications vary across ethno-communal lines, regional boundaries, societal class, or just the feeling of being relatively deprived vis-à-vis the general situation. For example, in the eastern Indonesian province of Maluku, the traditionally privileged Christian group felt relatively deprived compared to the rising Muslim community economically and politically, which resulted in the bloodiest Muslim–Christian conflict in the country's history (Tadjoeddin, 2003). Similar statements centring around unemployment could be made about the Catholic–Protestant cleavage in Northern Ireland. In Nepal, the lack of development in remote rural districts of the country fuelled the Maoist insurgency (Murshed and Gates, 2005).

Another form of conflict where relative deprivation may be applied concerns 'routine' violence, where the conflict is not chiefly directed against the state. It centres on vigilante violence/popular justice and inter-group/neighbourhood brawls. Routine violence covers group or collective violence, and it is different from individual violence, domestic violence, or homicide – which can simply be labelled as crime. The theoretical underpinnings for routine violence are similar to those utilized to explain mass political violence short of internal war in Hibbs (1973). Historical accounts suggest that in the earlier stages of development violence and increasing prosperity go hand in hand at first, but decline thereafter

(Bates, 2001). Traditional societies may have rules and norms that manage and contain violent behaviour. An increase in prosperity may encourage predatory behaviour in the form of private violence by the less fortunate. Once growth progresses further, violence has to decline to sustain the security of investment. Using panel data analysis of count data, Tadjoeddin and Murshed (2007) examine the relationship between routine violence on one hand, and growth, poverty and level of development (including education) on the other, in Java, Indonesia. The relationships between violence and the levels of education or income are non-linear in the form of inverted U–shape curves. The reasons for this are as follows: starting from low levels of average income and educational attainment, when these rise slightly there is much to compete over and quarrel about; this tendency, however, diminishes with further increases in income and education, as there is much more to lose from violence. Another explanation is the feeling of being relatively deprived, since rising education is not automatically accompanied by rising income.

3.3.1.2 Polarization
A related notion is that of polarization; see Esteban and Ray (1994) and Duclos, Esteban and Ray (2004) on this. Polarization occurs when two or a few groups exhibit great inter-group heterogeneity combined with intra-group homogeneity, or in other words, in any given distribution of characteristics, polarization refers to 'the extent to which the population is *clustered* around a small number of distant *poles*' (Esteban and Schneider, 2008, p. 133). This means that a society is more polarized (1) the wider the gaps are between groups; (2) the closer the population distribution is to perfect bimodality (demographic polarization), meaning that there are roughly two equal groups; and (3) the more internally homogeneous the group is (lower within-group inequality). Economic polarization, based on income or wealth, along with high vertical income or wealth inequality, can occur in culturally homogeneous societies. The same argument may be applied to social polarization, which is based on other social indicators, such as health or educational attainments.

Ethnic polarization (based on how society is divided up into different ethnicities) could, in principal, exist along with a degree of economic equality. In their original work on polarization, Esteban and Ray (1994), and Duclos, Esteban and Ray (2004) focus on the identification and alienation framework as the defining factors of polarization. Their idea is as follows: polarization is related to the alienation that groups of people feel from one another, and this alienation is fuelled by the feeling of within-group identity.

Furthermore, they argue that the traditional measures of inequality are only concerned with interpersonal alienation, but fail to capture the dimension of group identity. It is important to note that a high degree of ethnic polarization requires two or a few ethnicities. When a society has a very large number of identities, the term 'ethnic fractionalization' is more appropriate. Therefore, polarization is what may matter for conflict, rather than fractionalization and/or overall vertical (inter-individual) inequality.

In their seminal article on polarization, Esteban and Ray state, 'it is our contention that the phenomenon of polarization is closely linked to the generation of tensions, to the possibilities of articulated rebellion and revolt, and to the existence of social unrest in general' (1994, p. 820). Looking back further, the idea can be traced back to Marxian social class theory, as can be seen from Deutsch's (1971) account, quoted in Esteban and Ray (1994):

> As the struggle proceeds, 'the whole society breaks up more and more into two hostile camps, two great, directly antagonistic classes: bourgeoisie and proletariat.' The classes *polarize*, so that they become internally more homogeneous and more and more sharply distinguished from one another in wealth and power (Deutsch, 1971, p. 44).

Montalvo and Reynal-Querol (2005; 2007) find that polarization matters for both the incidence as well as duration of civil war. The former paper finds that ethnic polarization is a very robust determinant of the incidence of civil war, while the latter concludes that more ethnically polarized societies experience lengthier civil wars; in both cases, the degree of ethnic fractionalization does not matter. However, the theoretical work of Esteban and Ray (2008) argues in favour of a non-linear relationship between polarization and conflict; the overall degree of conflict is in its peak in societies with intermediate levels of polarization. In a highly polarized society, the potential cost of rebellion is extremely high and that can serve as a guarantor of peace. Therefore one may expect that overt conflict would be rare, but when it occurs, its intensity would be very severe. When polarization is extremely low, conflict becomes unattractive since there is little to fight about.

Other studies such as Fearon and Laitin (2003) on the onset of civil war, and Fearon (2004) on the duration of civil war, only consider ethnic fractionalization and do not include an ethnic polarization measure, and they find that ethnic fractionalization does not matter for both civil war onset and duration, which is consistent with Montalvo and Reynal-Querol (2005; 2007). However Collier, Hoeffler and Söderbom (2004) find that the effect of ethnic fractionalization is non-monotonic: the duration of conflict is at its maximum when ethnic fractionalization is around 50 on its 0–100 range. Although Collier, Hoeffler and Söderbom (2004) do not specifically include polarization measures, their result is consistent with the Montalvo and Reynal-Querol (2007) finding on polarization, since the relationship between ethnic fractionalization and ethnic polarization is curvilinear: ethnic polarization is low in the extreme high or low ends of fractionalization, and the peak of ethnic polarization coincides with median values of fractionalization. This situation corroborates the theoretical conclusions of Esteban and Ray (2008) that measures of fractionalization and polarization tend to move in opposite directions.

On the differences between demographic polarization and fractionalization, consider the following description given by Montalvo and Reynal-Querol (2007). Let us take a hypothetical example of two countries, A and B, each of which has three ethnic groups, say groups 1, 2 and 3. In country A the population distribution of the ethnic groups is the following, 49% for group 1, 49% for group 2 and 2% for group 3, while in country B, the distribution is virtually equal between the three ethnic groups, so the distributions are 33%, 33%, and 34% respectively for the three groups. Which country will have a higher probability of social conflict? Country A is more polarized, whereas ethnic fractionalization is greater in country B. Montalvo and Reynal-Querol's (2005 and 2007) cross-country empirical regressions find that polarization is more relevant to conflict risk.

3.3.1.3 Horizontal inequality

The notion of horizontal inequalities between groups, classified by ethnicity, religion, linguistic differences, tribal affiliations and so on, is thought to be an important cause of contemporary civil war and sectarian strife. The expression horizontal inequality originates in the work of Frances Stewart (2000), and should be distinguished from vertical inequality, which is the inequality within an otherwise homogeneous population. Vertical inequality, say in income or wealth, is the economic inequality that exists across a group assumed to be culturally homogeneous. It is also the most commonly measured type of inequality. The well-known GINI and Theil measures of income inequality – say within a nation state – define inequality across economic groups that differ from each other in one aspect only, income, but are otherwise assumed homogeneous.

Horizontal inequality aims to measure inequality across groups based on an ethnic group identity, such as between Catholics vis-à-vis Protestants, Hutus relative to Tutsis, and so on. Note that within each group relevant to horizontal inequality there will be rich and poor individuals or households. So, for example, if we are considering the Catholic–Protestant divide, within both the Catholic and Protestant groups there are some rich and some poor individuals and households. What really matters are the differences between the two groups, not the within group inequalities in each of these individual identities. As far as vertical inequality is concerned, within group inequalities are often as important as between group differences in decomposing changes in overall inequality between different time periods. It has to be remembered, however, that vertical inequality pertains only to one difference, income, wealth or some other social dimension such as health or education status. Thus, the differences between horizontal and vertical inequality mainly relate to group definition. In the horizontal case, ethnic groupings (based on racial, tribal, linguistic or confessional lines) are explicitly considered. This raises the issue of how to define ethnic groups, as in some countries groups can differ along several overlapping bases, such as language, religion and tribal affiliation. For example, two households in Indonesia may belong to the same linguistic group, but have different religious identities. With regard to vertical inequality, groups are defined only on the basis of a single socio-economic indicator; there will be richly and poorly endowed groups, but the only characteristic that distinguishes them are relative differences in the appropriate socioeconomic indicator. Vertical inequality is, therefore, more related to traditional socioeconomic class differences, and a very unequal society based on this definition can also be polarized in the economic or social sense, but not necessarily along ethnic lines.

Horizontal inequality usually stems from historical discrimination and can fuel group grievances; therefore Stewart (2000) argues that it is group horizontal inequality, not vertical inequality, that really matters for causing violent conflict. This is the reason why most cross-country conflict regressions, including two influential studies by Collier and Hoeffler (2004b) and Fearon and Laitin (2003), fail to find any significant relationship between vertical inequality and conflict. There is, however, support available for a significant relationship between conflict and horizontal inequality; Østby (2006 and 2008) on a cross-country basis, and Mancini (2008) in a cross-section regression at sub-national level in a single country (Indonesia). The idea of horizontal inequality may overlap with the notion of relative deprivation and polarization, as will be indicated by alternative measures discussed below. Four sources of horizontal inequality may be highlighted.

The first source is discrimination in public spending and taxation. Discrimination in the allocation of public spending, and unfair tax burdens, lead to serious unrest. Grossman (1991) develops a theoretical model of insurrection against the state by the peasantry reacting to over taxation, where the state is a tax farmer interested in maximizing the income of the rentier class. A peasant farmer household has a choice between agricultural production, soldiering for the state or engaging in rebellion against the state. A lot depends on the probability of the success of rebellion. If this is substantial, along with a high enough tax rate on peasant output, rebellion occurs. Even though rebellion reduces overall production and average income, it can increase the expected income of the peasantry.

Discrimination in the allocation of public employment is particularly resented in societies in which public employment represents the principal avenue for personal advance, as in Burundi. In addition, the over taxation of smallholders encourages insurrection, and indigenous peoples often face discrimination in access to schooling, health care, and public sector jobs; many of these factors were present in Nepal's civil war (see Murshed and Gates, 2005). Where there are inter-group fiscal transfers, which may take the form of spending on education and health for disadvantaged groups, or including them in government employment, commitment to the transfer by those in power may be imperfect. This lack of credibility can eventually lead to civil war.

The second source of horizontal inequality is high asset inequality. Agrarian societies with high inequality – for example El Salvador, Guatemala, Nepal, the Philippines and Zimbabwe – have high asset inequality, and are very prone to conflict, see Russett (1964) for an early view on this. Asset redistribution such as land reform to lessen inequality is more difficult than public finance reform. Besançon (2005), however, points out that purely ethnic conflicts, as opposed to revolutions and genocides, are more likely when a greater degree of income equality has been achieved between contending ethnic groups. Inclusion in the political process is crucial to preventing this type of conflict, which does not usually take the form of civil wars, as the state is not involved.

The third source is economic mismanagement and recession. In Africa, Latin America and the former Soviet Union conflict-ridden countries have also suffered prolonged economic mismanagement and growth collapse. Successive IMF and World Bank supported adjustment programmes in DRC/Zaire, Somalia and elsewhere not only proved incapable of promoting economic recovery, but given the level of corruption within the state, the programmes became targets for capture by elite groups. Economic mismanagement is often associated with an uneven and unfair distribution of the burdens of subsequent adjustment; public spending benefiting the elite and the military is protected, often favouring particular ethnic groups, with the burden of adjustment placed on expenditures of value to the poor and disadvantaged groups. Also, as Rodrik (1999) emphasizes, countries with weak institutions of conflict management, as well as high income inequality are less able to withstand economic shocks and experience growth failure. They are also more prone to the risk of civil strife and war, since their weak institutions, which are further weakened by shocks and lower growth, are unable to contain the resulting social pressure and distributional conflict.

Finally, the fourth source is grievances related to resource rents. Natural resource rents can by themselves become a source of grievance, if local populations feel that they are not getting a fair share of these, as in the Niger Delta region of Nigeria. In more than seven years of civilian rule in Nigeria, the state at all levels (local, state and federal) is perceived to have failed to bring tangible economic benefits for impoverished local residents of the delta. Even Nigeria's federal system indirectly encourages violence in the Niger Delta by rewarding those who pose the greatest threats to oil facilities with lucrative oil contracts and government positions (ICG, 2006). It can also cause secessionist tendencies among relatively rich regions, who no longer want to subsidize their fellow countrymen, as in the case of Aceh and Papua in Indonesia. During three decades of the relatively stable authoritarian regime of Suharto, rents from these natural resource-rich provinces were used to achieve equitable social development across the country, which was beneficial from a national point of view, but created grievances in the wealth producing regions. After the regime collapsed in 1998, such a policy could not be continued, and new schemes of revenue sharing were introduced under special autonomy settings in both provinces (see Tadjoeddin et al., 2003, and Tadjoeddin, 2007).

3.3.2   Measurement of Grievance

3.3.2.1   Relative deprivation
A simple starting point in measuring relative deprivation is to calculate the simple ratio (or difference) between two competing groups on particular socioeconomic indicators, as discussed in Gurr (1970), and examine their evolution over time. These may be subjective or perception based on what people have and what they would ideally like to have, or more objectively related to actual differences in achievement. A worsening ratio for one group means an improving ratio for the other, which may be perceived by the deprived group as unjust.[8]

Murshed and Gates (2005), in a cross-sectional study, calculate the gap in the human development index between sub-national entities (districts) in Nepal and its national capital, Kathmandu, which has the highest

---

[8]   Stewart (2000) applied this method to nine cases of internal conflict and social violence and showed that widening socioeconomic gaps contribute to ethnic violence. In this early work, however, a measure of what really is relative deprivation is referred to as horizontal inequality.

human development score.[9] Their measure, based on actual differences in attainment, is close to that proposed by Gurr (1970). In many ways, it implicitly points to the level of human development in the capital city as the level that may be desired if perception based surveys were conducted. The gap can be interpreted as the extent of deprivation relative to the capital's urban and modern economic development. However, this measure can also be viewed as spatial horizontal inequality, according to Murshed and Gates (2005). This gap measure can also be measured using national averages.[10] Within country, disaggregated data on the human development index is collected for many countries in Asia and Latin America. This data is usually available spatially – across provinces or districts. But in some cases we can impute group inequalities from spatial data, because certain ethnic groups chiefly reside in particular areas. In a few instances, household surveys also explicitly ask questions about the ethnicity of households. If that is the case, we can compute differences (gaps) in income, poverty incidence, educational and health status across ethnic groups. Such data, for example, is recently available for Indonesia.

3.3.2.2 Polarization

Esteban and Ray (1994) pioneered a polarization measure, called the ER polarization index (see also Duclos, Esteban and Ray, 2004). The index is more about economic or social polarization than identity based inequality. It can, however, be adapted to ethnic dimensions, as discussed above (see Montalvo and Reynal-Querol, 2005 and 2007). The formula contains a subjective measure of α, akin to an Atkinson inequality aversion measure, whose purpose is to increase the weight given to large groups, so that the index rises as the population is distributed among fewer and more equally sized groups.

Another polarization measure is proposed by Zhang and Kanbur (2001). The Zhang–Kanbur (ZK) polarization index is the ratio of the between group and within group inequality based on their respective Theil index. The ZK index emphasizes the role of within group inequality by implying that lower within group inequality would increase the polarization measure, an aspect that is missing in the ER polarization measure. Therefore, according to the ZK index, the same values of between group variance will lead to different measures according to the values of within group inequalities. Zhang and Kanbur (2001) apply the method to measure the rural–urban and coastal–inland polarizations of per capita expenditure

---

[9]   The human development index is an unweighted average of per capita income, educational status and longevity.
[10]   Analogies with the poverty gap measure are appropriate.

in China during 1983–95. They find that the magnitude of rural–urban polarization is much higher than that in the coastal–inland dimension. However, during the period, the coastal–inland polarization increases by 184%, compared to the −32.5 % decline in the rural–urban polarization.

Reynal-Querol (2002) proposes an ethnic polarization measure, a purely demographic polarization measure, referred to as the RQ index, that is intended to capture how far the distribution of the ethnic groups is from the (0.5; 0.0; . . .; 0.0; 0.5) distribution (bipolar), or a situation when society consists of only two ethnic groups with a 50% share each, representing the highest degree of polarization. This index is included as an independent variable in conflict regressions using civil war incidence and civil war duration as the dependent variables (Montalvo and Reynal-Querol, 2005 and 2007).

3.3.2.3 Horizontal inequality

Horizontal inequality is a relatively new concept; not only is its measurement thwarted by the paucity of data on relevant ethnic groups, but no real theoretical consensus exists as yet about a metric for its measurement. But for a variety of purposes, including cross-national comparisons, a single index number type measure of horizontal inequality is required, similar to the GINI coefficient for vertical inequality. We also need to be clear as to which groups we wish to apply this idea to: linguistic, tribal, religious and so on; as indicated above there may be some overlap across these categorizations. For example, in diverse countries such as India or Indonesia, horizontal inequalities across linguistic lines will be different from those along a confessional basis. A good summary of the literature can be found in Stewart, Brown and Mancini (2005).

As a starting point, such an index should be objective (descriptive) and not subjective (evaluative), as is the case, for example, with the Atkinson subjective measure of inequality aversion. Secondly, as far as its application to conflict is concerned we would probably be more interested in between group inequality than in the inequality within groups, as mentioned above. So, for example, if we want to examine the horizontal inequality between Hutus and Tutsis in promoting conflict in Burundi and Rwanda, we might be less interested in the inequalities that exist within each group, than between groups, but we would be concerned with group sizes. Stewart, Brown and Mancini (2005) distinguish between inequality measures that are specifically designed to measure differences across different identity based groups, and those that adapt existing measures of vertical inequality. Chief among the former are the ER index and the ZK index. In the second category of measures, those already in use in measuring vertical inequality, the two most promising are the group based coefficient of variation weighted by group size (GCOV),[11] and the population weighted group GINI coefficient (GGINI).[12] Stewart, Brown and Mancini (2005) argue that these two approaches (GCOV and GGINI) are the best ways to measure horizontal inequality since they do not involve any subjective measurement such as the value of α in the case of ER index, and are unconcerned with within group inequality as in the ZK index. Mancini (2008) uses the population weighted GCOV to measure horizontal inequalities in terms of several socioeconomic indicators at the district level in his study on communal violence in Indonesia.

In summary, each measure of grievance discussed above – actual or perceived achievement gaps related to relative deprivation, ethnic or social/economic polarization, group GINI or coefficients of variation – can be used to measure grievance based origins of conflict. There might even be some overlap between these measurements; for example if the α parameter is dropped from the ER formula, the ER and GGINI indices discussed above become identical. Given that most civil wars nowadays are ethnically based, indices of social polarization akin to traditional descriptions of class struggle are perhaps less salient in capturing grievances related to civil wars in developing countries, although its importance in explaining general mass political violence cannot be denied.

3.3.3   Some Empirical Findings

Relative deprivation has been found to affect conflict significantly in Nepal, which had a Maoist armed insurgency. Murshed and Gates (2005) find that HDI gaps with the capital Kathmandu, as well as greater landlessness, significantly explain the intensity of conflict-related fatalities across different districts in Nepal, whereas natural resources do not. Thus variables of enduring grievance such as landlessness are the most significant compared to more temporary income differences; at the same time the greed hypothesis is invalidated.

Indonesia is plagued by several conflicts, some of which are secessionist in nature, others are inter-communal. Four natural resource-rich provinces, Aceh, Riau, East Kalimantan and Papua, have wanted to separate, in different degrees, from the federation. Brown (2005) argues that the socioeconomic achievements (in terms of jobs and education) of the native Acehnese declined during periods when GRDP (regional income) rose substantially. This rise in GRDP took place because of the presence of

---

[11]   The coefficient of variation is the variance divided by the mean. Population weighting may be appropriate as they correct for large variations owing to small population groups.

[12]   The GINI coefficient compares differences between all groups.

oil and gas in Aceh. For example, poverty in Aceh rose by 239% during 1980–2002, whereas it fell by 42% in the rest of Indonesia. In Aceh, income (GRDP) per capita is 39% greater than the Indonesian average but expenditure per head, after redistribution through the fiscal system, was 18% below the national average. In Papua (rich in copper and silver), income per capita was 65% above the national average before the fiscal system came into operation. After taxes and subsidies, expenditure is 9% below the Indonesian average and there is a higher incidence of poverty, particularly among indigenous peoples. Thus, these separatist tendencies, in whole or in part, are a reflection of the dissatisfaction in some of the richer and natural resource endowed areas with the federal authority's redistributive policies taxing richer provinces to subsidize poorer regions.

Ethno-communal violence can be explained by differences in district health status, measured by a horizontal inequality index (population weighted coefficient of variation); see Mancini (2008). Tadjoeddin (2003) finds interesting results in this connection with regard to relative deprivation. Converging gaps in socioeconomic achievements of the two competing groups contribute to ethnic violence between Muslims and Christians in Maluku, whereas widening indicators have led to Dayak–Madurese violence in Kalimantan. The latter point has also been emphasized by Besançon (2005). What matters is the perception of change in the relative position of each ethnic group's rival community.

Østby (2008) manages to construct polarization indices and horizontal inequalities across 36 developing countries during 1986–2004 based on ownership of consumer durables (which she uses to calculate measures referred to as economic) and educational attainment (which she uses to calculate measures referred to as social), based upon household surveys. She employs a hybrid measure of polarization combining identity and economic polarities. The data is drawn from demographic and health surveys (DHS), and does not contain information on income or wealth. Be that as it may, this represents a pioneering application to the cross-country conflict debate. In her panel and cross-sectional analysis, she finds that social and economic polarization,[13] and social horizontal inequality based on education significantly contributes to conflict, whereas vertical inequality and purely ethnic or socioeconomic polarization do not. A priori, one would expect more enduring horizontal inequalities based on health, education, political exclusion and asset holdings to be more significant compared to transient income differences, as emphasized by Tilly (1998).

Østby (2006) utilizes the same data set on horizontal inequalities along

---

[13] Economic polarization becomes insignificant in the cross-sectional regressions.

with a variety of political variables ranging from democracy to political inclusiveness. The idea is that democracies and semi-democracies may facilitate the transformation of horizontal inequalities into conflict, by permitting protest. This theoretical assertion is supported by her empirical analysis. Inclusiveness implies an electoral system that has greater characteristics of proportional representation, and where minority groups are allowed to participate in elections. Inclusiveness, combined with high horizontal inequality and democracy, can exacerbate conflict at low levels of economic development. Thus, what is needed for peace is economic development and reduced horizontal inequalities in parallel with democratic development and inclusiveness. Despite the paucity of data on horizontal inequality, reasonable proxies show that it does matter in explaining conflict onset in a cross-section of countries, in contrast to the earlier assertions by many that inequality was immaterial to conflict risk.

Three further points are worth emphasizing at this juncture. First of all, horizontal inequality has to be measured at the level of the nation state. In a sense it refers to cross-sectional variation within a specific country. The data in different countries on horizontal inequality is still embryonic. Indices for horizontal inequality can be used for cross-country comparisons, whereas for a single conflict onset, gap measures may be sufficient. Secondly, most nation states do not keep detailed or systematic data on identity group based inequalities (say, between Catholics and Protestants, Hutus and Tutsis, Muslims and Christians) because of obvious political sensitivities. However, ethnic questions in future household surveys across the developing world will go a long way in helping us to enumerate data on inter-group differences in socioeconomic achievement. Finally, horizontal inequality as a cause of conflict can work in two directions: the rich may initiate conflict to extricate themselves from the relatively poor (the rage of the rich), or the poor may rise up in revolt against the rich (the rage of the poor). The former may be more likely in cases where a region suddenly discovers it can exist viably on its own resources, thus wishing to secede and not hand over revenues to the rest of the country. The latter is more likely to manifest itself in rebellions and revolutionary attempts to overthrow an oppressive state.

3.4   SYNTHESIS

Pure versions of the greed hypothesis are, on their own, unsatisfactory explanations for the causes of conflict. Addison, Le Billon and Murshed (2002), and Addison and Murshed (2003) construct a game theoretic model of contemporary conflict involving competition for resources combined with historical grievances, and a possible transfer from those in power that assuages the grievances of the excluded (see appendix to this chapter). In addition to resource rents or greed, grievances also play their part in fuelling conflict by explaining inter-group non-cooperation and serving to lower the cost of participation in conflict. Conflict can increase because of heightened intrinsic grievances, or because there are more lootable resources. Similarly, conflict may decline if historical grievances are assuaged by transfers from the party in power to potential rebel groups. In short, greed and grievances may exist simultaneously. Even if a conflict is initially based on grievance, it can acquire greedy characteristics, and the converse is also true. For example, a civil war originating in demands for land reform (Colombia, Nepal) can acquire greed based characteristics once the rebels begin to enjoy narco-rents or taxes from the peasantry. A civil war based on a desire to control lootable revenue rents can also produce grievances as people are killed.

In reality the competing greed versus grievance hypotheses may, after all, be complementary explanations for conflict. Insofar as they do provide alternative views, a fair test for their relative explanatory powers is best conducted at the level of a quantitative country case study, because cross-country comparisons of horizontal inequality are still at very early stages of development due to the lack of data. Indonesia's resource-rich regions that have had separatist conflicts with the federal government offer us a striking contrast in trying to gauge the relative explanatory power of the greed versus grievance explanations for conflict. When viewed via the lens of a detailed quantitative case study, the grievance and horizontal inequality explanations dominate any greed motivation. Yet, when looked at as one observation among many through the prism of a cross-country study, Indonesia's resource-rich regions become part of a modified form of the greed explanation (resources helping to prolong the duration of conflict and encouraging secession). It would appear, therefore, that the greed explanation for conflict duration and secessionist wars works in cross-country studies, but has to make way for grievance based arguments in quantitative country case studies. Grievances and horizontal inequalities may, after all, be better at explaining why conflicts begin, but not necessarily why they persist. The presence of neither greed nor grievance is sufficient for the outbreak of violent conflict, something that requires institutional breakdown, which can be described as the failure of the social contract, and is discussed in Chapter 5.

As yet, no empirical models at the level of cross-national analysis exist to test properly for the relative power of greed vis-à-vis horizontal inequality type grievances in explaining conflict onset. This is not just a result of constraints posed by insufficient data. Greed and grievance can and do co-exist; because one breeds the other a model of their simultaneous determination is required, along with the contribution of poverty (which is chiefly about the lack of growth) and institutional quality. Furthermore, the existing econometric literature regarding the causes of conflict allows us to infer little about the true nature of the causal links between the phenomena examined. Tests for causality require sufficiently long time series data; unless techniques of time series econometrics are employed, inferences about causality will remain limited in nature.

APPENDIX: CIVIL WAR WITH GREED AND GRIEVANCES

The model below is based on Addison, Le Billon and Murshed (2002) and Addison and Murshed (2003). There are two sides to the potential conflict: a government side and a rebel group. Both sides have access to a natural based rent or booty, which could be viewed as the greed motivation for conflict. The rebels have some historical grievances, based on relative deprivation and/or other forms of horizontal inequality against the government, which can be assuaged by a transfer from the government.

The Government Side

The expected utility of the government side (G) is given by:

$$G = \pi(a, e)G^P + (1 - \pi)(\cdot)G^C - C(a) \qquad (3.1)$$

Where G^P and G^C denote utilities or pay-offs in peace and conflict respectively, weighted by the probabilities of the two states, peace (π) and war $(1 - \pi)$. The pay-offs are endogenous in the sense that the probabilities of the two states depend on a strategic action (a) undertaken by the government. The strategic action parameter itself will depend on a number of variables described below. C is the cost of undertaking peaceful action, a.

Note that the government's income, (Y^G), defined in 3.2, is greater during peacetime, $\alpha > 1$. This is because income is derived from tax revenues, which in turn are related to output and the technology of production. During war, rising transactions costs, reduced investment and the flight of labour all combine to reduce output. And output losses are generally greater in resource diffuse economies than in 'point-sourced' ones, since the latter are easier (and more profitable) to defend. But even in the latter case, there are investments necessary to make extractive mining sectors function. In a state of war, there are certain lootable revenues (X^G) that can be obtained, and this corresponds to greed. The parameter a is the strategic choice variable of the government. T is the 'transfer' made by the government to the rebels in the state of relative peace and depends on government income. This can take a variety of forms, including broad based social and development expenditure extended to the rebels. F denotes military expenditure, this is clearly greater in wartime than during peace, hence $c > p$. The amount of F will depend on the objective function of the state (W), and whether or not the war or peace tendency is more dominant within the government. Note that even the peaceful outcome is a state of armed peace, as a minimum credible deterrent is required by the state.

$$G^P = \alpha Y^G - pF^G - T$$

$$\alpha > 1$$

$$G^C = Y^G - cF^G + X^G \qquad (3.2)$$

$$a = \frac{T(Y^G)}{F^G(W)}$$

$$c > p > 0, c + p = 1.$$

The probabilities of the two states are not related to a Tullock-type contest success function, as in Hirshleifer (1995), for example. This is because the low-intensity conflict is not a war of attrition. The rebels cannot expect to oust the government solely via a military victory and vice versa. Nor does the government have a Weberian monopoly over violence. We are concerned with a continuum of possible states of peace or war.

In fact, the strategic actions of the two players are a ratio of peaceful–belligerent behaviour, and are therefore mixed strategies. This is reflected in the ratio of transfers to military expenditure in the definition of a in (3.2) for the government. Thus, its strategic action depends on T, Y^G, X^G, W and F^G. Totally differentiating the expression for a in (3.2):

$$da = \frac{T_1}{F^G}dY^G - \frac{T}{F_1^{G2}}dW \qquad (3.3)$$

The first term on the right-hand side of 3.3 is positive, while the second term has a negative sign before it (T_1, $F_1^G > 0$). The first term is associated with a transfer to the excluded, and the second corresponds to a greater military effort against the rebels. W stands for the government's objective function with respect to military expenditure. The chances of the peaceful state in equation 3.1 are positively associated with a. In other words, $\pi_a > 0$, but $\pi_{aa} < 0$, due to diminishing returns. Peace is more likely if a transfer is made, including the excluded, rather than resorting to military expenditure with a view to overthrowing the rebels. There is a trade-off between transfers and fighting to generate the same level of expected utility indicated in 3.1. A more benevolent and developmental state may prefer making transfers to rebels to fighting them.[14] In equation 3.1, C is the cost function of undertaking the action, a, which increases the probability of

---

[14]   I refrain from making the distinction between democracies and military dictatorships in this regard, as democracies are occasionally 'militaristic' and dictatorships sometimes pacific, even inclusive.

peace, π. Both $C_a > 0$ and $C_{aa} > 0$. This cost function also incorporates psychological costs of making peace.

The Rebel Side

Turning to the rebel or excluded group, its expected utility (R) is given by:

$$R = \pi(a, e) R^P + (1 - \pi)(\cdot) R^C - E(e) \qquad (3.4)$$

where

$$R^P = \alpha Y^R - pF^R + T$$
$$R^C = Y^R - cF^R + X^R$$
$$e = \frac{T(Y^G)}{\theta} \qquad (3.5)$$

The pay-offs are endogenous in the sense that the probabilities of the two states depend on a strategic action (e) undertaken by the rebels. The strategic action parameter itself will depend on a number of variables described below. Its income may be greater during peace, at least for diffuse economies for the reasons outlined above. The income of the rebel group might be derived from voluntary contributions in rebel areas, or coercion of the local population, contributions from sympathetic citizens abroad or the export of narcotics and natural resources such as diamonds, particularly in the state of war (X^R). E is the cost of effort, e, which increases the probability of peace, π. Also, $\pi_e > 0$, but $\pi_{ee} < 0$, $E_e > 0$, and $E_{ee} > 0$. Peaceful effort increases as more transfers or broad based social expenditures are extended to the rebel group. I introduce an exogenous parameter, $\theta > 0$, which affects the level of peaceful action, and captures the horizontal inequality, polarization or relative deprivation dimension. It is based on the grievance measures discussed above, and is a non-pecuniary and intrinsic measure of historical and pure grievance. Rebel grievances therefore contain a pure or historical element (θ), and a component that can be mollified via pecuniary means through broad based spending (T). This grievance or sense of injustice serves to bind the rebels into a group, overcoming Olson's (1965) collective action problem. Furthermore, the presence of the grievance is what precludes cooperation or an effective social compact between the government and the rebels. A rise in θ could be caused by an increase in poverty or a greater perception of injustice; it serves to increase the cost of peaceful effort and raises belligerency levels among rebels. Alternatively, the parameter θ could reflect the relative income gap between the government and rebels. Thus the strategic action by the rebels depends on T and θ. Totally differentiating e, in 3.5:

$$de = \frac{T_1}{\theta}dY^G - \frac{T}{\theta^2}d\theta \qquad (3.6)$$

Thus peaceful efforts, e, increase with transfers from the state (the first term on the right-hand side of 3.6), and decrease with a rise in grievances (the second term on the right-hand side of 3.6).

Non-Cooperative Behaviour

Conflict (non-cooperation) occurs because neither side can cooperate or enter into a social contract due to the presence of historical grievances, low levels of transfers to the rebel group, imperfectly credible transfers to the rebel group or because the returns to peace relative to war are insufficient (greed). In the model, the strategies adopted by the two sides (a and e) in a Cournot–Nash non-cooperative one-shot game are endogenous. This in turn depends on disposable income and war booty (greed); transfers and fighting intensities hinge on the nature of the government as well as pure grievances on the rebel side.

Each side will maximize its own utility with respect to its own choice variable, and set it equal to zero. For the government it implies maximizing utility in 3.1, with respect to a as shown by:

$$\frac{\partial G}{\partial a} = \pi_a[G^P(\cdot) - G^C(\cdot)] - C_a = 0 \qquad (3.7)$$

Rebels maximize 3.4 with respect to e:

$$\frac{\partial R}{\partial e} = \pi_e[R^P(\cdot) - R^C(\cdot)] - E_e = 0 \qquad (3.8)$$

Equations 3.7 and 3.8 form the basis of the reaction functions for both sides, obtained by completely differentiating them with respect to a and e. Thus:

$$\frac{de}{da/R^G} = \frac{C_{aa} + \pi_{aa}[G^C(\cdot) - G^P(\cdot)]}{\pi_{ae}[G^P(\cdot) - G^C(\cdot)]} \gtreqless 0 \; if \; \pi_{ae} \gtreqless 0 \qquad (3.9)$$

and

$$\frac{de}{da/R^R} = \frac{\pi_{ae}[R^P(\cdot) - R^C(\cdot)]}{E_{ee} + \pi_{ee}[R^C(\cdot) - R^P(\cdot)]} \gtreqless 0 \; if \; \pi_{ae} \gtreqless 0 \qquad (3.10)$$

Note that $\pi_{ae} = \pi_{ea}$ by symmetry.

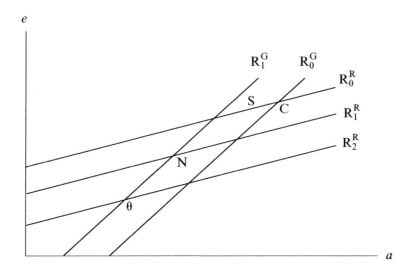

Figure 3.1   Strategic complements

The reaction functions are positively sloped if $\pi_{ae} > 0$, implying that the two strategies are complements (Figure 3.1). This is the standard assumption in the literature on conflict (see for example Hirshleifer, 1995). It means that increases in fighting or peaceful efforts by one side are matched in the same direction by the other side. In our model, however, we allow for the possibility that $\pi_{ae} < 0$, the choice variables are strategic substitutes and the reaction functions could slope downwards (Figure 3.2). This can only occur because the strategy space is defined in terms of peace. Thus if one side behaves more peacefully it increases the utility of both parties, and the other side may free ride on this action by actually reducing their own action. Note that the free riding does not necessarily lead to a rise in the equilibrium level of conflict, as the side raising its efforts may compensate more than proportionately for the group lowering their action. Recall that we are concerned with relative states of war and peace. Thus the two strategies can become substitutes the closer society is to complete peace, or the lower is the state of belligerency. The higher the intensity of war, the greater the likelihood of the two strategies being complements (Figure 3.1), as is conventional in the literature.

The non-cooperative solution to the model creates situations akin to moral hazard. From the viewpoint of domestic non-combatants and the rest of the world, the actions and efforts by the governments and rebels are not always observable or verifiable. Also, neither side has the incentive to engage in globally optimal levels of action or effort. Since the moral hazard

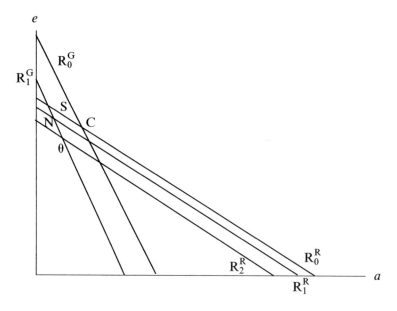

Figure 3.2　Strategic substitutes

is found in both parties, we have double moral hazard (see Murshed and Sen, 1995). In both Figures 3.1 and 3.2, the non-cooperative solution associated with moral hazard is given by point N. A more cooperative outcome is illustrated at point C. Also, in Figure 3.2, when the strategies are substitutes we have an additional 'equity' problem. In the non-cooperative equilibrium (point N) the government has effectively passed on some of the burden of action to the rebels. In fact the level of effort exercised by the rebels is greater than in the more cooperative solution. We could say that the government is free riding on the rebels. The positions could equally be reversed, so that the rebels pass on the burden of action to the government. The elimination of double moral hazard requires the design of mechanisms that induce cooperation and transparency.

What if one side, say the government, acts as a Stackelberg leader, as discussed in Azam (1995)? This means that the leader takes the followers' reaction function into account. A variety of multiple equilibria are possible under Stackelberg leader–follower situations. We depict some of the possibilities by the point S in Figures 3.1 and 3.2. These are associated with Pareto improvements on Cournot–Nash behaviour, but this is not necessarily always the case. In Azam's (1995) model the government pays the opposition a bribe, in the form of an unrequited fiscal transfer. This could also be easily construed as power sharing, or the promise of future income, and even privatizing a state asset in favour of the rebels. The theory therefore illuminates a recurring problem – that of credibility – which is frequently encountered in processes to end civil wars. I will return to this issue again in Chapter 4.

An Increase in Rebel Grievance

Recall that a rise in θ increases the costs to the rebels of engaging in peaceful activity, and is a result of rising intrinsic grievances related to horizontal inequality, polarization or relative deprivation. In both Figures 3.1 and 3.2 a downward movement in the rebels' reaction functions represents this increase in θ, and the new intersection points are denoted by θ from the original position at N (the rebel reaction functions move from R_1^R to R_2^R. There is less peaceful activity, and greater conflict. In Figure 3.1 when the two activities are strategic complements there is a clear welfare loss. In Figure 3.2, however, the two strategies are substitutes. The decrease in effort by the rebels is matched by an increase in government action. In the cases where the strategies are substitutes and the government had shifted some of the burden of action to the rebels (Figure 3.2), there could be a Pareto improvement on the earlier situation in terms of equity.

A Rise in Booty (Greed)

This raises the gains from conflict. In Figures 3.3 and 3.4 we consider the rise in available war loot, bearing in mind that this increase could be relevant to either or both sides. Figure 3.3 represents the case where the two strategies are complements. An increase in available booty to the government (X^G) shifts its reaction function leftwards, indicating a lower optimal choice of a for any level of e. For the rebels a greater availability of lootable resources (X^R) has the effect of a downward shift in its reaction function, pointing to reduced e for every level of a. When both sides have equal access to booty the shift is to point B with an obvious decline in activities to promote peace. When it is exclusive to the government point G becomes applicable, when it is only the rebels, point R is the new equilibrium. The side receiving the booty lowers its action or effort accompanied by a corresponding, but less than proportionate, decline in its opponent's strategic variable.

A qualitatively different picture emerges in Figure 3.4 where the strategies are substitutes. Greater loot shifts reaction functions in a downward direction. Here the greater endowment of booty by one side exclusively not only reduces its incentive to undertake its own relevant strategic action or effort, but also causes it to shift part of the burden of peaceful

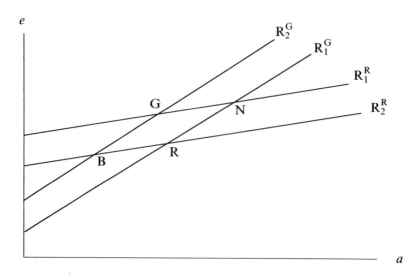

Figure 3.3   Booty (complements)

behaviour to its opponent. In general, the greater availability of booty or lootable resources to both sides (as opposed to one side only) reduces the equilibrium levels of peaceful behaviour as illustrated by point B in Figures 3.3 and 3.4.

Aid to the Government to Induce More Transfers to the Rebels (T)

Aid augments income. First, in terms of our model, if donors make foreign aid conditional on peace or transfers to the rebel group, the R^G curve moves rightwards in Figure 3.1 when the government receives aid in a state of peace only, and there is a rise in T to the rebels. In Figure 3.2 a similar gift causes the recipient's reaction function to move upwards. In both diagrams there is a shift from R_1^G to R_0^G. In either case there is greater peace and more a and e. Aid to parties that increases their utility in times of peace could even replicate the more cooperative outcome at point C, and solve the double moral hazard problem caused by non-cooperation. However, such aid conditionality is notoriously difficult to achieve. The recipient may accept aid and then renege on his commitment to work towards peace. If aid is fungible (unconditional) the recipient may transfer all or part of these resources to his military effort. If we examine equation 3.3 above, taking a derivative with respect to Y^G, we will notice that transfers to the rebels rise with an increase in government income. But belligerence towards the rebels declines unambiguously only if $dW/dY^G < 0$; so that

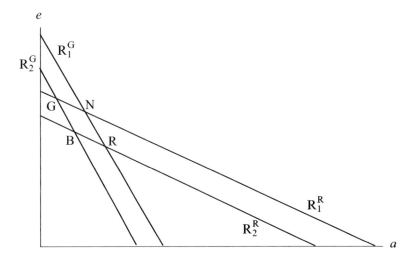

Figure 3.4   Booty (substitutes)

$da/dY^G > 0$. This $(dW/dY^G < 0)$ means that the state derives greater welfare from transfers to the rebels, aimed at lessening their grievances, rather than trying to emasculate them through military force. Unconditional aid to the government may result in an increase in both transfers to the rebels, as well as military efforts to suppress them, if $dW/dY^G > 0$ in equation 3.3, when the government side has a relatively stronger preference for military options.

4. The uneasy commitment to peace

4.1 INTRODUCTION

The previous chapter examined the immediate causes of civil conflict based on greed and grievance, whereas the chapter prior to that looked at the pre-conditions for conflict in terms of growth failure and underdevelopment. The purpose of this chapter is to analyse why it is so difficult to end ongoing conflicts. In particular, the aim is to understand why there are so many false promises claiming to end civil wars. Collier (2004) argues that countries that have just experienced a civil war are more likely to have further conflict, with a 38.6% post-conflict risk based upon an analysis of 21 countries during 1965–99. He characterizes this phenomenon of recurring war as the 'conflict trap', and this position is currently very fashionable amongst policy makers. Others, such as Walter (2004) are less pessimistic; she states that for all civil wars between 1945 and 1996, only 36% were followed by another war.

In civil war situations, negotiations often take place, bargains are struck, widely trumpeted peace treaties are signed, yet either one or more of the parties, or a newly formed splinter group or a faction unrepresented in the peace negotiations go back to war; see Table 4.1 on signed bargains to end internal conflict in the post-cold war era. Walter (2002) indicates that 62% of civil wars between 1940 and 1992 culminated in a signed peace treaty. Of these, only 57% were successfully implemented. The figure for the period after the cold war (Table 4.1) indicates that about 70% of treaties were implemented. Of 148 peace settlements signed between 1991 and 2005 some 103 appeared to be implemented. Table 4.1 also illustrates the multiplicity of peace treaties associated with civil wars involving the same country. This suggests that many attempts at negotiation are necessary to establish peace, and many signed treaties that emerge from these bargaining processes are reneged upon by some group. This requires several iterations at negotiation. The general context in which these events are taking place is one where the number of countries embroiled in civil war appears to be declining since 1994 (Hegre, 2004; Fearon, 2004).

Since the end of the cold war there has been no shortage of mediation by

Table 4.1   Peace agreements

Name	Peace agreement name	Year	Outcome
Afghanistan	Islamabad Accord	1993	1
Afghanistan	Jalalabad Agreement	1993	0
Afghanistan	Mahipar Agreement	1996	1
Angola	The Gbadolite Declaration on Angola	1989	1
Angola	The Bicesse Agreement	1991	1
Angola	The Lusaka Protocol	1994	1
Angola	Memorandum of Understanding or Memorandum of Intent	2002	0
Bangladesh (Chittagong Hill Tracts)	Chittagong Hill Tracts Peace Accord	1997	0
Bosnia and Herzegovina (Croat)	The Washington Agreement	1994	0
Bosnia and Herzegovina (Serb)	The General Framework Agreement for Peace in Bosnia and Herzegovina (the Dayton Agreement)	1995	0
Burundi	Arusha Peace and Reconciliation Agreement for Burundi	2000	0
Burundi	Accord du Cessez-le-feu entre le Gouvernement de Transition du Burundi et le CNDD-FDD	2002	0
Burundi	The Pretoria Protocol on Political, Defence and Security Power Sharing in Burundi	2003	0
Burundi	The Pretoria Protocol on Outstanding Political, Defence and Security Power Sharing Issues in Burundi	2003	0
Burundi	The Global Ceasefire Agreement between Transitional Government and the Forces pour la defence de la democratie (CNDD-FDD) of Mr Nkúrunziza	2003	0
Cambodia	Agreement on a Comprehensive Political Settlement of the Cambodia Conflict, 'The Paris Agreement'	1991	0
Chad	El Geneina Agreement	1992	1
Chad	Tripoli I Agreement	1993	1
Chad	Bangui II Agreement	1994	1
Chad	Abeche Agreement	1994	0
Chad	The Dougia Accord	1995	1
Chad	National Reconciliation Agreement	1997	0

Table 4.1   (continued)

Name	Peace agreement name	Year	Outcome
Chad	Donya Agreement	1998	0
Chad	Reconciliation Agreement	1999	1
Chad	Tripoli II Agreement	2002	1
Chad	Yebibou Agreement 2005	2005	0
Colombia	Acuerdo final Gobierno Nacional-Ejército Popular De Liberación	1991	0
Colombia	Common Agenda for the Path to a New Colombia	1999	0
Colombia	Los Pozos Agreement	2001	0
Colombia	Los Pozos Accord	2002	1
Comoros (Anjouan)	The Famboni Declaration	2000	1
Comoros (Anjouan)	The Famboni II Agreement	2001	0
Comoros (Anjouan)	Agreement on the transitional arrangements in the Comoros	2003	0
Congo	Accord de Cessez-le-Feu et de Cessation des Hostilités	1999	0
Croatia (Serb)	The Erdut Agreement	1995	0
Democratic Republic of Congo	Lusaka Accord	1999	1
Democratic Republic of Congo	Declaration of Fundamental Principles for the Inter-Congolese Dialogue	2001	0
Democratic Republic of Congo	Political agreement on consensual management of the transition in the Democratic Republic of the Congo	2002	0
Democratic Republic of Congo	Global and Inclusive Agreement on the Transition in the Democratic Republic of Congo	2002	0
Democratic Republic of Congo	Inter-Congolese Political Negotiations – The Final Act	2003	0
Djibouti	Accord de paix et de la reconciliation nationale	1994	0
Djibouti	Accord Cadre de Reforme et de Concorde Civile	2000	0
Djibouti	Accord de reforme et concorde civile	2001	0
Ecuador–Peru	Acta Presidencial de Brasilia	1998	0
El Salvador	Geneva Agreement	1990	0

Table 4.1   (continued)

Name	Peace agreement name	Year	Outcome
El Salvador	General Agenda and Timetable for the Comprehensive Negotiating Process	1990	0
El Salvador	Agreement on Human Rights	1990	0
El Salvador	Mexico Agreements	1991	0
El Salvador	New York Agreement	1991	0
El Salvador	The Compressed Negotiations	1991	0
El Salvador	New York Act	1991	0
El Salvador	New York Act II	1992	0
El Salvador	The Chapultepec Peace Agreement	1992	0
Eritrea–Ethiopia	Agreement between the Government of the State of Eritrea and the Government of the Federal Democratic Republic of Ethiopia	2000	0
Georgia (Abkhazia)	Declaration on Measures for a Political Settlement of the Georgian/Abkhaz conflict	1994	0
Guatemala	The Oslo Accord	1990	0
Guatemala	The Mexico Accord	1991	0
Guatemala	The Querétaro Agreement	1991	0
Guatemala	The Framework Agreement for the Resumption of Negotiations between the Government of Guatemala and the Guatemalan National Revolutionary Unity	1994	0
Guatemala	The Agreement on a Timetable for Negotiations on a Firm and Lasting Peace in Guatemala	1994	0
Guatemala	The Comprehensive Agreement on Human Rights	1994	0
Guatemala	The Agreement on the Resettlement of Population Groups Uprooted by the Armed Conflict	1994	0
Guatemala	The Agreement for the Establishment of the Commission to Clarify Past Human Rights Violations and Acts of Violence that Have Caused the Guatemalan Population to Suffer	1994	0
Guatemala	The Agreement on the Identity and Rights of Indigenous Peoples	1995	0
Guatemala	The Agreement on Socio-economic Aspects and the Agrarian Situation	1996	0

Table 4.1   (continued)

Name	Peace agreement name	Year	Outcome
Guatemala	The Agreement on the Strengthening of Civilian Power and the Role of the Armed Forces in a Democratic Society	1996	0
Guatemala	The Agreement on a Definitive Ceasefire	1996	0
Guatemala	The Agreement on Constitutional Reforms and the Electoral Regime	1996	0
Guatemala	The Agreement on the Basis for the Legal Integration of the URNG	1996	0
Guatemala	The Agreement for a Firm and Lasting Peace	1996	0
Guatemala	The Agreement on the Implementation, Compliance and Verification Timetable for the Peace Agreements	1996	0
Guinea Bissau	Abuja Peace Agreement	1998	1
Haiti	The Governor's Island Agreement	1993	1
India (Bodoland)	Bodoland Autonomous Council Act, 1993	1993	0
India (Tripura)	Memorandum of Settlement – 23 August 1993	1993	1
Indonesia (Aceh)	Cessation of Hostilities Framework Agreement	2002	0
Indonesia (Aceh)	Memorandum of Understanding between the Government of the Republic of Indonesia and the Free Aceh Movement	2005	0
Israel (Palestine)	Declaration of Principles on Interim Self-Government Arrangements/ Oslo Agreement	1993	0
Israel (Palestine)	Agreement on the Gaza Strip and the Jericho Area	1994	0
Israel (Palestine)	Agreement on Preparatory Transfer of Powers and Responsibilities Between Israel and the PLO	1994	0
Israel (Palestine)	Israeli–Palestinian Interim Agreement on the West Bank and the Gaza Strip/ Oslo B	1995	0
Israel (Palestine)	Protocol on Redeployment in Hebron	1995	0
Israel (Palestine)	The Wye River Memorandum	1998	1
Israel (Palestine)	The Sharm el-Sheik Memorandum Wye II	1999	0
Ivory Coast	Linas-Marcoussis Peace Accords	2003	1

Table 4.1 (continued)

Name	Peace agreement name	Year	Outcome
Ivory Coast	Accra II	2003	0
Ivory Coast	Accra III	2004	1
Ivory Coast	Pretoria Agreement on the Peace Process in Côte d'Ivoire	2005	0
Liberia	Banjul III Agreement	1990	0
Liberia	Bamako Ceasefire Agreement	1990	1
Liberia	Banjul IV Agreement	1990	1
Liberia	Lomé Agreement	1991	1
Liberia	Yamoussoukro IV Peace Agreement	1991	1
Liberia	Cotonou Peace Agreement	1993	1
Liberia	Akosombo Peace Agreement	1994	1
Liberia	Abuja Peace Agreement	1995	1
Liberia	Abuja II Peace Agreement	1996	0
Liberia	Accra Ceasefire Agreement	2003	0
Liberia	Accra Peace Agreement	2003	0
Macedonia	The Ohrid Agreement	2001	0
Mali (Azawad)	Tamanrasset Accord	1991	1
Mali (Azawad)	Pacte National	1992	1
Mexico	The San Andrés Accords	1996	1
Moldova (Dniestr)	Memorandum on the Basis for Normalization of Relations Between the Republic of Moldova and Transdniestria	1997	0
Mozambique	The Protocol on the Agreed Agenda	1991	0
Mozambique	Basic Principles	1991	0
Mozambique	Agreement on Establishment and Recognition of Political Parties	1991	0
Mozambique	Agreement on Principles of the Electoral Act	1992	0
Mozambique	The Acordo Geral de Paz (AGP)	1992	0
Niger (Air and Azawad)	Paris Accord	1993	1
Niger (Air and Azawad)	Ouagadougou Accord	1994	0
Niger (Air and Azawad)	Accord Établissant une Paix Définitive entre le Gouvernement de la République du Niger et L'Organisation de la Résistance Armée	1995	0
Papua New Guinea (Bougainville)	The Honiara Declaration	1991	1

Table 4.1 (continued)

Name	Peace agreement name	Year	Outcome
Papua New Guinea (Bougainville)	Honiara Commitments to Peace	1994	1
Papua New Guinea (Bougainville)	Bougainville Peace Agreement	2001	0
Philippines	GRP-RAM/SFP/YOU General Agreement for Peace	1995	0
Philippines (Mindanao)	Mindanao Final Agreement	1996	0
Philippines (Mindanao)	Agreement on Peace between the Government of the Republic of the Philippines and the Moro Islamic Liberation Front	2001	0
Rwanda	The N'SELE Ceasefire Agreement	1991	1
Rwanda	The Protocol of Agreement Between the Government of the Republic of Rwanda and the Rwandese Patriotic Front on the Rule of Law	1992	1
Rwanda	The Protocols of Agreement Between the Government of the Republic of Rwanda and the Rwandese Patriotic Front on Power-Sharing within the Framework of a Broad-Based Transitional Government	1993	1
Rwanda	The Protocol of Agreement Between the Government of the Republic of Rwanda and the Rwandese Patriotic Front on the Repatriation of Refugees and the Resettlement of Displaced Persons	1993	1
Rwanda	Same as above, with integration of armed forces, as well as a Protocol of Agreement on Miscellaneous Issues and Final Provisions	1993	1
Rwanda	Arusha Accords	1993	1
Senegal (Casamance)	Accord Général de Paix entre le Gouvernement de la République du Senegal et le Mouvement des Forces Democratique de la Casamace (MFDC)	2004	0

Table 4.1   (continued)

Name	Peace agreement name	Year	Outcome
Sierra Leone	Abidjan Peace Agreement	1996	1
Sierra Leone	Lomé Peace Agreement	1999	1
Sierra Leone	Abuja Ceasefire Agreement	2000	0
Somalia	Addis Ababa Agreement	1993	1
Somalia	Nairobi Declaration on National Reconciliation	1994	1
Somalia	The Cairo Declaration on Somalia	1997	1
Sudan (Southern Sudan)	Khartoum Agreement	1997	1
Sudan (Southern Sudan)	Machakos Protocol	2002	0
Sudan (Southern Sudan)	Agreement on Security Arrangements During the Interim Period	2003	0
Sudan (Southern Sudan)	Framework on Wealth Sharing During the Pre-Interim and Interim Period	2004	0
Sudan (Southern Sudan)	Protocol Between the GOS and SPLM on Power Sharing	2004	0
Sudan (Southern Sudan)	The Protocol Between the GOS and SPLM on the Resolution of Conflict in Abyei Area	2004	0
Sudan (Southern Sudan)	The Protocol Between the GOS and SPLM on the Resolution of Conflict in Southern Kordofan/Nuba Mountains and Blue Nile States	2004	0
Sudan (Southern Sudan)	Sudan Comprehensive Peace Agreement	2005	0
Tajikistan	Protocol on the Fundamental Principles of Establishing Peace and National Accord in Tajikistan	1995	0
Tajikistan	Agreement between the President of the Republic of Tajikistan, E. S. Rakhmonov, and the Leader of the United Tajik Opposition, S. A. Huri, on the Results of the Meeting Held in Moscow 23 December 1996	1996	0
Tajikistan	Statute of the Commission on National Reconciliation	1997	0
Tajikistan	Protocol on Political Issues	1997	0
Tajikistan	The Moscow Declaration – General Agreement on the Establishment of Peace and National Accord in Tajikistan	1997	0

Table 4.1 (continued)

Name	Peace agreement name	Year	Outcome
Uganda	Yumbe Peace Agreement	2002	0
UK (Northern Ireland)	The Good Friday Agreement	1998	0
Yugoslavia (Kosovo)	Kosovo peace Agreement I	1999	0
Yugoslavia (Slovenia)	Brioni Agreement	1991	0

Note: The Outcome indicator asks: Did the peace agreement end, i.e. did the implementation fail? 1: Yes, 0: No. The peace agreement is no longer considered fully implemented if the validity of the agreement is contested by one or more of the warring parties that signed. A peace agreement cannot, from the UCDP perspective, survive if the primary parties are no longer party to it. If a party officially withdraws from a peace agreement, it is considered to have ended.

Source: UCDP (Uppsala Conflict Data Programme) Peace Agreement Data Set Codebook Version 1.0, October 2006, http://www.pcr.uu.se/research/UCDP/data_and_publications/datasets.htm.

third parties aimed at ending civil wars.[1] Mediation aims to bring warring parties to the bargaining table. Often this is conducted through the good offices of, strategically speaking, smaller Western powers. These might be affluent nations with a large stake in the foreign aid business but without significant military power, for example, Nordic donors such as Norway. These countries may wish to exercise 'soft' power by helping to broker conflict resolution in 'fragile' states,[2] however, they lack the means to enforce militarily the stipulations of any signed bargain that may follow mediation. Similarly, regional powers (countries in the vicinity of civil war affected nations) who mediate face the same dilemma; they can facilitate negotiation but cannot always enforce any peace agreement that may ensue. Belligerent parties in a civil war may find the prospects of talks attractive because of the promises of aid that follow a signed bargain. This may be the case even if they are not really genuinely ready to make peace. If they do sign a peace agreement, is their commitment to this treaty credible, or do they face temptations to renege on it?

---

[1]   This may be because, unlike during the cold war, the dominant role of the superpowers in initiating, supporting and ending strategically or ideologically based civil wars is no longer as overwhelming in our uni-polar world.

[2]   Concern with fragile states, many of which are in conflict, and all of whom are in danger of slipping into civil war, have become the cornerstone of aid policy among both multilateral and bilateral donors (see Menocal, Othieno and Evans, 2008).

A peaceful end to civil war, without outright military victory by any one side, does involve making concessions to opponents. As Walter (2002) points out this raises issues as to whether the various parties to the conflict are ready to negotiate, willing to make deals and sign an agreement that stipulates the bargain that has been arrived at. The implementation of the treaty is also fraught with danger. These issues are discussed in section 4.2, and are chiefly to do with power sharing formulas in the post-conflict political order, and third party guarantees for the peace treaty. Section 4.3 concerns itself with the dangers of the peace treaty becoming 'cheap talk', because the interests of one or more of the warring factions make them first sign a treaty, which is effectively only an empty piece of paper to them, and then opportunistically renege on their commitment. Here the valuation of the future reputation becomes salient, because the various parties to the conflict often return to the bargaining process after a failed peace treaty, as Table 4.1 illustrates. It should be remembered that signing a peace treaty constitutes a signal of commitment to its stipulations; I will examine issues related to their credibility. Finally section 4.4 is concerned with policies that can aid commitment to peace treaties, especially the peacekeeping or monitoring arrangements that help sustain these agreements.

4.2 BARGAINING, SIGNING AND IMPLEMENTING PEACE TREATIES

What are the conditions that are conducive to initiating peace negotiations between warring parties? Walter (2002) highlights three factors. First of all, one or more parties to the conflict must become war weary in a manner that the expected utility or benefit from continuing in a state of war is considerably less than if a peace deal is struck, even if that requires concessions to erstwhile enemies.[3] Ultimately, war is irrational and inefficient, as pointed out in earlier chapters. It destroys output through direct and collateral damage, and peace is always globally Pareto optimal. Misperceptions, mistrust and coordination failure are responsible for conflict, as are political aims that cannot be achieved through peaceful means. But the costs of war imply that a negotiated settlement with concessions might be better. An obvious candidate that prevents peace in this category of explanations for civil war persistence is an overestimate of the probability of military victory (see Collier, Hoeffler and Söderbom, 2004, in this connection).

---

[3] See, for example, the government side in the signalling game in the appendix to this chapter.

This brings us to Walter's (2002) second point: a military stalemate between the two sides is conducive towards commencing negotiations. Finally, Walter (2002) suggests that democracies are more likely to arrive at settlements with enemies; accountable democracies may find it easier to make credible commitments to treaties, and as they are more used to sharing power than are autocracies. There are loopholes in this last argument, as democracies need to be well functioning and not the flawed democracies endemic in developing countries (a Polity score of at least 6, but more likely 8). Democracies in factional states may not be used to sharing power with other ethnicities or groups in a winner-take-all electoral system, and commitments made by long-standing autocrats may be more credible than promises made by politicians in imperfect democracies.

Secondly, there are issues related to the granting of concessions that ultimately lead to formal peace treaties. Two factors merit mention here, following Walter (2002). There is, first of all, the crucial importance of mediation in solving the coordination problems that prevent disputants from negotiating. This is mainly to do with informational problems, and often boils down to the inability of two sides to get together to talk, as this could politically be an extremely costly gesture for the leadership, without the good offices of a third party. Mediators often directly bear the various costs of warring parties getting together and negotiating. As pointed out earlier, there is no shortage of mediation at the moment.

Furthermore, concessions leading to a peace treaty are more likely if what is at stake is more divisible. Fearon (2004) points out that of all types of civil wars those with secessionist tendencies and 'sons of the soil' dynamics are the most difficult to resolve, and tend to last the longest. This could be because of an overlapping interest and attachment to the inviolability of land and territorial sovereignty by both parties to the conflict. But the indivisibility of war aims, symbols or land can also make certain civil wars intractable. Wood (2003) highlights indivisibility as a major impediment to peace deals. This arises when territory, symbols or revenue in a post-conflict situation cannot be divided up so as to achieve peace. The problem can be most acute when religious sites such as Har'm El Sharif or Temple Mount in Jerusalem are involved. Also, considerable difficulties arise when it is problematic to achieve compromise over a war aim such as land reform (Colombia), or deep constitutional change (future of the monarchy in Nepal). There can also be seemingly irreconcilable disputes over post-war power sharing. Secessionist wars where territorial sovereignty is contested can be tricky to resolve too. Compared to these, disagreements over sharing resources may be less challenging.

Wood (2003) considers non-cooperative strategies of actors in a conflict, and whether their strategies to fight or compromise are self-enforcing without third party mediation. The decision to compromise is based on the pay-off in the peaceful state, as well as beliefs about the strategy that will be adopted by one's opponent. There also has to be bargaining over the share of the post-war pie that each side gets. The Nash equilibrium can involve either fighting or compromise; multiple equilibria are possible. If each side's expected post-war share is greater than what they can get from fighting, feasible compromise equilibria exist. But that depends upon beliefs about the other side's strategy. The feasible compromise equilibrium and the sharing it involves may not coincide with beliefs about the opponent's strategy. In general, there will be an optimal share of the post-war pie for each side that will maximize the robustness of a peaceful settlement (the agreement lasting or being self-enforcing), given beliefs of the two sides about each other. Within each group there may be factions or spoiler groups with more pessimistic views about their opponent's strategies. This will depress their value of any share of the post-war pie. Indivisibilities regarding the issues contested, and the post-war pie, also lower the expected worth of any share of the post-war settlement, making self-enforcing compromises difficult.

Additionally, Walter (2002) emphasizes the vital nature of the implementation of a peace treaty. Even when signed bargains are struck, the road to their implementation is fraught with danger. These relate to: (1) the stability of power sharing deals entered into during the peace process; (2) external guarantees and enforcement of both the disarmament process and the stipulations of the peace treaty in general; and I would add (3) the adequacy of post-war aid.

With regard to the first point, it is crucial that the immediate post-war political arrangement includes positions of power for all warring factions represented at the negotiating table, otherwise the peace accord is simply not incentive compatible for the excluded groups. Most importantly, post-war political power must not be left to a winner-take-all electoral system as this will discourage compromise. Even when a treaty is cajoled upon the various factions, the absence of assured positions of power will encourage some belligerents to renege on the treaty. Thus, the post-conflict constitution is of importance. There would be a preference for more federalist structures, parliamentary as opposed to presidential systems, proportional systems of representation rather than majoritarian Westminster-type systems, and effective checks and balances on the executive (separation of powers as discussed in Chapter 2). As such these ideas behind power sharing constitutions can be traced back to the ideas (consociationalism) and work of Lijphart (1977, 1997). Issues related to the longer-term effects of power sharing are examined in more detail in Chapter 5.

With regard to external guarantees, Walter (2002) makes a strong conceptual case for the risks associated with disarmament in the immediate aftermath of a war being covered by external guarantees. The various warring parties to a conflict are at greatest danger in the initial phases of disarmament, because they are vulnerable to surprise attacks by an enemy who has not fully disarmed (see the appendix to this chapter for an analytical model of surprise warfare). To prevent these apprehensions, and to facilitate the smooth functioning of the disarmament process, we require both external verification of disarmament phases and external sanctions (including military ones) that punish violators. A similar argument can be applied to the enforceability of the peace treaty. Furthermore, for peace to be sustainable, growth must restart, and this requires overseas development assistance (aid) to poor countries.[4] I will employ the short-hand term 'sanctions' to denote this policy package. Moreover, as the model in the appendix shows, a state of peace in the absence of external sanctions and aid is simply not a self-enforcing or sustainable outcome in many poor developing countries, even if the parties to a conflict have been cajoled into signing a peace agreement by powerful donors.

Walter (2002), econometrically tests some of the hypotheses mentioned above on civil wars between 1940 and 1992 (the cold war era). She finds that the presence of mediation, a military stalemate and the absence of territorial goals augur well for a lasting peace. Interestingly the presence of executive constraints, non-total goals (divisible aims), the length of the war and ethnic divisions are statistically insignificant. Most important for a successful resolution are third power guarantees, as well as territorial and political pacts. The latter two refer to power sharing. In a nutshell, the two most crucial factors for obtaining a credible commitment to peace (a treaty that is not violated) are sanctions and power sharing. Furthermore, power sharing deals in a peace treaty without third party guarantees fail in 80% of cases, while those with external guarantees succeed in 90% of cases. This implies a degree of inseparability between external sanctions and power sharing deals, even if both exercise an independent influence on the chances of a peace treaty lasting. Finally, there appears to be a trade-off between the degree of power sharing and the strength of external guarantees or sanctions. For example, the militarily very powerful NATO guarantees to the peace treaties in Bosnia were accompanied by relatively weaker political power sharing arrangements according to Walter (2002). The saliency of the huge amount of aid in Bosnia and Kosovo, per capita of the population, cannot be overemphasized; this factor is often neglected in the purely political science literature.

---

4   This last issue on aid to post-conflict countries is examined in Chapter 6.

In a similar vein, Hoddie and Hartzell (2005) find that territorial and military power sharing arrangements reduce the risk of peace treaty failure by 99% and 95% respectively. Military power sharing was insignificant in Walter's (2002) empirical analysis. Also, unlike Walter (2002), Hoddie and Hartzell (2005) find that the duration and intensity of conflict is significant, but central government level power sharing appears less important in their analysis.

It is, therefore, important to note that there are a variety of power sharing agreements, with differing impacts on the sustainability of peace agreements. First, there are political power sharing agreements that chiefly divide cabinet positions among erstwhile antagonists in the immediate aftermath of the peace accord, and stipulate arrangements for elections. Secondly, there may be military pacts that aim to integrate forces that were battling each other prior to the treaty (in addition to any disarmament process). Thirdly, there may be so-called territorial pacts that bring about a degree of decentralization and regional autonomy.

Jarstad and Nilsson (2008) argue that of the three types of power sharing mentioned above, military and territorial sharing deals involve the most costly and time consuming concessions, as they necessitate sacrificing command and control. This sends out a 'costly' signal to former enemies, as they involve concessions that are deeper and more costly. In these circumstances, peaceful overtures are perceived to be more sincere by other parties because genuinely costly concessions appear to be made. By contrast, political power sharing is more likely to be seen as cheap talk; this is because political commitments are easier to renege upon. As Dixit (2003) points out, the political process in any society, irrespective of whether there is violent large-scale conflict or not, is fraught with opportunistic behaviour where it is difficult to sustain political commitments except through costly constitutional safeguards that act as commitment devices.[5] A similar point is made by Acemoglu, Johnson and Robinson (2005), and it even applies to the rules of the game (the constitution itself).[6] Jarstad and Nilsson (2008) conclude that military and territorial (decentralization) power sharing pacts are more likely to contribute towards the longevity of a peace accord. Secondly, they distinguish between promises of power sharing that might be written into accords, and their actual post-accord implementation (see the multiperiod signalling model in the appendix to this chapter).

Jarstad and Nilsson (2008) employ data related to political, military and territorial pacts and their implementation in 83 peace agreements between

---

[5]   This is modelled as the signalling game in the appendix to this chapter.
[6]   See Chapter 2 on institutions and their implications for growth.

conflicting dyads[7] in the post-cold war period (1989–2004). They point out that 77% of political power sharing agreements were actually implemented, and quite quickly. Whereas 34.5% of military pacts are fully implemented, and a high percentage (55%) are partially implemented, making the total implementation figure for this type of power sharing accord greater than for political deals. The same is true for territorial arrangements: as much as 55% are fully implemented and a further 27% partially executed. Thus it appears that in recent times these two kinds of deals have a greater chance of partial or complete implementation, albeit more slowly, than purely political pacts. In their statistical analysis power sharing deals that are purely political (both the commitment to it and the actual implementation) have no significant impact on the duration of peace. By contrast, territorial pacts and their implementation significantly increase the sustainability of a peace agreement. Military pacts may not exert a significant effect on the duration of peace, but their implementation does. Furthermore, the greater the intensity of conflict, the lesser are the chances of a peace accord lasting. Surprisingly, peacekeeping operations (UN or regional) seem to exert no significant impact on the duration of peace.

These results are in sharp contrast to Walter's findings about the cold war era (1940–92) where the joint effect of political pacts and external security guarantees exercised the most significant impact on the chances of peace. Perhaps, with the end of superpower rivalry, political power sharing pacts may be quickly and imperfectly cobbled together by mediators, and without superpower sanctions they may be more quickly reneged upon. It should be pointed out that Jarstad and Nilsson's findings about the insignificance of peacekeeping interventions do not vitiate the importance of external security guarantees. It is just that many contemporary peacekeeping operations simply lack teeth, and this makes them look like cheap talk to rogue groups looking to restart the conflict, as the model in the appendix analyses. Secondly, the production or financing of peacekeeping and financial aid to post-conflict societies may provide little benefit to those who pay for peace (Western donors) in distant lands; I analyse this in the last theoretical model in the appendix. Thirdly, neither of the two studies (Walter, 2002, or Jarstad and Nilsson, 2008 and the voluminous literature they cite) picks up on the centrality of the financial aid and reconstruction package that accompanies external guarantees of peace accords. This must follow a peace deal to kick start economic growth.

The conflict abating property of economic growth and poverty reduction is perhaps the most significant factor in building lasting peace, and for

---

[7] A dyad refers to conflict between the government and each one of several rebel groups.

this reason I will discuss post-conflict economic reconstruction, and the role of aid in this regard separately in Chapter 6. Finally, power sharing and the institutions that anchor commitments to lasting peace (in the sense of peace not just as the absence of war) are very much part of the long-term social contract, which will be discussed in Chapter 5. The next section is devoted to the idea that no matter what kind of accord is in place there are always temptations for some to renege on these.

4.3   CREDIBLE COMMITMENT TO PEACE[8]

Being party to a treaty sends out a signal of commitment. The difficulty arises when it is in the interest of one side to renege on the promise of peace, and the actions that peace involves. For example, in the model contained in the appendix to this chapter based on Addison and Murshed (2002) one side to a peace treaty may wish to renege on its commitment to peace because it allows them then to loot valuable natural resource rents. We could easily add unresolved grievances or the absence of a credible power sharing deal, as discussed in the previous section. The expropria-tion of these gains cannot take place without one side fooling the other, by feigning to make peace and later reneging on this undertaking. Thus, the model predicts a temptation to engage in surprise war by at least one group who are signatories to the peace treaty. Knowing this to be the case, other groups will not find the peace deal credible and the civil war recurs. Clearly, this means that the peace treaty does not have the characteris-tic of a final settlement that resolves all potential disputes, removing all temptations for conflict to re-emerge. In that situation and when peace is not incentive compatible, commitments lack credibility, thus the peace is not self-enforcing or renegotiation proof and it acquires characteristics of cheap talk. Cheap talk refers to a signal without commitment.

Sometimes agents or groups cannot commit credibly because there are no institutions or mechanisms upon which to anchor their promises. In that situation they are not believed, even when they are honest. For governments, this is more likely in the context of weak state capacity, as it is difficult for a state to guarantee pledges when its own legitimacy and power base is fragile.

An aspect of the commitment problem that has received scant attention is the very high discount rates, or the short time horizons of some of the parties involved (Addison and Murshed, 2002). With high enough discount

---

[8]   This section is a non-technical presentation of the ideas behind the signalling game in the mathematical appendix to this chapter.

rates, the model in the appendix predicts that peace treaties (even those incorporating costly signals) may not be self-enforcing. The same argument can be applied to reputation, a factor that is central to the credibility of peacemaking. This is because the same parties often renegotiate. Breaking an agreement damages future reputation, but with a high enough discount rate it might pay to renege because the cost comes in the future. Each failure of the peace process raises the discount rates of the belligerents, thereby increasing the difficulty of making peace. Given the tarnished reputations of belligerents it becomes increasingly difficult to establish credible peace.

In a multiperiod framework reputation evolves, but initial reputation does matter, and there is some path dependence; see the appendix. My theoretical analysis makes an important analytical innovation. We are able to distinguish between innately good and bad types of agents, and also sub-divide the rebel group, say, into relatively honest and dishonest types in the multiple-period framework of analysis. The former is more interested in the revelation of its true type; the latter derives greater utility from concealing its intentions. Uncertainty and imperfect information about rebel types makes zero warfare untenable even with only an honest type of rebel. It also serves to create a wedge between current promises of peace and its future implementation, as highlighted by Jarstad and Nilsson (2008). Walter (2002) refers to the immediate post-war period as one where the signals of commitment are noisy or blurred. This may make the costly signals mentioned above difficult to read, in the absence of clear signals that distinguish between honest and dishonest types. Even a dishonest type negotiator will not engage in the full range of surprise conflict in the first period; as a rational but selfish negotiator he will want to keep his reputation intact for use in fooling his opponent at a later stage of the game. Of course, an honest type will pick a lower equilibrium level of conflict than his more dishonest counterpart. In multiple period analysis the less important the future, the greater is the chosen level of present conflict. Even a more honest type of negotiator will choose more current conflict for low (high) values of the discount factor (rate). This is indeed a serious problem in societies where poverty is endemic.

With regard to commitment and commitment technologies there are four factors that deserve further consideration: the separation of economic life and politics, time horizons, institutional settings and the presence of excluded parties from the agreement, or the emergence of spoiler groups.

4.3.1 Economics and Politics

When we assess why some 'post-conflict' countries returned frequently to war (Angola) while others have managed to sustain peace (Mozambique), economic motivations may lie at the root of the problem – Mozambique has few valuable resources over which to fight while Angola has several – and this may help explain several peace commitment failures in Angola. In fact, Angola is one important case of a peace treaty with power sharing and external guarantees that failed because of the intransigency of Savimbi, and his presumed greed. There may be situations when conflict and business entrepreneurs are one and the same, as in many cases in Africa. That is when rulers themselves are directly engaged in appropriating lootable mineral resource rents. This makes the commitment to peace less likely to hold, compared to societies with a relatively stricter dichotomy between those who rule (politicians) and those who conduct economic affairs. This is because in the former case the political and economic interests are one, and clearly pro-war. Economic interests in this instance centre around war contracts, and the harnessing of resource or illicit drug rents. In the latter case, there is some room for competition between different interests; business activities such as the exporting of manufactured goods from Sri Lanka or Nepal may be disrupted by the war. Even when there are links between the two groups, the greater the institutional separation through parliament and the political process, the better are the chances for lasting commitments to peace. But these interventions refer to long-term institution building.

4.3.2   Time Horizons

This turns out to be a crucial feature in individual decisions. When the future is seen to be feasible, it results in more peaceful attitudes, even in situations where deep-seated historical grievances are present. Generally speaking, investment, which only bears fruit in the future, requires a long time horizon. More secure and affluent societies tend to have a longer time horizon and recognize the path dependence of current actions. By contrast severely war torn, insecure and poorer societies have shorter time horizons, with a very strong preference for current consumption even at the expense of future consumption. This applies equally to wars motivated by grievance, as well as greed. Short-term income may be readily obtainable in a war situation, even if war destroys future earning prospects. In the language of economics, this is referred to as a high discount rate applied to future income, as opposed to the high value put on present consumption. All of this means discounting the future cost of conflict, as well as undervaluing the tarnished future reputation, which arises from an excessive zeal for short-term profit.

Furthermore, societies with faulty and degenerating institutions of governance and democracy tend to have a high discount rate, as the future is uncertain. New and fledgling democracies are often characterized by these high discount rates, as the future is uncertain due to the fact that the political system may collapse. The state apparatus in this situation runs the risk of descending into kleptocracy. The important point here is that many groups in these situations are also characterized by similar short-term mindsets, making them often prefer current profits in a war situation when compared to investing for a far greater income that peace might bring in the future. Also, investment in trying to bring about future peace can have substantial current costs in terms of forgone profit.

4.3.3   Institutions of Commitment

Even when all parties agree to and recognize the benefits of peace they need to commit credibly to peace, and the conditions stipulated therein. Generally, this requires institutions that help parties to credibly anchor their commitment to the peace treaty. The fear of reversal in the context of poor commitment mechanisms leads to a peace treaty being imperfectly credible even when costly signals are imbedded. And if it is not credible, the peace agreement will not last. Leaders of various groups and factions will then tend to behave like roving bandits, with little concern for the country, unlike stationary bandits who have an encompassing interest in nurturing the tax base from which they obtain rent (Olson, 1996). A poor environment for commitment often arises when the government or the rebel leadership's power base is weak and/or lacks legitimacy. Solutions here lie in devising better mechanisms to engender credible commitment via institutional improvement. This includes better constitutional safeguards, greater respect for the rule of law and superior regulatory capacities. This may even be a part of a society's democratic transition. Existing domestic institutions often degenerate beyond redemption in many conflict-ridden societies, making externally enforced methods of commitment imperative in the interim before domestic institutions can once again evolve. I address these issues in greater detail in Chapter 5.

4.3.4   Spoiler Groups and Multiple Rebel Groups

One problem that arises in sustaining commitments to peace is the emergence and formation of spoiler groups who have an incentive to gain from surprise warfare. Another recurring problem is the presence of multiple groups, especially on the rebel side. The existing literature, as summarized in Nilsson (2008) argued that peace treaties that do not include all rebel groups in any single dispute are at a greater risk of failure. Her study of conflict dyads in the 1989 to 2004 post-cold war period suggests that this is indeed the case for overall peace. Peace between any dyad (or pair) of conflict parties can, however, be sustained and stable even in the absence of peace treaties with other groups. Thus, a partial peace between limited numbers of parties to a conflict is sustainable, because each group of co-signatories to a treaty will take into account the intentions of excluded groups, which will not impact on their interaction. Some form of power sharing facilitates this process. Peace deals ending protracted and intense wars suffer from a greater risk of breaking down. Agreements are more sustainable if what is at stake is territory rather than control over the central government.

4.4 SUSTAINING COMMITMENTS TO PEACE

Is ending a civil war in a distant land something that is of benefit to the average global citizen? Or is it something that should only concern neighbouring countries or the great powers?

If global peace is an international public good[9] (all inhabitants of the planet benefit from it), then attention has to be given to sustaining peace accords through credible peacekeeping missions and interventions. The motivations behind securing peace may be altruistic, but strategic factors such as the negative externalities that Western nations may suffer from the consequences of civil war – such as refugee spillovers – and the costs of meeting complex humanitarian disasters such as famines may make peacekeeping an action that is not only a palliative, but also preventive in nature.

I have argued that externally devised commitment is crucial to ending conflicts where the peace treaty is otherwise not self-enforcable, as is usually the case in contemporary civil wars in many poor countries that are differentially described in the literature as failed, fragile or bottom billion states. Sanctions and aid, if effective, might help to eliminate the temptation to re-ignite conflict. This means that the financial aid package must be adequate and long lasting (over several years), and the commitment to punish those who violate the peace treaty must be credible. These peacekeeping missions (as well as the associated aid package) have to be adequately financed, manned and mandated. The external sanctions,

---

[9] A public good is non-rivalled and non-excludable. That is, one citizen's ability to obtain utility from a public good does not detract from another citizen's ability to also consume it; also the enjoyment of a public good has nothing to do with an individual's ability to pay for it, rather it is society's total willingness to pay for it that matters. Security in terms of defence and law and order, are the best examples of a pure public good, which are financed by general taxation.

themselves, must not be perceived by potential combatants as cheap talk. In other words, the sanctions must also have credibility. If the cost of effective sanctions is too high, or it yields little security benefit to the sponsor as is likely to be the case for conflicts in distant lands, there is under-production of the sanction, making it more likely that it really is cheap talk (see the appendix). In that case conflict will re-ignite, as I demonstrate in the appendix. A weak and inadequately devised package of post-conflict sanctions and aid can not only cause conflict to re-emerge, but might even be worse than no intervention at all.

Perhaps that is why we see such a slow and painful end to many civil wars in Africa, where large territories as in the Congo are policed by relatively small and weakly empowered peacekeeping forces. Civil wars in Europe, such as in the Balkans, by contrast, are quickly concluded, with a huge relative (to population and geographical size) commitment in peacekeeping forces and aid. Aid per capita and the trooping levels per square kilometre are greater in the Balkans compared to commitments in Africa. This is because conflicts in the European neighbourhood are more important to the West, particularly the European Union. The will and resources to end more distant wars by external powers may be more strictly limited, and it is difficult to sell prolonged and expensive conflict ending projects to the average official in a Western finance ministry, and to the median taxpaying voter or their elected representatives who ultimately finance these ventures.

I will leave the issue of aid to countries in conflict to Chapter 6. With regard to the peacekeeping operations part of the sanctions that prevent conflict restarting, a question remains as to whether they should be ad hoc, or conducted by a multilateral global agency such as the United Nations (UN), or some regional organization. Ad hoc peace missions are conducted by the great powers, such as the UK in Sierra Leone in 2001, or by a neighbouring country such as India in Sri Lanka in the mid-1980s. The activities of UN peacekeeping missions are well known, and in recent times there has been the growth of regional associations in Africa who are mandated to undertake peacekeeping. Interventions mandated through the UN or regional bodies may, however, have a greater degree of legitimacy than purely ad hoc missions.

Furthermore, there are arguments based on economic efficiency for a global public good (global peace in this instance) to be managed through a common pool[10], such as the UN peacekeeping operations. Recent years have seen growing optimism in the ability of African organizations to intervene and manage the continent's security crises with the cooperation of international

---

[10] See Kanbur, Sandler and Morrison (1999) on common global pools to tackle global public goods issues.

organizations, as well as the European Union (EU) and the USA (see Klingebiel, 2005). Chief among these organizations are the newly created African Union (AU) formed in 2002 to succeed the erstwhile Organization of African Unity (OAU) and the Economic Community of West African States (ECOWAS). While ECOWAS operations in the past met with very limited success, greater optimism pervades for the AU's missions in the immediate future, and external donors in the West are increasingly financing AU operations. The success of AU missions requires agreement among member states on the principles, mechanisms and instruments for intervention.

It has been argued, for instance by Heldt and Wallensteen (2006), that regional organizations and ad hoc coalitions may have greater knowledge of local conditions, and may be able to act faster than the UN (where mandate seeking is time consuming), thereby successfully pre-empting conflict. UN operations, on the other hand, have greater legitimacy, experience and better access to logistical support. In many ways the two types of operations could be complementary to each other, with regional interventions leading the way and the UN following. They also do not find great differences in their success rates.[11]

To take the example of Africa, in 2005 nearly 77% of all UN peace-keeping forces (or 50 000 out of a total of 65 000) were deployed in that continent. In terms of finance, African missions accounted for nearly 75% of the UN's peacekeeping budget (US$2.9 billion out of US$3.9 billion in 2004–5).[12] This makes the African continent the most important region for UN peacekeeping. African troops have been involved in all but 10 of the 54 UN peacekeeping operations in the continent since 1948. The experience of UN peacekeeping in the continent has been mixed. UN peacekeeping has had some success in West Africa in cooperation with regional organizations, but failed utterly in Somalia and Rwanda (1994), with limited success in the DRC, Ivory Coast and Darfur.[13] Improving the quality of peacekeeping is an important policy issue.

The short-term solutions to civil wars require externally enforced peace treaties along with sustained financial assistance. Economic and political interventions in this regard are therefore inseparable.[14] In the ultimate

---

[11]   Nilsson (2008) finds non-UN peacekeeping less able to affect the duration of peace positively in comparison with UN peacekeeping.

[12]   United Nations, Department of Public Information.

[13]   In the DRC, UN peacekeepers fought with Katangan rebels in the early 1960s; more recently UN peacekeepers have been accused of gross human rights abuses.

[14]   For example, Walter (2004) in a paper entitled 'Does Conflict Beget Conflict' argues that the most significant causes of recurring civil war between 1945 and 1996 are poor living conditions (the quality of life) combined with an inability to participate politically. Both these factors are highly correlated with economic growth.

analysis, credible commitments to peace must be found in effective domestic constitutional restraints and delegation. These domestic commitment mechanisms require deep interventions in institution building, something that is notoriously difficult to achieve because of the persistence of vested interests in conflict. I will address some of these issues related to long-term peacebuilding in the next chapter. Furthermore, the best antidote to conflict is economic growth, and issues related to reconstructing conflict affected economies are analysed in Chapter 6.

APPENDIX: SIGNALLING, CREDIBLE COMMITMENT, MECHANISM DESIGN AND SANCTIONS PRODUCTION

The models in this appendix are drawn from Addison and Murshed (2002), as well as Cuesta and Murshed (2008).

Credibility and Reputation in a Single Period

The basic set-up of the model involves two sides who are referred to as government and rebels. One side is either tired of fighting or it has an interest in peace. This group is the government in our example. The other side, the rebels (or a rebel faction or spoiler group), may have something to gain from the resumption of fighting. The roles of the government and rebels in the games that follow can be reversed without altering the results. Both sides have entered into a peace deal. The government side derives no benefit from breaking this agreement. Consider the utility function of the rebel group (U^R):

$$U^R = -(1/2)c_1 w^2 + E\theta c_2(w - w^e) \qquad (4.1)$$

where $c_1 > 0$, w, w^e, θ, $c_2 \geq 0$.

$$\theta = B + \varepsilon, B \geq 0$$

$$\varepsilon = \varepsilon_{t-1} + \eta, \eta(0, \sigma^2)$$

The expectation operator (E) is introduced for the value of a random variable within the function, and a superscript e is used for an expectation of a variable on which information is incomplete. The first term on the right-hand side of equation 4.1 is the pure cost of conflict in quadratic (squared) form, where w represents warfare or belligerent behaviour and c_1 is the parameter measuring the direct cost of warfare. The negative sign before it is to indicate the cost or disutility from fighting. The quadratic form of the cost indicates that the costs of war rise more than proportionately as the level of w rises. The parameter $(1/2)$ is introduced for analytical tractability. The second term on the right-hand side of 4.1 indicates the gains to the rebels from reneging on a peace agreement, or the benefit from a 'surprise' war, where the level of actual conflict (w) exceeds the amount of conflict expected by the opposition, the government in our example (w^e). The parameter c_2 captures the magnitude of this effect; the higher c_2 is the greater is the gain from pretending to make peace first and fighting later. It may also be viewed as a subjective measure of either greed or grievance. The gain from surprise war is measured by the expected value (E) of the parameter θ which captures the rent (B) from disputed natural resources such as oil, diamonds and so on.

Alternatively, θ might be a parameter measuring historical grievances or the pecuniary value of post-conflict political power to be shared among erstwhile antagonists. It could include financial contributions from non-residents, and during the cold war period fungible military aid from superpowers. The rent or grievance is subject to random shocks (ε) with a first-order auto-regressive process resulting in shocks persisting for some time. The purely random component (η) has zero mean and constant variance. Random shocks could arise from terms of trade fluctuations, changes to the valuation of grievances or sudden increases in outside contributions to the war chest. Equation 4.1 is the utility function of the rebel leaders, or a splinter faction after the peace treaty emerges, and their followers whose participation and incentive compatibility constraints have to be satisfied to induce them to follow warlords.

The gains from surprise war are part of a process of income generation for the rebels:

$$y^R = y^N + E\theta(w - w^e) \tag{4.2}$$

Here the income of rebels is equal to some pre-arranged rate (y^N) plus an additional component arising from surprise warfare. The income associated with the pre-arranged rate is received with certainty following a peace treaty. In contrast, the gains from the surprise element are based upon driving a wedge between actual and expected levels of belligerence.

The rebels maximize their utility in 4.1 subject to w, which leads to optimal w^*:

$$w^* = E\theta c_2/c_1 \tag{4.3}$$

Proposition 1:   The equilibrium choice of warfare is greater the higher is the element of greed or grievance, c_2, the higher the expected availability of greed or grievance based valuation, θ, and the smaller the direct cost of fighting, c_1.

As far as the government (G) is concerned, a simple version of their utility function is:

$$U^G(w^e/w) = -(w - w^e)^2 \tag{4.4}$$

The meaning of 4.4 is that government's utility is declining in surprise warfare, when w diverges from w^e. In case actual fighting levels are in excess of the government side's expectation it is clearly caught less than fully prepared for war. In the event that actual fighting is less than expected, the disutility arises because the government has to engage in unplanned military expenditure that diverts income from other types of expenditure. Maximizing 4.4 with respect to w^e yields:

$$w = w^e \qquad (4.5)$$

The government reacts at the same time as the rebels. Substituting 4.3 into 4.1 for the rebels, and 4.5 into 4.4 for the government gives us:

$$U^R = -(E\theta c_2)^2/2c_1$$
$$U^G = 0 \qquad (4.6)$$

This is the outcome when the rebels have an incentive to renege on an announcement of complete peace, but do not have a first mover advantage. Both announcements by the rebels and expectations formation by the government take place simultaneously. What if the rebels pursue a policy of no warfare with $w = 0$? Then:

$$U_P^R = 0$$
$$U_P^G = 0 \qquad (4.7)$$

This is the Pareto optimal outcome and superior to the result in 4.6. In the optimal state there is no war, and $y^R = y^N$.

Now we assume that the rebels enjoy a first mover advantage and can announce complete peace and then engage in surprise warfare. In this case the actual and expected levels of warfare would diverge, $w = E\theta c_2/c_1$ and $w^e = 0$ in equation 4.1. This involves cheating on a pre-announced commitment:

$$U_C^R = (E\theta c_2)^2/2c_1 \qquad (4.8)$$

Note that the rebels' utility is greater in this case than under 4.6. At this juncture we introduce reputation. Following Barro and Gordon (1983) the reputation of the rebels is all or nothing, and it hinges on their behaviour in the past. The opposition believes the announcement if the rebels acted honestly in the previous period and kept their commitments. Otherwise they are not believed, and their actions are predicted to be that of a rogue group. This implies that there exists a future cost of cheating in the context

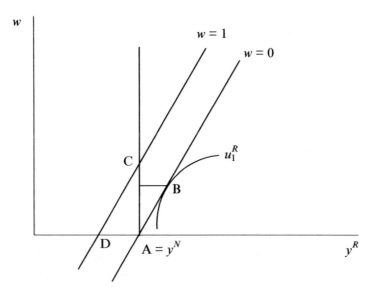

Figure 4.1 Credibility and reputation

of a low-intensity conflict. The cost is equal to the loss of reputation and the inability to create surprises, but this cost (C) is in the future:

$$C = -((E\theta c_2)^2/2c_1) \qquad (4.9)$$

Hence the penalty for cheating (which is the loss of reputation) appears exactly to cancel the gain from cheating in 4.8. But the punishment comes in some future period. If the rebel group discounts this future loss, the cost of cheating is always less than the gain from reneging on a fixed commitment. Typically in conflict situations in many developing countries the future is heavily discounted. The upshot is that the socially optimal policy of zero warfare ($w = 0$) is time inconsistent or incentive incompatible, and thus will not be an enforcable outcome. The optimal policy of no conflict is not self-enforcing, as it is not consistent with the incentives and expectations of the parties to the game. More particularly, the government knows it is in the interests of the rebels to renege on a pre-announced policy of total peace, and thus will not find any peace offering credible. Hence, the peace treaty is simply cheap talk.

Furthermore, there will be a range of possible conflict intensities that are feasible equilibria. The results are depicted in Figure 4.1 in y^R and w space. The upward sloping linear aggregate supply curve has a slope exactly equal to $E\theta$, from equation 4.2, and is steeper the greater the value of greed or grievance. The rebels' preferences are shown by the concave indifference curves with a slope = $E\theta c_2/c_1$, obtained from 4.1. The greedier or more aggrieved the group (the greater is θc_2) the steeper is the indifference curve. The rebels could announce zero conflict at point A. They could then cheat on their commitment and try to move to point B. The aggregate supply curve schedule would shift leftwards because of the process of expectation formation. The vertical distance between B and C gives the range of multiple equilibria depending on the time horizon of the game and the discount rate used to obtain the present value of future reputation losses. The point B defines the lowest feasible rate of conflict. Following Barro and Gordon (1983) it is described as the best enforceable outcome, given the objectives of the rebels and the expectations of the government. To reiterate, a no war situation (point A) is simply not incentive compatible for the rebels, or credible to the government.

An increase in the value of greed or grievance, $E\theta$, shifts the aggregate supply function leftwards and makes the indifference curves steeper, pointing to an expansion in the range of fighting. Note that this could arise due to random fluctuations on θ and its lingering effects over time. Also situations where the future is heavily discounted (a low discount factor) are likely to raise the fighting threshold associated with the best enforceable outcome.

Commitment Technologies

We now consider external policies to reduce conflict, an exercise in mechanism design. This implies manipulating the attitudes of the rebels via sanctions, arms controls, trade restrictions and foreign aid. Consider a reformulated version of the rebel utility function where we embed external conflict prevention policy parameters:

$$U^R = -(1/2)c_1(M)w^2 + E\theta c_2(A,T)(w - w^e) - c_3(S)(w - w^e)$$
(4.10)

where: $c_1 > 0, c_2 \geq 0, c_3 \geq 0; c_{11}, c_{31} > 0; c_{21}, c_{22} < 0$

Also:

$$c_1(M) \geq c_1 \forall M, c_2(T) \geq c_2 \forall T, c_3(S) \geq 0 \forall S^e \geq 0, c_3(S) < 0 \forall S^e < 0$$

In equation 4.10 the behavioural parameters of the rebel group, c_1, c_2 and c_3 are made functions of actions undertaken by external actors; it is therefore an exercise in mechanism design.

Aid (A) may be utilized by a foreign power to reduce greedy attitudes or assuage grievances, c_2. Similarly, trade sanctions (T) on items such as 'conflict' diamonds, money laundering and the activities of foreign entrepreneurs in supplying arms and finance might have the same effect. International controls on arms transfers (M) and/or sympathetic assistance from non-residents could be utilized to raise the direct cost of war, c_1. In either case, the indifference curve in Figure 4.1 will flatten out, and lower equilibrium ranges of fighting will emerge. All of these interventions represent indirect effects emanating from the manipulation of the behavioural parameters of the rebels.

Another way of reducing conflict and belligerent behaviour is through a direct and enforceable international agreement or understanding. Although this method does not always eliminate conflict, it does raise the costs of war and reneging on peace deals. The last term in 4.10 represents such a commitment technology or delegation, and c_3 measures the costs of reneging on peace agreements as a function of sanctions (S) imposed by other signatories or parties to the agreement. Maximizing 4.10 with respect to w yields the optimum level of w with commitment ($w_c{}^*$):

$$w_c{}^* = (E\theta c_2 - c_3)/c_1 \tag{4.11}$$

Proposition 2:   The presence of external commitment technologies in the form of sanctions lowers the optimal level of belligerency amongst rebels, if and only if $S^e > 0$.

The proposition can be verified by noting that w_c^* in 4.11 is less than w^* in 4.3 if $c_3 > 0$ when $S^e > 0$. If so, these commitment technologies lead to lower levels of warfare when compared to 4.3. Even though the commitment technologies and sanctions are independent of actual w in 4.10 for simplicity, our result will hold through if T, M and S are increasing in w. For high enough values of c_3 the temptation to renege on the peace treaty may vanish. Note, however, that the production of sanctions and policies are a result of external intervention, and involve costs to outside parties, which is something we turn to below.

Corollary 1:   If sanctions are expected to be ineffective, because the level of force and developmental aid is inadequate, making the sanction cheap talk, $S^e < 0$, and $c_3 < 0$ in 4.10 and 4.11. A half-hearted sanction package will be a failure, and the levels of conflict that ensue are greater than without the cheap talk sanction.

Corollary 2:   The temptation to engage in conflict could even be completely eliminated ($w = 0$) if the 'largesse', θ, is redistributed to become part of pre-arranged income (y^N) in 4.2. Then the gains from capture and surprise war will vanish in rebel utility functions, as $E\theta = 0$. Such a redistribution of θ is more likely in cases where resource rents accrue to a societal fund, and post-war power sharing arrangements mentioned in section 4.3 are credible.

Reputation in a Multiperiod Framework

Here the period of analysis involves more than a single time period, and consists of two types of rebels. I leave out commitment technologies for the sake of analytical tractability. There will be honest (H) and dishonest (D) types, where the former is more dependable. The government knows that there are two types of rebels, but is imperfectly informed about their true type, because of noisy signals. This also captures situations where the rebel groups are divided, and splinter factions constantly appear. Perceptions about reputation will be inherited from the past and updated using Bayes's rule. The Baysesian priors are common knowledge to both sides. A central finding will be that even dishonest groups, operating over a multiperiod time horizon, may not break agreements at early stages of the game so as to leave their reputation intact for manipulation at later stages. Yet the discount rate, or the impatience to consume at present, could act against future reputational considerations. A generic objective function for both rebel types can take the following form:

$$U^{H,D} = -(1/2)c_1w^2 + E\theta c_2(w - w^e) + \delta[-(1/2)c_1w^2 + E\theta c_2(w - w^e)] \tag{4.12}$$

Here we have extended the single period utility in 4.1 to two periods applying a discount factor δ to weight the future period. Note that the discount factor $\delta = (1/1 + r)$, where r is an indicator of time preference. Thus the higher the discount factor the lower is the rate of discount. In other words, a higher value of δ implies a greater concern for the future. Observe that we have reduced a multiperiod game to a two-period problem. This is because sub-game perfection allows solution by backward induction, and what matters are the penultimate and last periods.

It is instructive to examine decision making by the two types in the final period of analysis. A dishonest (D) type group in the second and final period of the game will simply choose the level of surprise warfare indicated by 4.3 above. This is because no discounting is involved in the last period, and the second term on the right-hand side of 4.12 vanishes with $\delta = 0$.

The honest type maximizes utility (first term on the right-hand side of equation 4.12) with respect to two constraints (see Cukierman, 2000). The first is a dependability constraint; the honest type wants to appear to be true to its word:

$$w^H(2) = w^A(2) \qquad (4.13)$$

the superscript H stands for the dependable or honest type, H's announcements or offers are indicated by the superscript A, while the 2 in parenthesis indicates the second period. This constraint states that the actual outcome equals the announcement.

The other constraint concerns the government's beliefs about the type of rebel group. The government will assign a probability, γ, that the other side is the honest type and a probability $1 - \gamma$ that it is the dishonest type. Its expectation of the level of conflict in period 2 will be a linear combination of the two strategies weighted by the corresponding probabilities:

$$w^e(2) = \gamma(2)w^A(2) + (1 - \gamma(2))[E\theta c_2/c_1] \qquad (4.14)$$

Substituting 4.14 in 4.12, using 4.13, $\delta = 0$, maximizing with respect to w^H, yields:

$$w^H(2) = w^A(2) = (1 - \gamma(2))[E\theta c_2/c_1] \qquad (4.15)$$

Note that the level of conflict picked by the H type in 4.15 is lower than that chosen by the D type in 4.3. Observe, however, that even the 'better' type of group engenders conflict, as it is also non-altruistic. Knowing the group to be non-altruistic, the government will not regard over-optimistic levels of peace as a credible offer even from an honest type of group. Levels of w chosen in 4.15 vary proportionately with the poorness of equilibrium reputation $(1 - \gamma(2))$. This is akin to classic adverse selection problems in insurance markets, where the high risk type exerts a negative externality on the pooled contract offered to both categories.

Proposition 3:   Given previous assumptions, if the government is imperfectly informed about rebel type then the level of warfare is strictly positive for each type of rebel.

This can be seen from 4.15: if $\gamma(2) = 1$, $w^H(2) = w^A(2) = 0$, and there is no warfare. It amounts to perfect information on the government side.

Corollary 3:   The level of warfare by the honest type is zero, if and only if, the government is fully informed about the rebels' type.

If there was full separation of the two types of rebels, implying no uncertainty about the H or D type, then $\gamma(2) = 1$ or 0. Otherwise in the presence of uncertainty (unclear signals), the government will use Bayes's law to update its prior beliefs about the rebel type (see Cukierman, 2000).[15] In that case, in period 2, we will have:

$$\gamma(2) = \frac{\gamma(1)}{\gamma(1) + (1 - \gamma(1))p_1} \tag{4.16}$$

This is the equilibrium value of the probability of the rebels being of the honest type in the second and final period of the game. It therefore captures reputational equilibrium. It also states that reputation in the second period is higher the greater it was in the first period and the lower is the probability of type D pretending to be H (p_1). Intuitively, this means a degree of path dependence or hysteresis. Some groups might wish to invest in a very good reputation in initial stages following a peace accord, causing them to make large temporary concessions. Point D in Figure 4.1 would illustrate such an outcome.

Moving on to decision making in the first period, denoted by parenthesis 1, this is the period involving intertemporal choices over the two periods. This will mean discounting future utility levels, and choices about promoting and preserving a good reputation for use in future surprise warfare. Most importantly, the party making the offer will have to take into account the chance that its true type (either H or D) may be revealed in advance. This possibility implies that the other side knows for certain the type of group making the offer, an outcome known as 'separation'. By the same token, no separation (NS) means that the governments are left guessing about the rebel type that they are dealing with in the final period.

To develop the above point more fully it is worthwhile examining the utility levels of the two types of rebel groups in the final (or second) period under no separation and separation respectively. For the dishonest type under NS this is derived by substituting w from 4.3 into 4.12, $w^A(2) = w^H(2)$ from 4.15 into 4.14 and then in 4.12 with $\delta = 0$:

$$U^D_{NS}(2) = \frac{[2(\gamma(2))^2 - 1](E\theta c_2)^2}{2c_1} \tag{4.17}$$

With complete separation (S) the government knows that its opposition is of the dishonest type so that the second term on the right side of 4.12 vanishes, and there is no surprise war. All that is applicable is the first term:

$$U^D_S(2) = -\frac{(E\theta c_2)^2}{2c_1} \tag{4.18}$$

---

[15]   Equation 4.16 is the posterior probability that the rebel is the H type, given that the H type has been played in period 1.

Note that for the dishonest type non-separation from 4.17 yields a greater utility than separation in 4.18. It will pay the D type to keep the government guessing about its type and therefore it will conceal its true nature.

For the honest rebels, utility in the second period with no separation involves inserting 4.15 into 4.12, with $w = w^e$, and $\delta = 0$:

$$U_{NS}^{H}(2) = -\frac{[(1 - \gamma(2))E\theta c_2]^2}{2c_1} \tag{4.19}$$

With full separation the above expression reduces to zero. Note that, unlike in the case of the D type, the utility of the H type is greater under separation, as the expression in 4.19 is negative. Consequently, the honest type actually wants its type revealed.

We can finally move to consider equilibrium in the first period. This will involve discounting the second period's utility (see Addison and Murshed, 2002, for the details). For the D type the equilibrium level of conflict in period 1 is:

$$w^D(1) = \frac{E\theta c_2}{c_1} - \frac{\delta(2(\gamma(2))^2 - 1)(E\theta c_2)^2}{4c_1^2} \tag{4.20}$$

This demonstrates that even a dishonest type negotiator or rebel group will not engage in the full range of surprise conflict in the first period provided that there is a multiple period time horizon. This can be understood by comparing 4.20 with 4.3 above. The intuition is that a rational but selfish negotiator will want to keep his reputation intact for use in surprises at a later stage of the game. Another implication follows from 4.16 above, which states that the higher the initial reputation $\gamma(1)$, the greater is the second period reputation, $\gamma(2)$. When this result is combined with 4.20, it makes the more dishonest type less belligerent in the first period. Equally, if a bad reputation were inherited from the past, it would make this type of negotiator more reckless.

Turning now to the more honest type, the utility from full separation for the honest type in period 2 is zero, and the first period equilibrium conflict level is:

$$w^H(1) = \frac{E\theta c_2(1 - \gamma(1))}{c_1} - \frac{\delta(1 - \gamma(2))^2(E\theta c_2)^2}{4c_1^2} \tag{4.21}$$

Thus, the honest type will pick a lower equilibrium level of conflict than the dishonest rebel in 4.20. Also, inter-temporal considerations will make the honest type moderate initial period belligerency as well; compare 4.21 with 4.15.

Proposition 4:   The greater the valuation of future reputation the less is the amount of conflict chosen by both rebel types.

The centrality of the discount factor cannot be overemphasized. The higher is δ, the discount factor, the more important is the future, and less conflict is chosen by both types of rebel groups from 4.20 and 4.21. In poor countries the future is heavily discounted (δ is very low), and conflict persists because of the relative lack of concern for the future.

The Production of Sanctions

The production of sanctions, S, a global public good as argued in section 4.4, involves costs to outside powers and agencies, as it is they who initiate them. The external powers could be NATO, the European Union or the United Nations. By sanctions, I mean the enforcement of a peace deal via peacekeeping forces. Normally, it also includes some conditional development assistance or aid. Either way, the production of sanctions and the aid that accompanies it costs money. Here, I examine situations where the finance and production of the sanction, S, is not carried out by the same party. The separation of finance and enforcement of peace deals is quite common, as discussed above. The idea here is that the sponsor or financier of peacekeeping derives some utility from peace in other parts of the world due to security considerations (terrorism, refugee influxes), humanitarian considerations or because promoting peace enhances the sponsors' international prestige. But how much is the external sponsor of the peace willing to pay, and how far are they willing to go in this respect?

The sponsor or financier of the sanction can be regarded as the principal, and the implementer of the sanction the agent, in a principal–agent framework (Laffont, 2005). Since the principal takes into account the agent's objectives, we can add the utility of the agent to that of the principal to obtain the grand utilitarian welfare function, W (see Cuesta and Murshed, 2008 for details):

$$W = Q(S) + \lambda SP(S) - (1 + \lambda)[(h - a)S + F + f(a)] - \lambda Z \tag{4.22}$$

Here Q represents the benefit from the sanction in deterring the onset of war to the external sponsor, $P(S)$ is the inverse demand function for sanctions given its price or cost which is paid to the agent, P, λ captures the distortionary taxation needed to finance the transfer and Z is the agent's utility. There are diminishing returns to the benefits of the sanction. The revenue from the sanction to the agent is $SP(S)$, F represents a fixed cost of sanctions production, the production of the sanction (S) depends on the qualitative type of the agent, h and the effort exercised by him (a) and $f(a)$ represents the cost or disutility of (output increasing) effort to the agent.

Note that a higher value of h implies a more productive agent, his cost of producing sanctions is correspondingly lower. Maximizing 4.22 with respect to S yields:

$$Q'(S^*) + \lambda[P'(S^*)S^* + P(S^*)] = (1 + \lambda)(h - a^*) \qquad (4.23)$$

Asterisks (*) indicate optimal values, and the solution in 4.23 refers to a full informational outcome.[16]

Proposition 5: From 4.23, the lower the marginal utility of sanctions to the sponsor $Q'(S)$, the more expensive the aid-cum-military sanctions package is in terms of 'price', $P'(S)$, the greater the shadow cost of the distortionary tax, λ, that has to be levied to finance it and the greater the effort levels (a) needed to produce a unit of sanction, the lower is the optimal level of sanction chosen.

This result relates to the 'cheap talk' result in corollary 1 above. If the optimal level of sanctions-cum-aid is low in 4.23, then the peacekeeping force's sanction is ineffective cheap talk, as $S^e < 0$ in 4.11. This is likely to happen if the conflict is in some distant land. Also, the financing of such projects through taxation might be hard to sell to the ordinary median voter in the sponsoring country. Finally, the effort level required on the part of the sponsor's agent might just be too great to make it worthwhile, and the probability of the agent's success in this regard may be too uncertain. Hence, the saliency of the expression, 'cheap talk', implying that in the absence of a willingness to pay by external sponsors many peace deals in far flung places of the world are doomed to failure.

---

[16] When the agent's efforts are non-verifiable, even when final output is observable, we have moral hazard. When the sponsor or principal cannot observe the intrinsic type of the agent we have adverse selection. In this situation the better type agent will extract a private informational rent.

5. The social contract and lasting peace

5.1 MOTIVATION

The previous chapter analysed the difficulties in sustaining peace accords that aim to end wars. Its concern was mainly with the aftermath of war, which is chiefly about the difficulties of arriving at credible pacts or accords that lead to the cessation of hostilities. A variety of factors, including the imperfect nature of the commitment to peace amongst domestic actors, and the flawed nature of external peace enforcement, were to blame for these difficulties. I also examined the various types of power sharing agreements that could be devised. A viable peace treaty, if it does not lead to partition of the erstwhile nation state, must give former belligerents some share in the future government of the country. Equally, rights of minority or excluded groups require some guarantees, and they need to have a voice in the formulation of policies and decisions that affect them, otherwise they may revolt again. This may imply a federal or decentralized mode of government, buttressing the power sharing peace treaty that ends war. In this chapter I will be concerned with issues related to the sustainability of peace in the long term. These turn out to be the very factors that characterize a well-functioning polity in the long-run.

Chapter 3 suggested that if the forces behind either greed or grievance are to take the form of large-scale violence there must be other factors at work, mechanisms in the middle, related to the institutional failure to resolve conflict peacefully. Addison and Murshed (2006) call these mechanisms the 'social contract' (see also Murshed, 2002a). Thus, even if capturable resource rents constitute a sizeable prize, violent conflict is unlikely to take hold in states with a framework of widely agreed rules, formal and informal,[1] that govern the resource allocation and the peaceful settlement of grievances. Such a viable social contract can be sufficient to restrain conflict, and following its collapse, on the road to violent internal conflict,

---

[1] North (1990) highlights the difference between formal rules as in a written constitution, and informal rules or norms or conventions that can become equally institutionalized and embedded into social interaction.

rebuilding and reconstructing a new social contract is key to peacebuilding and conflict resolution. Addison and Murshed (2006) indicate that a social contract could contain three dimensions. The first is political (the rules that govern political representation, consultation, and decision making), the second consists of moral values (the rules that govern personal conduct and society's sense of justice), and the third is economic (the rules that govern production, market exchange and government intervention).

In this chapter, section 5.2 contains a brief sketch of the idea of the social contract, and how its functioning may become undermined. Distributional theories related to conflict resolution arising from the social choice literature are discussed in section 5.3 on fair division, which has moral dimensions, grounded as it is on principles of equity. Section 5.4 is concerned with the difficulties of maintaining power sharing agreements that end civil wars in the long run, which may require power dividing structures. Section 5.5 deals with issues related to federalism (mainly fiscal issues) that are crucial for solutions to the material basis for greed and/or grievance motivations for conflict. Finally, section 5.6 provides a brief synthesis of the diverse issues discussed earlier.

5.2 THE SOCIAL CONTRACT AND ITS BREAKDOWN

War implies the absence or breakdown of contractual interaction. A state of anarchy, where groups intermittently predate on one another characterizes its absence (the state of nature as described by Thomas Hobbes in 1651). Insecurity, reflected in mutual mistrust and the prospect of short-term gain, causes groups to predate on others. This is due to the lack of a sovereign regulatory authority or a self-enforcing contractual mechanism that binds groups peacefully together. In political thought, the idea of a contract, as the basis of the modern state, can be traced back to political philosophers, including Hobbes and Locke (see, Sabine, 1961, for example). Within a society, contracts can be vertical if they are authoritarian in the sense of Thomas Hobbes, or they may be horizontal if fashioned by a greater degree of consent, as advocated by John Locke (see Sabine, 1961). The former may be described as autocratic, and the latter as a more democratic contract.

According to Hobbes, the state of nature was characterized by anarchy akin to perpetual war,[2] with each man taking what he can and with no

---

[2] Chapter 1, 'Bellum Omnium Contra Omnes', or war by all against all.

legal basis for right or wrong. Life was: 'solitary, poor, nasty, brutish and short'. Consequently, it was in the interest of individuals collectively to surrender their personal freedom of action to a ruler (absolute monarch) in return for personal security and rule based interactions in society. His arguments may be interpreted as a defence of absolute monarchs. If Hobbes regarded war as the natural state of man, John Locke had a more felicitous view of the state of nature (see, Sabine, 1961). Locke regarded the right to life and property (often just access to common resources) as a natural right, which existed in the state of nature. These rights could not be properly enforced in the state of nature, except through mutual self-help. In civil society it was the duty of the sovereign to enforce these natural rights; rule ought to be based on consent; society should have the right to oust a tyrant or failing ruler. Rousseau spoke of the general will (volonté générale) in fashioning civil society. In general, political theories of the social contract base authority and the exercise of power on rational self-interest, as well as consent, and as such their aim is the avoidance of large-scale violence in a well-ordered society.

At this point, we may ask how the social contract is codified. The answer would be that it is partly, but not exclusively, in the country's written constitution. There are other norms of behaviour that are not in any way formalized, but which nevertheless constitute a strong element of how society functions. On the one hand, written rules and laws are flouted in many cases, so that a country may have all the panoply of constitutions and laws but not a working social contract. These occur most frequently in 'failing' states, sometimes leading to violent conflict. On the other hand, the social contract of a peaceful society may have elements that have never been written down.

An additional question arises about the use of coercive force in societies with a functioning contract.[3] In well-functioning democracies the use of force derives its legitimacy from democratic oversight. There are also authoritarian or semi-authoritarian states in which people acquiesce to constraints on political freedom because they derive other benefits. These may include protection from external aggression or economic benefits. People are offered the prospect of rising living standards in return for acquiescing to limited freedom. They may dislike their lack of political freedom, but any desire to rebel is held in check by the prospect of losing the economic gains that the authoritarian system delivers. In this sense, there is a measure of agreement to the rules of the game, and order is not maintained by coercion alone. This type of social contract has

---

[3]   As Hobbes in his *Leviathan* (chapter 17) remarked: 'And covenants, without the sword, are but words, and of no strength to secure a man at all' (Hobbes, 1651 [1998], p. 111).

been characteristic of the South-East and East Asia regions (Malaysia, Singapore, South Korea, Taiwan and later China). Still another group could include nations held together largely by terror: authoritarian states that fail to deliver economic prosperity generally resort to intensifying state violence to discourage large-scale rebellion. These states may not have outright civil war, but that does not mean that some major breakdown will not occur in the future.

So what factors lead to the breakdown of the social contract within a nation state? What circumstances create incentives for groups within societies to choose war rather than resolve disputes peacefully? Clearly these seem to occur in failing societies. Yet, the term 'failed state' may be too vague and unhelpful in this regard. Contemporary civil wars are more often related to the breakdown of explicit or implicit mechanisms to share power and resources, rather than the complete absence of an agreement to govern these. This is true even in the most extreme cases, such as in Somalia. Among the various factors in question,[4] two domestic reasons may be highlighted. The first is to do with breakdowns in the agreements to share resources in the context of economic decline, and the second refers to malfunctioning political institutions. Both of these factors produce what Ghani and Lockhart (2008) describe as the sovereignty gap (the wedge between the state's legal status and its ability to provide basic public goods such as security so essential to the social contract) and the accountability gap (when it is unaccountable to the people).

The first point refers to the resource sharing agreements that the state, or those in power, have with various stakeholders, and the breakdown of these arrangements that can produce greed and/or grievance. Within nation states, the fiscal system will secure a workable social contract if the allocation of public expenditures and the apportionment of taxes are judged to be fair, or at least not so unfair that some groups judge taking resources by force the better option. There are many examples of conflicts emerging out of fiscal disputes. Côte d'Ivoire, for instance, became unstable with the collapse of the social contract engineered by the late President Houphouët-Boigny, in which he allocated public spending across the regions to, successfully, buy the loyalty of the country's ethnic groups. Disputes over the apportionment of revenues from natural resources are especially common and, as in Nigeria (see, ICG, 2006), these take on ethnic and regional dimensions.

One reason that a contract to share revenues encounters difficulties is the imperfect credibility with which the side that controls the 'pot'

---

[4] Cold war rivalries in third countries and the interventions of external powers in the domestic affairs of other countries may also undermine an existing social contract.

honours its commitment. There may be two parties to the potential armed conflict: a government and a rebel group, say, where the government party has access to revenues and royalties, but is threatened by the excluded rebel group, which may violently overthrow the government as in Addison and Murshed (2001, 2003) or Azam (1995). On the other hand, the rebels may choose not to fight if they receive a transfer from the government. Similarly, the government has a choice between fighting the rebels and offering it a fiscal transfer. This includes broad based public expenditure, fairer taxation, inclusion in government jobs and allowing potential rebel groups a share of locally generated resource rents. Also, the social contract is less likely with regimes that prefer repression over making a fiscal transfer (broad based development) to potential rebels, including allowing resource-rich regions partially to control locally generated revenues; these phenomena are formally modelled in the appendix to this chapter.

Secondly, there is the political system. Hegre et al. (2001) point out that the risk of conflict is lower in both well-established democracies and autocracies. It suggests that conflict risk is at its greatest during transitions to and away from democracy, when state capacity is weak, and also in fledgling and imperfect democracies (anocracies). This is when the violent expression of grievance is most likely. Autocracies are adept at suppressing dissent, and established democracies deal with the same problem in a more peaceful fashion. Also, state capacity (the state's ability to both police citizens and provide public goods) is greater in established autocratic or democratic societies, rather than in those somewhere in the middle. The functions of the state are important in maintaining the cohesiveness of society, which in turn is central to a functioning social contract.

Besides its legitimate Weberian monopoly over violence as discussed above, a functioning state must be able to enforce laws, property rights and contracts, as well as have the fiscal capacity to raise revenues and provide public goods (Mill, 1848). A modern state must also be able to provide a wider range of public goods (health, education for example), in addition to a capacity to regulate and manage markets. The list grows longer with economic prosperity and progress; more affluent nations have bigger governments (as measured by the share of government consumption in national income). Economic decline in a 'failing' state severely undermines the state's fiscal capacity, something which makes it heavily aid dependent (Ghani and Lockhart, 2008). Aid dependence, in turn, further diminishes state capacity. Furthermore, a 'failing' state's ability to guarantee personal security, property rights and laws is often limited, leading to the gradual privatization of violence between predatory and defensive elements within society. All of these circumstances combine to produce a degenerating social contract, where individuals rely on kinship based groups and local warlords for security and public good provision; this heightens the risk of civil war as society descends towards an anarchical, Hobbesian, state of nature.

5.3   FAIR DIVISION

The post-war or post-accord economic, political and territorial pie needs to be fairly divided among erstwhile antagonists if the agreement is to be sustainable. A necessary condition for the viability of a peace treaty may lie in meeting the participation constraints of those involved, and ensuring that its stipulations are enforced. But it will never fulfil incentive compatibility constraints, which are to do with the exercise of effort to ensure that the accord lasts, unless it is perceived to be just, fair and equitable. If a peace agreement, inclusive of the divisions and compromises it entails is perceived to be unfair, then the deal itself will not be robust. The social choice theory literature on mechanisms for sharing and division offers us several insights on how to sustain peace agreements. For example, Brams (2006) points out several allocation rules for a single divisible good, many divisible goods and several indivisible goods. All of these have implications for durable peacemaking involving compromises over issues and post-war economic stakes. Sharing, in this regard, must be equitable as well as efficient. That is why envy-free allocative outcomes are so important.[5] In an envy-free outcome each participant does not regard the allocation achieved by another player to be superior to what he has achieved. All the various allocative mechanisms considered by Brams (2006) require monitoring or intervention by an outside agency, mediator and/or external power. These are all the more so in the case of allocations in a post-war situation.

In the case of a single divisible good the analogy with cake cutting is applicable. This may, for example, concern the division of the post-war peace dividend. The application of the envy-free criterion may entail several slices or divisions that may be inefficient and in excess of the

---

[5]   This also includes inclusiveness. A historical example may be in order (see Armstrong, 2003, pp. 81–2). Repairs were being conducted in the sacred temple known as the Ka'ba in Mecca in circa 605 AD. A sacred black (meteorite) stone had to be removed so that the renovations could progress. Once completed, each of the clans in Mecca wished to have the privilege of transporting the object back to its original location, leading to a serious dispute. Muhammad (who was later to found the Islamic religion) suggested that the stone be placed on a cloth and one member of each clan be represented in a party that would drag the object back to its original resting place. The solution to the dispute has the property of inclusiveness (each clan is represented), as well as being equitable; only one (and no more than one) member of each interested party participates in the event.

number of parties to the conflict. This will be all the more true if what is being divided up is not homogeneous. One can visualize situations to do with the division of the expenditure of post-war aid, and the dividing up of land that may require a great deal of parcelling.

A second situation considered by Brams (2006) entails several items to be divided, each of which is, in principle, divisible. Peace negotiations usually involve several issues, including regional autonomy, sharing of resource rents (such as oil revenues in the Sudan), constitutional changes, power sharing in the federal government and so on. Typically these issues will involve a long period of extended bargaining. The procedure behind the settlement, if reached, is described as the adjusted winner mechanism. Negotiations on the issues may involve placing upper and lower limits on the values of each issue, bearing in mind that assigning pecuniary values is more amenable in quantifiable matters such as resource rents rather than for non-monetary matters involving status, such as who should be president. Each side will allocate weights on the different issues at hand, and – given that each side has a similar number of bargaining chips – each party will win on some of the disputed issues. These will tend to be in areas most highly valued by the concerned parties. So, if a rebel group prizes regional autonomy more highly than resource rents, the group will put a higher weight on it and secure that goal under the adjusted winner mechanism. But one side can end up with wins on many high-value issues, and the consequent allocation could be inequitable to the other side. So this mechanism requires an equitability adjustment. Basically, this means sharing on high-value issues where the two sides' preferences are close, or the weights assigned to them out of their bargaining chip allocation are similar. So, if the government and the rebels assign a close and high weight to resource rents, they must share these. In other words, if the government and the rebels both value resource rents highly, one side cannot, equitably, be allowed to be a sole winner. There has to be a revenue sharing mechanism on this issue.

Other issues, where values diverge considerably, tend to be winner take all based on which side places the higher bid. This adjusted winner mechanism gives both sides an allocation that is roughly equal, and more than 50% of the assigned weights from the bargaining chip pile. The problem with applying this equitability included adjusted winner mechanism is that many issues are not easily divisible, such as which side first occupies a rotating presidency. A further difficulty can arise if the two sides do not have similar bargaining power, something that external actors need to engineer.

Thirdly, and most importantly, Brams (2006) considers mechanisms for allocating several indivisible issues, such as cabinet positions. The allocation of indivisible goods requires the application of the envy-free principle for any allocation to endure. A unique envy-free allocation may not be Pareto efficient. Pareto efficiency means that one side cannot be made better off without making another side worse off. One can make an envy-free allocation Pareto efficient by improving the utility of one side without lowering the utility of the other. But such allocations may not remain envy-free as one side could have a lower allocation of relatively more highly prized items (yielding the same utility) that are being allocated, and consequently resent the other side's allocation. Generally, allocations involving indivisible items are more difficult to achieve.[6] The answers, in the most intractable cases, must lie in sharing: joint access, equal user rights and other 'federal' constructions, as the recent arrangements between the North and South in the Sudan, and immediate post-apartheid South African dispensation (with a rotating presidency) suggest.

5.4 POWER SHARING AND POWER DIVISION

Power sharing is an important part of framing any peace agreement that ends civil war, as discussed in Chapter 4.[7] Peace is incentive incompatible if leaders of warring groups do not get positions of power in the settlement that follows. Power sharing can take several forms (political, territorial, military and fiscal, as analysed in Chapter 4). It is a way of reassuring weaker parties after a conflict via a signal of inclusiveness (see Rothchild, 2005, 2008). A great deal of thought and attention goes into designing post-war power sharing mechanisms, where the principles behind fair division can be applied. A successful mechanism brings about a balance of power among former belligerents. At first a transitional government and legislature is devised, with shared cabinet positions and even rotating presidencies on occasion, as was the case in South Africa. Its success or failure, as Sisk (1996) states, rests on the individual parties' commitment

---

[6] Sometimes there may be intractable integer problems. Ali-ibne-Abi Taleb (the fourth Islamic caliph or leader to succeed the Prophet Muhammad and his cousin and son-in-law), was confronted with the problem of dividing 17 camels among a man's three sons (an account of the story may be found in http://imamezaman.com/AHLEBAIT/1IMAM/camels.htm). The man had willed that his eldest son receive half, the second a third and the last a ninth; a weighting system that does not sum to one. Ali temporarily added one of his own camels to make the sum momentarily 18; consequently the first son received nine, the second six and the last two, which sums exactly to 17. When each son calculated his own share he felt he had received more than his fair share, so the result was perfectly envy-free and Pareto efficient. The mathematical solution to the problem involves normalizing the sum of the denominators; see query.nytimes.com/gst.

[7] Unless the country is partitioned into more than one nation state.

to the stipulations and mechanisms of power sharing (the rules of the game), as well as the presence of external mediation and guarantees for these. A road map is usually prepared with mechanisms that devise a more lasting political and governance structure. The ultimate aims are democratization and economic reconstruction. Is it a good idea that power sharing agreements remain in place in the longer-term political dispensation, particularly in ethnically fractionalized societies, which is the case in most civil war countries?

In the longer run, power sharing by being inclusive (consociationalist as described by Lijphart, 1977, 1999), may be a form of workable democracy preferable to majoritarianism, which is a system where the winner takes all. Power sharing is not only inclusive, as minorities are part of government, but may dampen harmful and potentially conflict producing elite competition. It has been argued that it is a superior mode of government (with proportional representation in elections) to the more traditional Westminster-style majoritarian systems[8], as the majority has to accommodate the minority. This is certainly relevant to ethnically fragmented developing countries, and has historically supported peace and democratic development in fragmented, yet industrialized, societies such as the Netherlands.

While power sharing is necessary for the peace agreement initially, there may be a trade-off between short-term power sharing and long-term institution building that leads to a stable peaceful democracy. This has been described by Rothchild and Roeder (2005) as the power sharing dilemma. Rothchild (2008) cogently demonstrated that while power sharing may constitute a convenient short-term mechanism for achieving a peace accord that ends hostilities, it may become a source of long-term tensions. Power sharing arrangements crafted together with the best of intentions may go through an uneasy post-war phase, eventually descending to a stage where it is only partially inclusive (as is the case in the Sudan with the Darfur dispute unresolved at the same time as there is a North–South peace accord; or in Rwanda prior to the genocide of 1994 with Habyarimana playing a mixed strategy of simultaneously working with Hutu moderates as well as pandering to extremist elements). The ultimate denouement could be the collapse of power sharing and a return to violence (Ivory Coast in 2003, say).

The factors that contribute to the demise of power sharing formulas include first the problem of asymmetric information in the peace accord.

---

[8] Even in certain Westminster-style governments in former British colonies power sharing has involved sharing ministerial positions among groups delineated along regional, confessional, tribal and other identity based lines.

Each side to the peace treaty may have private information regarding their own strengths, the presence or absence of spoiler groups within it, as well as its own military capabilities; this is information that is unknown to other parties and external guarantors of the agreement. This includes some groups or militias attempting to retain an outside option of returning to war by only partially disarming. Secondly, there may be an imperfect commitment to the treaty, as analysed in Chapter 4, because of the paucity of domestic and international anchors to the peace. To this list we may add the all-pervading atmosphere of mutual distrust and suspicion that characterizes many fragmented societies.

Thirdly, we have the underproduction of external sanctions and guarantees of the peace accord (Chapter 4), including inadequate external assistance to augment the peace dividend in war-torn societies where the economic pie has shrunk considerably as a consequence of war. Power sharing may also break down if external guarantors are biased, and show excessive favour to one group (the French in the Ivory Coast or erstwhile Zaire). Fourthly, the power sharing deal may be incomplete and not include all relevant groups, as in the case of the Sudan. In the Ugandan case, the leader of the rebel Lord's Resistance Army's (LRA) initial motivation may have been related to his non-inclusion in the arrangements following the struggle against Idi Amin. Power sharing may not, therefore, prevent the formation of splinter groups who act as spoilers towards the peace process.

Fifthly, Roeder (2005) argues that leaders of certain ethnicities have an incentive to escalate the tensions and disputes along ethnic lines that are bound to reappear at some future juncture, thereby undermining the federal government. Various parties to a power sharing deal could try to act as veto players, thereby undermining the system. The stability of power sharing relies on a delicate balance of power. Each side must be deterred from using violence by the belief that it will bring about retaliation or through a cost–benefit calculation that informs their minds that the costs of violence exceed potential gains. In this connection, Brams and Kilgour (2007a) argue that power sharing is unstable because different players have incentives to eliminate partners in order to grab the entire prize, unless the prospect of simultaneous destruction deters this type of behaviour (Brams and Kilgour, 2007b). There are many situations of bounded rationality that induce leaders to choose violence rather than negotiation, or to negotiate and use violence at the same time (mixed strategy).

Sixthly, power sharing based on ethnicity is bad for long-term democratization because all issues risk becoming 'ethnicized', and it produces incentives to make demands in favour of ethnic groups, particularly when there are resource rents at stake. Power sharing formulas may even become obsolete if the population's ethnic composition changes over time (Jarstad, 2006). Most societies are dynamic, and the ethnic mix is subject to change. For example, in the Lebanon the allocation of seats in Parliament reflects an obsolete ethnic composition dating back to the 1920s. Finally, power sharing formulas may give too much weight to those enamoured of violence, and place too little emphasis on moderate voices. This not only endangers the peace accord, but may also retard the future evolution of democracy.

For all these reasons, power sharing formulas need to be carefully designed. One way forward is to have temporary power sharing mechanisms that are dismantled later as democracy takes root, as was hoped for in recent peace accords in Burundi (ethnic parties initially were to share power and later the constitution apportioned Hutu and Tutsi representation) and Sierra Leone (where the Revolutionary United Front (RUF) were initially part of a power sharing deal up to the elections of 2002, when they withered away as a political force) (see Jarstad, 2006). Secondly, mechanisms to prevent opportunistic behaviour by one party or the formation of violent splinter groups have to be considered. Thirdly, the voice accorded to moderate elements has to be increased. Cognizance also needs to be taken of the fact that a future democratic system may have to take on a different configuration to an immediate post-war power sharing agreement. Including all of these elements in any one power sharing peacebuilding design is well-nigh impossible, and the relative weight placed on the various factors needs to be judged on a case-by-case basis.

The long-term solution, according to Roeder (2005) lies in 'power dividing' institutions, akin to the Constitution of the USA. Its characteristics include first, certain limitations on the powers of government. So, for example, the USA has a Bill of Rights that the state cannot tamper with, and Europe has a Human Rights convention. Secondly, it is important to devise multiple majorities. This means separated decision making at various levels. This may include a federated form of governance. But power division can take place even without a politically federal structure in smaller nations. For example, even in a city government, one committee decides on finance, another on education policy, another on police and yet another on street lighting. Power division occurs if the composition of each of these bodies is different, leading to varying decisive majority configurations, so in one committee one group may have a majority, but not at all levels. Power division also means the separation of powers, as first discussed by Montesquieu (1748), and later by James Madison in the Federalist Papers (1787–8). This means the separation of executive, legislative and judicial branches. Thirdly, none of the multiple majorities should have veto powers. This means checks and balances (also proposed by Madison in the Federalist Papers of 1787–8) and constraints on executive power. In the USA, for example, Congress can pass a bill and the president can veto it unless there is a two-thirds majority in Congress. The president's cabinet appointments require Congressional approval. The Supreme Court can declare a statutory law or executive action unconstitutional, through judicial review.

One interpretation of the above idea is that there should be more layers of political and economic decision making than there are ethnicities. This is likely to lead to more cooperative behaviour and several overlapping coalitions between groups. Decentralization of the decision making processes may be relevant here. A federalist construction with provinces or states, rather than a unitary system, could be desirable. A bicameral rather than unicameral legislature would be superior. The electoral system, whether proportional or majoritarian, should succeed in returning representatives of different ethnicities.

Finally, constraints on the exercise of executive power are highly important also for long-run growth, as stressed in Chapter 2. The idea of limits to sovereignty can be traced back to Jean Bodin (Sabine, 1961) and later to Madison in the Federalist Papers. The saliency of an independent judiciary in this regard cannot be overemphasized. Table 5.1 lists the average constraints on the executive for conflict countries over a period stretching from 1960 to 2005. This figure, derived from Polity IV, ranges from 0 to 7, with 7 implying the highest level of checks on the executive. Substantial constraints on the executive only begin from 5 and upwards. Clearly, we would expect some variation in these checks and balances on the executive in societies experiencing civil war and struggling with democratic transitions in the post-cold war era. In other words, we would expect a degree of fluctuation in the levels of checks on the executive. The emergence of multiparty elections is no guarantee of sufficient checks on executive power, particularly in new democracies. The mean value for all countries experiencing conflict is 3.4 during this 45-year period. This figure includes many nations that are part of Europe, the former Soviet Union and Latin America. If we exclude these nations only Papua New Guinea, India, Sri Lanka and South Africa have average scores exceeding 5. The average figure during this time period for non-conflict countries is higher at 4.7, along with a smaller coefficient of variation. Thus, conflict-ridden countries have weaker checks on executive power.

Crucially, Roeder (2005) argues that the very long-term survival of power sharing mechanisms in ethnically divided societies requires the construction of power dividing rules, as described above. Only then will it be stable in the long run. So, power division is essential to the sustainability of power sharing. Roeder (2005) provides empirical evidence in support of his argument.

Table 5.1   Constraints on the executive in conflict countries (1960–2005)

Country	Conflict years	Mean executive constraints	Coefficient of variation
Afghanistan	28	2.083	0.450
Algeria	15	1.721	0.599
Angola	35	3.000	0.000
Argentina	6	3.911	0.579
Azerbaijan	6	2.231	0.197
Bangladesh	17	3.394	0.570
Bolivia	1	4.422	0.615
Burkina Faso (Upper Volta)	1	2.045	0.494
Burundi	15	1.471	0.653
Cambodia (Kampuchea)	30	2.036	0.662
Cameroon	1	2.289	0.200
Central African Republic	2	1.933	0.864
Chad	36	1.351	0.358
Chile	1	4.222	0.608
Colombia	40	6.089	0.047
Comoros	2	3.310	0.530
Congo	6	2.727	0.414
Congo, DRC or Zaire	17	1.000	0.000
Croatia	4	4.154	0.366
Cuba	1	1.000	0.000
Cyprus	1	6.850	0.053
Djibouti	5	2.214	0.189
Dominican Republic	1	4.585	0.288
Egypt	6	3.000	0.000
El Salvador	14	4.375	0.169
Equatorial Guinea	1	1.378	0.396
Eritrea	4	2.667	0.185
Ethiopia	83	2.125	0.429
Gabon	1	1.500	0.337
Gambia	1	4.100	0.366
Georgia	7	5.000	0.000
Ghana	4	2.405	0.774
Guatemala	39	3.341	0.456
Guinea	3	1.533	0.549
Guinea-Bissau	2	3.034	0.311
Haiti	3	2.000	0.994

Table 5.1   (continued)

Country	Conflict years	Mean executive constraints	Coefficient of variation
India	144	6.956	0.030
Indonesia	36	2.711	0.501
Iran (Persia)	34	2.238	0.539
Iraq	44	1.000	0.000
Israel	46	7.000	0.000
Ivory Coast	3	1.537	0.684
Kenya	1	3.429	0.267
Laos	15	3.000	0.000
Lebanon	16	3.333	0.146
Lesotho	1	3.429	0.773
Liberia	12	2.278	0.387
Macedonia (FYR)	1	5.429	0.157
Madagascar (Malagasy)	1	3.841	0.368
Malaysia	8	5.089	0.217
Mali	2	2.545	0.696
Mexico	2	3.689	0.288
Moldova	1	6.714	0.108
Morocco	16	2.070	0.386
Mozambique	16	3.000	0.290
Myanmar (Burma)	183	2.311	0.560
Nepal	13	3.156	0.577
Nicaragua	11	3.209	0.771
Niger	6	2.909	0.646
Nigeria	6	3.093	0.869
Oman	4	1.311	0.357
Pakistan	8	3.707	0.688
Panama	1	3.778	0.561
Papua New Guinea	8	7.000	0.000
Paraguay	1	2.844	0.942
Peru	20	4.119	0.539
Philippines	68	4.227	0.520
Romania	1	3.636	0.432
Russia		3.923	0.265
Rwanda	13	1.302	0.428
Saudi Arabia	1	1.000	0.000
Senegal	14	3.341	0.288
Sierra Leone	10	3.333	0.373
Somalia	19	2.742	1.010
South Africa	31	7.000	0.000
Spain	5	4.857	0.599

Table 5.1   (continued)

Country	Conflict years	Mean executive constraints	Coefficient of variation
Sri Lanka (Ceylon)	25	5.844	0.167
Sudan	37	2.707	0.802
Syria	5	1.409	0.723
Tajikistan	7	3.357	0.148
Thailand	11	3.714	0.638
Togo	2	1.605	0.474
Trinidad and Tobago	1	7.000	0.000
Tunisia	1	1.756	0.532
Turkey	25	6.136	0.271
Uganda	32	2.775	0.650
United Kingdom	22	7.000	0.000
Uruguay	1	5.256	0.360
USSR	15	3.094	0.096
Uzbekistan	2	1.000	0.000
Venezuela	2	5.689	0.082
Vietnam, Republic of	5	2.726	0.212
Yemen	13	2.761	0.283
Yugoslavia (Serbia)	4	3.205	0.347
Zimbabwe (Rhodesia)	8	4.235	0.435

Source: Polity IV project and author's calculations.

5.5   FEDERALISM

What is the role of federalism in reducing conflict and maintaining the peace in post-accord societies? In addition to power sharing it can act as a mechanism for power division as discussed in the previous section; the appendix to this chapter applies these ideas to a simple analytical model of ethnic conflict and peace between government and an excluded group. If federalist mechanisms function, there will be a working social contract.

Federalism is defined as the system in which the power to govern is shared between the national and sub-national governments, creating what is often called a federation. The term originates from the Latin word foedus (treaty or agreement). The term federalism usually denotes a system of government in which sovereignty is constitutionally divided between a central governing authority and constituent political units such as states or provinces.[9]

Much of the historical analysis of federalism surrounded the federalist construction of the USA in the 1780s (see the Federalist Papers, 1787–8), as penned by Alexander Hamilton, John Jay and James Madison. Prominent federalists argued that the risk of tyranny was diminished, and individual rights better protected, in larger republics where sub-units with shared interests pooled or shared sovereignty, and could check each other with no veto players; also the basis of the power dividing ideas enumerated previously. Most believed that crucial issues such as foreign affairs, defence and the regulation of commerce should be matters for the federal level of government. The list can grow longer as government functions increase, and has been a matter of debate between centralizers and decentralizers, historically (federalists and anti-federalists in the early USA), and at present. The anti-federalists (such as Thomas Jefferson) were fearful of centralizing powers. In contemporary speak, parties with greater capitalist economic interests would favour greater centralization.

Classical liberals argued that federalism could prevent internecine warfare within the federation; Mill (1861), for example, argued that federations created stronger states, reducing the temptation of aggression and allowed for the maximization of the gains from trade within the federation. He, too, favoured allowing the centre sufficient power to secure the benefits of union, particularly powers to prevent internal cross-border duties that could diminish inter-regional trade. His necessary conditions for a successful federation include overlapping characteristics in race, language, religion, political institutions and rough parity among sub-units to prevent excessive domination by any. Following his logic, modern-day ethnically fragmented federations in developing countries should encounter difficulties on account of their seemingly irreconcilable ethnic diversity, and the vested economic interests of some sub-units (locally generated resource rents or apprehensions of its industries being eliminated by larger competition[10]) might make it wish not to join a federation. Tackling these problems will require judiciously designed fiscal federalism and resource sharing when forming federations. It should be pointed out that free trade and financial flows can produce highly integrated economies

---

[9]   In a confederation, such as the European Union, sovereignty is pooled via a consensus or majority of members.

[10]   Krugman (1991) points out that economic integration results in more concentrated production in fewer locations; this produces winners and losers. Thus not all sub-units of an economically integrated area may gain.

(globalization) without political union, however, it is difficult to imagine a political federation without a degree of greater economic integration.[11]

More recently, three processes of federalism have been identified by Stepan (1999): (1) independent states may 'come together' by ceding or pooling sovereign powers in certain domains for the sake of benefits otherwise unattainable, such as security or economic prosperity; (2) 'holding together' federations developed from unitary states, as governments respond to alleviate threats of secession; and (3) 'put together' federations by a strong centre such as the former Soviet Union. The coming together federations are typically arranged to constrain the centre and prevent majorities from overriding a sub-unit, as in the USA, Switzerland and Australia. These may be more relevant to developed countries. Coming together federations are largely irrelevant in poor developing countries where the gain from shared sovereignty seem limited. Holding together federations often grant particular sub-units particular domains of sovereignty over language and cultural rights in an asymmetric federation, while maintaining broad scope of action for the central government and majorities (India, Indonesia and Spain). They may be regarded as cases where the object is to appease certain minorities and prevent secession in an otherwise powerful centre, with relevance for most contemporary developing country situations. Put together federations are also of importance to post-conflict countries, where external powers interested in the peace often behave as the powerful centre, devising federal arrangements (Iraq, Afghanistan) that become unstable over time because of the absence of sufficient power dividing mechanisms and the general paucity of public goods, which intensifies the competition for scarce resources.

Federalism implies decentralization of powers and functions of the state; the degree of decentralization may be at issue (a strong centre in holding together federations or a weaker centre in coming together constructions), but its salience in ensuring lasting peace through power sharing and dividing is almost indisputable. This is not to deny that flawed federations can implode, as the examples of the disintegration of Yugoslavia and the USSR painfully demonstrate. Certain federal constructions can become very unstable, if territorial (local) majorities have interests in undermining federal government, in the absence of stable dividing mechanisms.

The linking of decentralization to conflict is a fairly new area of

---

[11]   We could view the European Union as a political project aimed at confederation and the avoidance of wars in the sense of Mill (1861), employing economic instruments such as common customs duties and the free movement of labour and capital as means towards the objective of confederation.

research, with the international donor and policy community strongly in its favour. From an academic viewpoint, Brancati (2006) summarizes two contrasting political arguments about the effects of decentralization in general on secessionist ethnic conflict. On the one hand, decentralization may curtail ethnic tensions and secessionism by bringing the government closer to the people, increasing opportunities to participate in government and ultimately giving groups control over their political, social and economic affairs. On the other hand, decentralization may exacerbate ethnic conflict and secessionism for the following reasons. First, decentralization reinforces ethnic identities by recognizing certain groups in countries, and giving them a sense of legitimacy. Secondly, it enables groups to enact legislation that discriminates against regional minorities. Thirdly, it provides regions with mechanisms, such as regional legislatures, local media and regional police forces that make engaging in ethnic conflict and secessionism easier. Brancati (2006) conducts a cross-country statistical analysis and concludes that decentralization is a useful device for reducing both ethnic conflict and secessionism, but the effect is undermined by the growth or emergence of regional parties. Roeder (2005) also points out that the risk of conflict escalation (from ethno-politics to national crises) is not diminished in territorial federations. One interpretation of this phenomenon is to say that these situations imply that some minority voices are insufficiently included in federal constructions. What is missing in many of these studies is the economic dimension, specifically the fiscal devolution of powers to local authorities, which can be argued to be of greater significance than the mere creation of democratically elected sub-national legislatures where greater local competencies are meaningless without economic teeth.

Fiscal federalism means decentralized government expenditure decisions and/or revenue raising powers to sub-national entities.[12] The revenue aspect may be important, particularly for regions with natural resources as in Indonesia or Nigeria, as it appeases local discontent about regionally generated revenues being siphoned off to central government. Other regional governments may be better able to raise local revenues, or even conduct their own borrowing. Decentralization may also increase the utility of regions that can take their own decisions about local public expenditure. It is important, therefore, to distinguish between the revenue and expenditure side of fiscal decentralization and its relation to conflict, although the two are always connected in practice. Note that one can have

---

[12] The measurement of fiscal decentralization is problematic; does it mean the relative size of local expenditures vis-à-vis central expenditures, or the proportion of locally generated revenues etc.?

fiscal decentralization without elaborate political federalism[13] and vice versa. However, a modicum of local decision making has to be in place for fiscal decentralization, albeit solely through an administrative (executive) arrangement.

On the expenditure side, a citizen is normally indifferent to who (federal, state or city government) provides public goods, as long as provision is adequate. Citizens may care about the type of provision in some instances, for example about what languages are taught in school, which might vary over different education authorities. Nevertheless, many expenditure priorities are subject to political processes and the formation of public policy. Then, it may matter which executive authority (regional or national) or which legislature (regional or national) decides on public finance and spending priorities.

Related to this is the theory of club goods (see Cornes and Sandler, 1996 for a succinct survey). As the name suggests, club goods are excludable and voluntary. Only members can benefit from the club good, and membership is voluntary. The provision of club goods does not always require state intervention, as members' incentives do not lead to under-provisioning. As with a public good, members of a club do share something, so the rule for the optimal provision for public goods based on the vertical summation of individual preferences for the common good or service applies. But here there is an additional requirement, related to membership. This is to do with the fact that on the one hand increased membership can reduce per unit costs (because of economies of scale or scope); but on the other hand, more people sharing leads to congestion and may crowd out benefits. So, both of these factors need to be taken into account in the pricing and provision of club goods. The important point here is that many government services are closer to the characteristics of club goods (or at least they are impure public goods) rather than pure public goods, particularly at the local level. Furthermore, an outcome closer to the club goods optimum may be achieved with greater local control over public expenditure. Since this implies volition, it may be conflict reducing.

What role does fiscal federalism have for ethnic conflict resolution? Besides outright war involving the state, ethnic violence can also take the form of peaceful protest by ethnic groups, or sectarian violence that is not targeting the state or rebellion against the state.

Tranchant (2007) points out that fiscal federalism, by decentralizing public expenditure decisions, is in principle violence reducing if different ethnicities are concentrated in the different geographical entities of

---

[13] In many political federations, the provinces or states have relatively weak fiscal powers, as in Pakistan.

the federation. In other words, if each group is the majority in one of the sub-national units that make up the federation, the likelihood of peace is increased. Fiscal federalism, however, will not reduce conflict if minorities are thinly spread across the whole country because these minorities are not a majority anywhere. More generally, there are other problems as well; fiscal federalism can cement ethnic cleavages, it can act as a method of appeasement only for resource-rich regions, and fiscal federalism can generate veto player functions where blocking by a region does not abate conflict.

What is the empirical evidence across countries? In Tranchant's (2007) study the results vary between ordinary least squares (OLS) panel regressions and regressions emphasizing country fixed effects.[14] The empirical strategy looks at the risk of conflict onset, and also the intensity of the conflict once there is onset. Fiscal decentralization increases the intensity of protest, but not the risk of protest onset for dispersed groups. As far as rebellion is concerned, decentralization reduces the risk as well as the intensity of this phenomenon when minorities are a majority in some jurisdictions of the federation, and even reduces rebellion in some dispersed cases. Sectarian violence rises with decentralization in OLS estimates, but once unobserved country heterogeneity is controlled for, fiscal decentralization reduces this type of violence.

By contrast, Alemán and Treisman (2005) in their case studies of four countries (India, Pakistan, Nigeria and Yugoslavia) find no systematic evidence to support the idea that fiscal decentralization lowered the risk of secessionist violence. They suggest that fiscal appeasement (which allows some regions more resources or to keep more locally generated revenues) may help in conflict abatement. Fiscal appeasement may have more to do with the revenue or income side compared to decentralized expenditure decision making.

Badly conceived fiscal federalism, or the failure to adapt federalist rules to new and emerging situations (such as natural resource discoveries or debt burdens) can exacerbate latent conflictual tendencies in federations. In countries where minorities are dispersed, other forms of functional federalism or power dividing mechanisms are necessary in addition to fiscal federalism. Fiscal decentralization might work better in middle-income countries with greater revenues to spend on public goods, and in countries where resource-rich regions demand financial autonomy. Indeed, Tranchant (2008) empirically demonstrates that fiscal federalism is more successful at reducing conflict risk in countries with superior institutions

---

[14]   The latter method is in principle superior because it takes into account specific country characteristics, or unobserved heterogeneity.

using the international country risk guide (ICRG) data, implying that better institutional quality means the country has superior governance, and more durable political institutions. In particular, nations with malfunctioning institutions often have weak central governments, which encourages violent challenges, and fiscal decentralization may fail to mollify potential rebels.

5.6   SYNTHESIS

In this chapter, I have been concerned with factors that help sustain the peace in the long term. When war is ongoing, the stipulations of any peace treaty need to be made incentive compatible to belligerent parties; otherwise they will never agree. This includes a share of the post-war economic and political pie for each party to the conflict. Afterwards, there may be opportunistic behaviour by some belligerents threatening or actually returning to war, and imperfect enforcement of the security aspects of the peace treaty (Chapter 4). The present chapter analysed aspects of what holds a nation together; a convenient short-hand for which is the expression 'social contract'; rebuilding the 'contract' is crucial to long-term peacebuilding.

The preceding sections have identified three factors that contribute to long-term peace and the reconstruction of the social contract. These also correspond to the three dimensions of the social contract, identified by Addison and Murshed (2006). The first is an equity consideration, or a dimension of distributive justice.[15] Here we can draw on the social choice literature on fair division. Fair division can be across a single divisible, several divisible and several indivisible issues or items. In each case equity considerations apply, especially the principle of envy-free allocations. Without it, any post-war settlement is unlikely to endure.

Secondly, we have more realist notions about the balance of power that maintains peace among potential adversaries. In ethnically divided societies, power sharing may be insufficient to sustain peace if the leaders of different ethnicities have incentives to escalate conflicts, or 'ethnicize' future conflicts. In some cases, power sharing may become the source of future conflict. In these circumstances, power dividing formulas that devise multiple decision making layers, with no single veto player, may be necessary. These arrangements point to a federal political system, although federalism is not essential to power division. In the end, multiple sources of

---

[15]   There are many other aspects of distributive justice, including Rawls's (1971) maximin principle, which maximizes the utility of the least fortunate.

power (power division) may facilitate and stabilize power sharing among different ethnicities. Many federalist constructs are imposed by outside powers or donors following a conflict. These arrangements may not hold together, unless they are domestically incentive compatible. A similar argument applies to various agendas for democratic development. Unless democratization and power sharing (dividing) formulas are *sui generis* (endogenous), they will not withstand the test of time.

The third aspect concerns decentralization in the allocation of public expenditure and revenues – fiscal decentralization. Revenue sharing can be important to many settlements following a civil war, particularly when there are valuable local resource rents at stake, and certain groups are disaffected by their inability to control effectively what they regard as rightfully theirs. Equally, expenditures may be important, and decentralized decision making about public expenditure may yield greater utility to local communities. So, potentially, we have two issues here concerning peacebuilding. The first is to do with appeasing potentially disaffected groups about controlling locally generated revenues; giving these groups greater fiscal powers over revenue amounts to fiscal appeasement via increased regional public sector income, and this may be necessary to avoid conflict. Secondly, there is local control on the nature of public expenditure in ethnically divided societies. This is, broadly speaking, conflict reducing if each fiscal sub-unit has a substantial and different majority ethnic group. If ethnic minorities are thinly spread across the federation, other means of addressing potential public expenditure grievances have to be devised by the central government, leading to a broad based and inclusive provision of public goods with the special needs of certain groups (language, say) met. Decentralized decision making about public expenditure may be more relevant for middle-income developing countries, as there the share of government consumption as a proportion of GDP is greater and more significant than in low-income developing countries.

Finally, the social contract is between citizens, individually or in groups, with the state or sovereign authority. Consequently, the failure of the state to fulfil its functions leads to the breakdown of the social contract, and in many instances civil war. Once an uneasy peace is established, besides the restoration or reconstruction of the social contract, state capacity needs to be rebuilt. Of the functions of the state, four areas may be highlighted, the first two of which constitute the primary functions of the state in classical liberalism.

First, the state must be able to enforce laws, contracts and to ensure the personal security of its citizens. Otherwise violence becomes privatized, and the state loses its legitimate Weberian monopoly over violence.

Bates (2001) highlights that historically very often the traditional means of social control are undermined by economic progress; prosperity, however, cannot be sustained unless the state assumes responsibility for security. In many failing states, people have to rely on kinship ties to fill the sovereignty gaps left behind by a failing state. Secondly, the state must have fiscal capacity, both at the central and decentralized levels, to raise revenue and provide public goods (this list grows longer with economic progress). In states that are at a post-conflict reconstruction phase this hugely important task of rebuilding state capacity is often thwarted by the manner in which external assistance is provided (see Ghani and Lockhart, 2008). The state's role is often supplanted by donor provision of public goods (including particularist procurement practices), and the presence of financial aid stunts the development and need for domestic resource mobilization. Besides official aid donors, the activities of development non-governmental organizations (NGOs), both domestic and foreign, retard the development of state capacity.

Thirdly, the state has to provide the framework within which long-term economic growth is made possible. Long-term growth may depend on institutional quality, but more immediately the right policies have to be followed. The latter involves identifying the constraints on growth, and then removing them, as Rodrik (2006) suggests. These could include inadequate infrastructure, the paucity of financial capital, restrictive trade policies, and so on. Sound macroeconomic management that results in sustainable fiscal deficits, inflation control and balance of payments equilibrium is also part of a growth enhancing strategy.

Finally, the state needs to be able to regulate the (free) market. Just as the market can provide the basis for prosperity that ultimately diminishes the chances of conflict, the unregulated activities of the market can not only produce major economic downswings (the prime examples of which are financial crises, which inordinately impinge on the real economy), but the workings of the free market can enhance conflict risk, as will be shown in Chapter 7 on globalization and conflict. Also, governments need to ensure that growth needs to be broad based in order for it not to ignite conflict. Despite the fact that growth ultimately reduces conflict risk, the road to prosperity along its path increases the risk of conflict, unless measures are taken to address poverty and inequality, which in turn breed the greed and grievances (resource rents, polarization, horizontal inequality and relative deprivation) that produce conflict. The inevitable structural changes to the economy that emerge in the wake of growth always produce winners and losers, as some become richer and others become, relatively, poorer. For conflict to be avoided, the losers must not be allowed to fall too far. Therefore, the donor focus on poverty reduction is simply not enough; the presence of conflict risk enhancing horizontal inequalities also needs addressing. We are now in a position to examine strategies to reconstruct war-torn economies, with the aim of broad based and inclusive reconstruction in mind.

APPENDIX: A SIMPLE MODEL OF POWER SHARING AND POWER DIVIDING SOCIAL CONTRACT

The following is based on Cuesta and Murshed (2008), and builds on the model presented in the appendix to Chapter 3.

The Government Side

$$G = \pi(a, e) G^P + (1 - \pi)(\cdot) G^C - C(a) \tag{5.1}$$

Here expected utility of the government is denoted by G, where G^P and G^C denote utilities or pay-offs in peace and conflict respectively, weighted by the probabilities of the two states, peace (π) and war ($1 - \pi$). The pay-offs are endogenous to the strategic actions (a) undertaken by the government. The net income of the government (Y^G) includes fungible aid as well as resource rents.

$$G^P = Y^G - pF^G - T$$
$$G^C = Y^G - cF^G \tag{5.2}$$
$$c > p > 0, c + p = 1.$$

T is the 'transfer' made by the government to the rebels in the state of relative peace and depends on government income. This can take a variety of forms including broad based social and development expenditure extended to the rebels, power sharing, revenue sharing and the inclusion of the otherwise excluded group in government jobs and state contracts. F denotes military expenditure, this is clearly greater in wartime than during peace, hence $c > p$. The parameter a is the strategic choice variable of the government and determines quantities of F and T chosen. C is the cost of undertaking peaceful behaviour as hawkish constituencies within the state need to be appeased. This depends on the grand objective function of the state, involving a trade-off between war and peace:

$$a = -bG^C + (1 - b) G^P \tag{5.3}$$

Here b refers to the relative welfare from war, and $1-b$ the relative social utility of peace. We can simplify the expression into:

$$a = -bF^G + (1 - b) T \tag{5.4}$$

The above expression is justified by the fact that war involves fighting, and peace implies transfers to the rebels.

A more benevolent and developmental state may prefer making transfers to rebels to fighting them. In that case $b < \frac{1}{2}$; if $b > \frac{1}{2}$ fighting is preferred to transfers; in the limit if $b = 0$ then there is only peace, and $b = 1$ implies only war, $b = \frac{1}{2}$ implies indifference. Observe that, when $b = 0$, we have a social contract from the government's point of view, and when $b = 1$, we have war, in the intermediate region we have an imperfect social contract. Thus, it is possible for the state to be both benevolent or developmental and repressive at the same time, and various degrees of benevolence (repression) are possible as b declines (rises). The parameter b may also be regarded as a measure of power and revenue sharing. If $b \rightarrow 0$, we have greater power and revenue sharing. A rational decision maker who maximizes expected utility will decide to share power and revenues ($b = 0$) if:

$$F^G > T + C \tag{5.5}$$

This means that the cost of fighting the rebels must be high compared to the revenue lost from power and revenue sharing with rebels, and the political costs of appeasing hawkish elements in the government party must not be too high.

The Rebel Side

The rebel or excluded group's expected utility (R) is given by:

$$R = \pi(a, e)R^P + (1 - \pi)(\cdot)R^C - E(e) \tag{5.6}$$

$$R^P = Y^R - pF^R + (1 - \delta)T$$
$$R^C = Y^R + B(F^R) - cF^R + \delta S \tag{5.7}$$

The pay-offs are endogenous to the strategic action (e) undertaken by the rebels, which as with the government raises the probability of peace. The income of the rebel group in the state of war is supplemented by contributions from sympathetic citizens abroad (S), as well as exports (B) of narcotics and/or natural resources such as alluvial or blood diamonds. The role of diasporas (or alternatively, simply the more hawkish segment of the rebel group) is modelled through the parameter δ, which is a measure of the credibility of the government transfer vis-à-vis the transfer from diasporas or the hawkish element in the rebel group. If $\delta = 1$, then the state's transfers are not credible, but the rebels have diasporas finance S to use in a relatively more conflictive state. For the sake of analytical convenience, transfers (T) from the government occur only in peacetime, and diaspora finance (S) happens only in the state of belligerence. Ultimately, the inverse of δ captures the credibility of the state's power and revenue sharing offer to the rebels, particularly to the hawkish element or outside belligerent diaspora group; here for simplicity I only let δ take on 0, 1 values. As Roeder (2005) argues, the power sharing agreement with the rebel group will be sustainable over time only if there are power dividing arrangements in place; this implies federalism in most cases. So, if $\delta = 0$, federalist and power dividing structures are enabling the power and revenue sharing agreements in place.

E is the cost of effort, e, which increases the probability of peace, π. This means the cost of appeasing the more belligerent (diaspora) rebels. Turning to its determination:

$$e = -kB(F^R) + (1 - \delta)T - \delta S \qquad (5.8)$$

where k is the relative weight given to wartime booty. If $\delta = 0$ the state is perfectly credible, implying federalist structures are in place. If $k = \frac{1}{2}$, the rebels are indifferent to war or peace; preferring peace when $k < \frac{1}{2}$, war if $k > \frac{1}{2}$; only war if $k = 1$, and only peace when $k = 0$. As $k \to 0$, the rebels have stopped valuing wartime booty, and are instead content with their share of fiscal revenues and power within a federalist structure; $k = 0$ requires:

$$T - B > E\dots with\, \delta = 0 \qquad (5.9)$$

This implies fiscal federalism, or at least fiscal appeasement, so that the rebels get to keep locally generated resource revenues, and do not have to seize them through violence. They become part of the transfer (T), and B obtained from fighting the state becomes largely irrelevant. Also, the costs of appeasing the hawkish or diaspora rebels (E) must not be too high. Observe that the closer b, δ and k are to zero, the more proximate the working social contract is to fruition. This means power and revenue sharing within federalist structures, including a degree of fiscal federalism. Finally, it should be noted that b, $\delta = 0$ in 5.5 and 5.9 respectively also necessitates the resolution of historical grievances, otherwise the cost of concessions to enemies (C and E) will potentially remain high.

6. Post-war economic reconstruction

6.1 INTRODUCTION

The previous chapter was concerned with political institutions that foster lasting peace. In order to sustain peace, however, it is simply not sufficient to devise political mechanisms, be they power sharing arrangements or more long-term constitutional instruments, without ensuring that economic growth also ensues in the post-war period. In other words, securing lives without guaranteeing livelihoods will, like faith without charity, come to nothing. Political restructuring is meaningless without economic reconstruction. Nowadays, most civil wars take place in poor low-income economies; it is also widely accepted that growth failure, economic vulnerability and endemic poverty enhance conflict risk, as discussed in chapters 2 and 3. Reintegrating ex-combatants through successful demobilization policies, known as disarmament, demobilization and reintegration (DDR) also requires economic recovery (see Humphreys and Weinstein, 2007). Successful, sustained and broad based economic growth has also come to be regarded as the ultimate antidote to conflict. The previous chapter on refashioning the social contract touched upon economic dimensions of the contract. These included fair division and a degree of fiscal decentralization; aims that cannot be realized without economic reconstruction and an expanding economic pie.

For all these reasons, the policy maker in a post-conflict or post-accord situation must be concerned with rebuilding the economy.[1] This objective has three dimensions, which need to be addressed simultaneously. There is, first of all, a reconstruction phase where it is necessary to rebuild not just damaged physical infrastructure, but also the framework within which economic policy is conducted, including fiscal, monetary and regulatory institutions. This is because modern warfare in developing countries is particularly destructive towards institutions. Then there is the phase where economic growth must be restarted. In Chapter 2, I have pointed out the growth costs of war. War, particularly civil war, can distort economic

---

[1] The term post-conflict may be somewhat inappropriate; Chapter 4 demonstrates the empirical regularity with which conflict restarts following a peace accord; as a rule economic reconstruction policies cannot await the establishment of a more lasting peace.

activity away from growth enhancing pro-poor long-term sectors towards the direction of short-term profit. Finally, economic reconstruction must be broad based so as to avoid the risk of conflict re-igniting. Policy makers need to be mindful of the distributive consequences of reconstruction, taking into account the vertical and horizontal inequality effects of policies, as well as their poverty dimension.

This chapter is organized as follows. In section 6.2 I will consider macroeconomic issues, including broad based reconstruction, imbalanced recovery and the role of aid. Political economy issues connected with financing reconstruction and rebuilding economic institutions are dealt with in section 6.3. Section 6.4 will be concerned with the political economy of post-conflict economic reconstruction, and matters related to managing windfall rents that may arise either because of substantial, but temporary, aid inflows, or the advent or increase in natural resource revenues. Finally, section 6.5 presents a brief synthesis of the ideas contained in the chapter.

6.2 MACROECONOMICS OF RECONSTRUCTION, GROWTH AND AID

As we saw in Chapter 5, a peaceful social contract becomes unviable when the credibility of a transfer is low relative to the probability of rebel success in armed conflict. Also, in Chapter 4, the commitment to peace may be subject to temptations to renege on the agreement. Peace is more likely to endure if the economic pie can be made to grow. Growth, by raising the tax base, increases the possibilities of redressing grievances, and even stifling greed, through fiscal transfers. Furthermore, growth tightens the labour market, thereby reducing the attractiveness of joining a warlord or rebel group.

Addison and Murshed (2005) point out that the initial years of peace may offer considerable scope for growth. But just as economic growth in general can distribute broadly or narrowly its benefits across society – depending upon the initial distribution of assets and skills – so too does reconstruction-led growth. Pre-war asset and skill distributions that may have been highly unequal can worsen dramatically during wartime. The already poor often lose the few assets they have; looting adds to the numbers of the poor. In contrast, warlords and their followers accumulate assets, and so while the early years of peace may see quite rapid GDP growth it can be very narrow in its benefits – unless policies are put in place to restore the productive assets and human capital of the poor. The immediate post-conflict reconstruction phase may also offer a golden opportunity for pro-poor asset redistribution, although this can be impeded when 'winners' from war block the necessary measures, as in the case of Afghanistan where warlords are still protected by the Western (mainly American) coalition forces because of their role in the war on terror.

The 'post-conflict' economy will be initially distorted, and this can impose an unfortunate path dependence on reconstruction and growth (Addison and Murshed, 2005). One source of distortion is the sharp increase in transaction costs resulting from war, including the destruction of transport, the planting of land mines, and institutional collapse, which drive a wedge between producer and consumer prices. Typically, production is more vulnerable, leading to a sharper increase in its transaction costs compared to other sectors such as urban based trade and services. Services and trade, including profitable smuggling and other rent seeking, dominate wartime economies.

The result is shown in the production possibilities diagram in Figure 6.1, where short-term activities (S) are measured along the vertical axis and long-term activities are depicted along the horizontal axis (A). Three production frontiers are indicated: PP (peace), WW (war) and RR (recovery). A peace equilibrium could exist with growth along a ray such as G_p, as aggregate investment pushes the production frontier outwards over time. The wartime production frontier must therefore lie within the peacetime frontier. Long-term activities (A) are hit harder than short-term activity (S), and the production frontier changes shape (to form WW, reflecting the greater difficulties of A production). And the relative price shift in favour of services causes a structural shift to the new equilibrium E_w. There may be periods of growth during wartime – from a point below the peacetime production frontier – but it will be S-biased (along the ray G_w) and is therefore unlikely to be sufficiently poverty reducing.

If a peace deal is signed then transaction costs start to fall. Accordingly, A sector output recovers as relative prices shift back in its favour, and as infrastructure is rebuilt; the economy moves through a series of reconstruction frontiers such as RR. Although this reconstruction is characterized by a more than proportionate rise in A – which includes subsistence agriculture, the main livelihood of the poor – recovery's benefits may still be too narrowly distributed due to the loss of assets and skills among the poor. Moreover, the economy's pre-war structure may have been far from optimal for growth, poverty reduction or peace, due to policy distortions. Hence, significant economic reform must take place alongside reconstruction if broad, rather than narrow recovery, is to take place. In Figure 6.1, reform is shown as raising the return further on A relative to S activities (i.e. to the relative price line b so that the economy recovers along G_b).

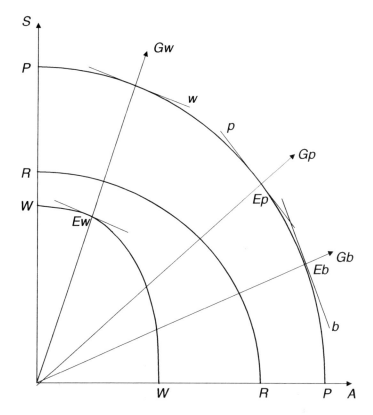

Source: Addison and Murshed (2005).

Figure 6.1   Broad versus narrow reconstruction

There is wide agreement on the need for fiscal reform in order to raise public spending on pro-poor basic health care and primary education, although implementation is often fraught with difficulties

Restarting activity in pro-poor production activities such as agriculture can therefore be especially hard after war when the peace is uneasy. Consequently the reconstruction–growth path may create insufficient income and employment, its narrowness leading to frustration amongst large sections of the excluded population. If grievances, however, are the main source of conflict then broad based reconstruction (along G_b) is necessary to recreating a sustainable social conflict. This growth path, however, may be slower in achieving national income associated with the production frontier, *PP*, compared to an alternative growth path described by *Gp*. This could represent a trade-off between faster economic recovery and political stability. One of the positive effects of growth, however achieved, is that it raises wage levels and reduces the attractiveness of predation as a livelihood.

The stylized macroeconomic model presented in the appendix to this chapter distinguishes between two sectors: one (N), which is mainly related to subsistence consumption, non-traded goods and unprocessed natural resource exports; with the other being the more dynamic growth enhancing sector (M), which includes manufactured exports. In the short-term the objective of aid donors may be humanitarian assistance, which requires an expansion in the N sector; this may, however, require careful targeting so that the subsistence consumption of the poor actually increases. Secondly, long-term growth, including the broad based growth alluded to above, may require greater expansion in the tradable part of the M sector in the longer term. This requires domestic investment in infrastructure and social services such as health and education, which can be financed by aid but also out of domestic tax revenues. Aid to the tradable sector requires domestic absorptive capacity, something which is weak due to wartime destruction of infrastructure as well as institutions; this fact is also highlighted by Demekas, McHugh and Kosma (2002).

Domestic resource mobilization is particularly difficult to achieve in the short term after a conflict, not just because of poverty, but also due to diminished fiscal institutional capacity following war. I will return to these issues in the next section. Finally, there could also be Dutch disease-type effects from aid and also natural resource rents in a post-conflict situation, and this too may crowd out the more dynamic growth sector. Policies should counteract these effects (see Murshed, 2001, for details); basically this involves encouraging the traded sector through subsidies, and discouraging excessive demand for non-traded goods. Eldbadawi, Kaltani and Schimdt-Hebbel (2008) also present evidence suggesting that aid does benefit growth in post-conflict societies, but at diminishing rates due to the fact that aid can cause real exchange rate appreciation.

Collier and Hoeffler (2004a) argue that aid has a particularly crucial role in restarting growth in post-conflict societies.[2] They make two crucial points. First, the capacity to absorb aid may be weaker at the initial post-conflict phase of up to three years. Indeed, Table 6.1 below does demonstrate a surge in aid in the immediate post-conflict period for countries such

---

[2]   Although issues pertaining to aid effectiveness are beyond the scope of this book, it is useful to note that there is a difference between the macroeconomic impact of all forms of aid on growth, and the impact of different types of aid such as project aid, food aid in kind and technical assistance, including institutional support. Furthermore, if one looks at the impact of aid on certain sectors rather than the general economy, aid is usually much more effective in achieving its goals.

Table 6.1   *Aid allocation (ODA net disbursements) in 40 conflict countries*

Countries	Total in five-year period (in constant 2006 US$ millions)			Individual share of the disbursement to 40 countries			Aid as % of GDP (five-year average)		
	1991–5	1996–2000	2000–5	1991–5	1996–2000	2000–5	1991–5	1996–2000	2001–5
Afghanistan	1777	1098	9286	1.6	1.2	5.9	–	–	32.43
Algeria	1679	1706	1780	1.5	1.9	1.1	0.57	0.54	0.41
Angola	2301	2418	3183	2.0	2.7	2.0	6.59	5.11	3.51
Azerbaijan	503	880	1428	0.4	1.0	0.9	2.24	3.34	3.49
Bosnia-Herzegovina	1648	5701	3586	1.4	6.4	2.3	–	21.56	7.65
Burundi	1716	527	1464	1.5	0.6	0.9	27.16	9.70	37.27
Cambodia	1696	2142	2784	1.5	2.4	1.8	10.94	10.23	10.11
Central African Rep.	1036	687	453	0.9	0.8	0.3	14.51	11.07	6.62
Chad	1465	1258	1607	1.3	1.4	1.0	15.21	12.87	9.10
Congo, Dem. Rep.	1712	988	11925	1.5	1.1	7.6	3.56	2.88	35.07
Congo, Rep.	1071	1197	1876	0.9	1.3	1.2	8.29	7.79	6.57
Côte d'Ivoire	6118	3978	2369	5.4	4.4	1.5	9.97	5.25	2.93
Djibouti	720	499	418	0.6	0.6	0.3	24.50	15.86	11.21
Egypt	19921	11045	6797	17.4	12.3	4.3	7.15	2.23	1.37
El Salvador	2159	1330	1286	1.9	1.5	0.8	5.00	1.95	1.43
Eritrea	482	1004	1715	0.4	1.1	1.1	–	22.49	42.06
Ethiopia	6715	4303	8921	5.9	4.8	5.7	11.15	8.18	16.48
Georgia	659	1446	1668	0.6	1.6	1.1	3.94	7.39	6.97
Guatemala	1277	1541	1395	1.1	1.7	0.9	1.79	1.37	1.07
Guinea	2460	1771	1474	2.2	2.0	0.9	12.08	7.91	7.36
Guinea-Bissau	779	685	507	0.7	0.8	0.3	50.15	44.00	35.18
Haiti	2191	1975	1462	1.9	2.2	0.9	13.83	8.92	6.93
Iraq	1887	1090	30174	1.7	1.2	19.3	–	–	–
Lebanon	973	1430	1705	0.9	1.6	1.1	2.11	1.41	1.46
Liberia	743	596	711	0.7	0.7	0.5	62.87	37.45	26.50
Macedonia, FYR	224	1081	1534	0.2	1.2	1.0	–	4.50	5.76
Mali	2789	2500	3134	2.4	2.8	2.0	18.79	15.61	13.17
Mozambique	7772	6036	8324	6.8	6.7	5.3	54.87	23.48	28.06
Nepal	2470	2335	2382	2.2	2.6	1.5	10.93	7.80	6.16
Nicaragua	3809	3908	5134	3.3	4.4	3.3	30.15	17.86	19.89
Niger	2132	1605	2401	1.9	1.8	1.5	18.08	13.12	15.76
Pakistan	6950	4579	9437	6.1	5.1	6.0	2.30	1.23	1.97
Rwanda	3111	2254	2415	2.7	2.5	1.5	40.40	20.30	21.61
Senegal	3788	3109	3523	3.3	3.5	2.2	12.16	9.95	8.92
Sierra Leone	1159	863	2132	1.0	1.0	1.4	22.65	17.74	36.07
Somalia	3224	626	1146	2.8	0.7	0.7	–	–	–

Table 6.1 (continued)

Countries	Total in five-year period (in constant 2006 US$ millions)			Individual share of the disbursement to 40 countries			Aid as % of GDP (five-year average)		
	1991–5	1996–2000	2000–5	1991–5	1996–2000	2000–5	1991–5	1996–2000	2001–5
Sri Lanka	3 893	2 011	3 308	3.4	2.2	2.1	6.45	2.35	3.01
Sudan	3 214	1 347	4 370	2.8	1.5	2.8	9.08	1.90	3.67
Tajikistan	216	751	1 103	0.2	0.8	0.7	–	11.03	12.13
Uganda	4 533	4 694	5 821	4.0	5.2	3.7	19.50	11.68	14.92

Source: OECD statistics.

as Mozambique and Uganda in the early 1990s, and Afghanistan, Congo (DRC), Sierra Leone, Tajikistan, Georgia and Macedonia more recently. We might expect aid dependence (aid as a percentage of GDP) to taper off as post-conflict growth restarts. As pointed out also by Eldbadawi, Kaltani and Schimdt-Hebbel (2008), this happens when aid pledges and flows are at their peak. Therefore, donor aid efforts should be phased and sustained for a sufficiently long period of time, instead of focusing pledges in the first year after the peace accord.

Secondly, they argue that the growth (and by implication the poverty reducing) elasticity of aid is greater in post-conflict countries relative to comparably poor non-conflict developing countries. Thus, donors principally interested in poverty reduction should focus their attention on post-conflict countries. This plea for a greater re-orientation of growth enhancing and poverty reducing aid towards post-conflict situations has been challenged by Suhrke, Villanger and Woodward (2005), who among other things criticize the atheoretical nature of the Collier–Hoeffler (2004a) policy recommendations. After recoding the data to reflect civil wars accurately, they find the growth effects of post-conflict aid to be less than half of the Collier–Hoeffler (2004a) claim. As far as the policy implications are concerned, Suhrke, Villanger and Woodward (2005) argue that the donor focus on the initial humanitarian aid in post-conflict societies relative to aid for long-term growth may not be as misplaced as believed by some, because the growth recovery effects are not as substantial as Collier and Hoeffler (2004a) allege.

A great deal depends on how aid is utilized. Most aid is fungible because it eases the government's budget constraint, even if it is not direct budget support, in which case it can take a variety of forms such as food aid (in kind), project aid, technical assistance (this includes institutional support such as building a new army, police force, judicial capacity etc.) or external debt relief. There is no doubt that aid can help ease financial constraints in post-war situations, when the government budget can be severely constrained. One problem is that aid, or for that matter debt relief, may be used to bolster military expenditure rather than finance spending on subsistence consumption by the poor or rebuilding infrastructure and institutions (Addison and Murshed, 2003). Military expenditure is not growth enhancing, as it detracts from more productive growth, such as increasing spending on the education and health sectors.

The main negative macroeconomic consequences of aid emanate from real exchange rate appreciation or rising real interest rates that can crowd out the international competitiveness of traded goods (akin to Dutch disease) and private sector investment respectively. Eldbadawi, Kaltani and Schimdt-Hebbel (2008) point out that both trade openness and financial development ultimately ease the constraints on growth in post-conflict economies. Addison, Chowdhury and Murshed (2002), however, demonstrate that the intensity of conflict detracts from financial development, as measured by financial deepening (the ratio of the monetary aggregate M2 to GDP, say), where governance also matters. Real exchange rate appreciation, which crowds out exports and hence lowers growth, is most likely if the demand for non-tradable goods rises, in common with Dutch disease mechanisms. Humanitarian aid, in the immediate aftermath of conflict, which is spent on productive activities such as subsistence consumption, demobilizing ex-combatants, rebuilding infrastructure and institutional capacity (such as the state's ability to govern) is unlikely to cause real exchange rate appreciation, particularly if the money is spent on imported goods (Gupta, 2008). Gupta goes on to argue that there may be a case for 'frontloading' some post-conflict assistance, particularly humanitarian aid, to fragile and post-conflict states where the conflict has been deeply destructive of the economy (substantial GDP contraction and a history of negative growth). This means giving more aid at the initial phase and less at later stages, in contrast to the arguments of Collier and Hoeffler (2004a) and Eldbadawi, Kaltani and Schimdt-Hebbel (2008), who focus mainly on the growth enhancing aspects of aid.

In general, a great deal would depend upon the ability of countries to 'absorb' the aid, and Gupta (2008) makes a distinction between absorption and spending aid. Here absorption should lead to an expansion in the current account deficit, and also implies the willingness of the central bank actually to sell the foreign exchange in which aid is denominated. Spending aid ought to lead to a rise in government expenditure, or the budget deficit. In some cases, aid is neither absorbed nor spent, in which case it only serves to build up foreign exchange reserves for use in the future. In other cases, aid is absorbed but not spent. It is then used instead to reduce the level of public debt. There can be instances where aid is spent but not absorbed, when the government's spending rises in proportion to aid but the foreign exchange is not used. This implies printing money or borrowing from the domestic credit market; in the former case it can be highly inflationary and in the latter instance raise domestic interest rates. Lastly, aid may be both absorbed and spent, which is what donors would desire after conflict. This would require coordination between the central bank, which sets interest rates and controls foreign exchange reserves, and the budgetary (fiscal) authorities. The lack of coordination between monetary and fiscal authorities often results in post-conflict aid not being fully utilized (neither absorbed nor spent, Gupta, 2008). Sometimes the state's fiscal and monetary institutions may have degenerated so much that the immediate post-conflict aid has to be off-budget, which means that donors or other development agencies have to spend the money directly. This, however, may have the unintended consequence of stifling the renaissance of state capacity, as Ghani and Lockhart (2008) have demonstrated in the case of Afghanistan.

Adam, Collier and Davis (2008) point out that aid may assist post-conflict monetary reconstruction by precluding the need for hyper-inflation. During conflict, and immediately after, the government faces many large spending priorities: initially in prosecuting the war, and later to finance reconstruction and social services, as well as keeping up a military deterrent. During war, and soon afterwards, it is tempting to resort to seigniorage[3] taxes to finance government expenditure relative to borrowing. But the ability to raise these types of revenues depends on the willingness of the public to hold domestic currency. During conflict the income elasticity of money demand may decline as production falls, and as economic activities move offshore, including capital flight (the greater holding of foreign currency and foreign currency denominated assets). Thus, the state's post-war ability to levy seigniorage taxes is diminished, making this avenue of raising revenue even more inflationary. Attempts at such policies, by causing greater inflation, may even destroy any remaining confidence in the domestic currency. In these situations, aid by financing government expenditure may preclude the need for seigniorage taxes and

---

[3]   Seigniorage refers to the inflationary tax that states can levy because of their monopoly over the issue of currency. Very often it means directly borrowing from the central bank who issue currency. The ability to impose the seigniorage tax depends upon the public's willingness to hold the currency. Addison, Chowdhury and Murshed (2005) cite evidence that seigniorage revenues are between 5% and 25% of all government revenues in developing countries.

hence further inflation, thus assisting post-war money reconstruction by preventing faith in the domestic currency from diminishing further.

6.3 FINANCING RECONSTRUCTION AND REBUILDING ECONOMIC INSTITUTIONS

We expect diminished productive capacity and damaged infrastructure in the wake of war. But, as noted above, contemporary civil wars (unlike many of the inter-state wars of the past) undermine institutions of govern- ance, and the rules (formal and informal) that bind society together. Both rulers and rebels deliberately debase institutions because of the incentive structures they face in furthering their (often kleptocratic) aims, and in their efforts to mobilize manpower and resources for conflict. The task of contemporary post-conflict economic reconstruction is therefore made more arduous than in the past, as it involves rebuilding institutions and being conscious of the fact that war may once again break out. This means that not only is it important to pay attention to revenue mobilization, public expenditure management and the overall macroeconomic balance, but long-standing grievances must also be addressed along with economic recovery strategies that are broad based so as not to exacerbate (horizon- tal and vertical) inequality. To this end, this section is divided into three sub-sections dealing with fiscal reconstruction, monetary reconstruction and sectoral priorities respectively.

6.3.1 Fiscal Reconstruction

The history of modern European (inter-state) warfare is replete with examples of fiscal and other forms of economic innovation (see Addison, Chowdhury and Murshed, 2004). In the UK, for example, the income tax was instituted during the Napoleonic Wars by William Pitt as a device for raising additional revenue. Generally, the need to raise revenues in order to prosecute wars compelled sovereigns both to delegate some of their absolute powers (Tilly, 1992), as well as to superintend the economy wisely such that it would become an expanding revenue source (Bates, 2001). By contrast, contemporary civil wars are often characterized by a leadership bent on looting or pure extraction; roving bandits, as described by Olson (1996), have no encompassing interest in nurturing a tax base (see Chapter 3).

After war, whatever form the political settlement takes, it invariably has a fiscal dimension; people will expect some new and a greater range of public services and infrastructure. This new pattern of public spending must be financed and therefore tax and revenue generation, including some measure of political agreement on their incidence, are imperative for a working peace agreement. In some instances, parties to the conflict may insist that the peace deal include an explicit set of fiscal commitments such as resource rent sharing or a degree of fiscal decentralization. In addition to that, there are costs of disarmament, demobilization and reintegration. Sometimes this leads to bloated, but temporary and unsustainable, public sector employment (Addison, Chowdhury and Murshed, 2005).

Addison, Chowdhury and Murshed (2003) demonstrate that the presence of conflict is costly in terms of the government's ability to generate revenue in the long run. They divide conflicts up into high-, medium- and low-intensity wars, following the PRIO-Uppsala convention. The presence of high-intensity conflict is, for example, responsible for a long-term reduction in tax receipts by 4.46%. The corresponding reductions in countries with medium- and low-intensity conflict are 3.54% and 2.98%, respectively. More interestingly, a reduction in the intensity of conflict from high to medium would lead to a 20.6% drop in tax receipt reduction. A similar shift from a medium- to low-intensity conflict would lead to a 15.8% reduction of tax receipt dimunition. Hence, any policy measures that reduce the intensity of conflict will go a long way in enhancing fiscal revenue capacities in developing countries. Governance indicators, as described by Kaufmann, Kraay and Mastruzzi (2006), also impact on the ability of the state to raise revenues. Among these, government effectiveness and the regulatory burden have the most significant effects on fiscal capacity.

During a civil war some of the losses in the government's ability to raise revenue are transferred to rebel groups, typically in wars of secession, as in the case of the Tamil held parts of Sri Lanka (see Addison, Chowdhury and Murshed, 2004, 2005). This is because a loyal local population would rather pay taxes to a rebel group that they identify with than to the central government. Secondly, quasi-criminal activity and revenues from these generally replace government revenues. As formal (taxed) activity shrinks during conflict, so the state loses its revenue base and the resources at the disposal of criminals (including warlords) may become greater than those of any legitimate post-war authority. Criminal resources can be used to thwart government attempts to collect revenues; for example, extensive rackets are run to evade excise duties on petrol, alcohol and tobacco in the countries of former Yugoslavia, and to corrupt and control the political process (including tax concessions for 'legitimate' businesses acting as fronts for organized crime). In Afghanistan, warlords are very reluctant to cede their local tax raising powers to the Kabul government, and some of their revenue is derived from the lucrative opium trade. However, the scale of this problem varies significantly depending on the history of each country's conflict. Thirdly, the state itself becomes more and more reliant on easier to levy trade taxes and inflationary seigniorage taxes. A heavy dependence on these two sources of finance is frowned upon, as it is considered unsustainable in a 'normal' economy.

Addison, Chowdhury and Murshed (2004) point out that just after conflict a country's fiscal institutions may have degenerated so much that it may be unable to gather revenues, conduct expenditures or even receive the aid money and debt relief that donors deliver. The worst cases have been in countries such as Afghanistan and Somalia where state collapse was, or is, almost complete. Gupta (2008) indicates that nations regarded as 'fragile' (using several definitions) have the weakest fiscal institutions among developing countries. He suggests that, in rebuilding these fiscal institutions, the priorities should be in the following order: (1) ensuring a legal and regulatory framework; (2) establishing a new fiscal authority or strengthening a weak existing authority; and (3) adopting appropriate revenue and expenditure systems.

6.3.2 Monetary Reconstruction

Addison, Chowdhury and Murshed (2002) point out that conflict has two major effects on the domestic financial system. First, it lowers confidence in the domestic currency: people fear the high inflation, often hyperinflation that is frequently associated with conflict, as the authorities loosen fiscal and monetary policy to finance war, or lose control of the supply of currency. The currency also tends to depreciate in these circumstances, either through devaluation of the official exchange rate or, if the latter is inflexible, through a depreciation in the parallel market rate. The demand for domestic currency therefore falls, and the demand for other stores of value (precious metals, foreign currency and real assets) rises. Examples of the loss of confidence in the domestic currency during civil war include the Confederacy in the American Civil War and, more recently, Afghanistan, Angola, the Democratic Republic of the Congo and the former Yugoslavia. Conflict, therefore, undermines faith in the currency, and protracted large-scale conflict is even more damaging in this regard.

In Addison, Chowdhury and Murshed's (2002) econometric work, the presence of conflict is found to be extremely costly in terms of a long run reduction in financial depth (M2 over GDP or with an alternative measure emphasizing the risk sharing and information services that banks are most likely to provide). This result is similar to their work on the state's diminished fiscal capacity due to conflict. The presence of high-intensity conflict is, for example, responsible for a long run reduction in financial depth by 5.18%. The corresponding falls in countries with medium- and low-intensity conflict are 4.32% and 3.70%, respectively. More interestingly, a reduction in the intensity of conflict from high to medium would lead to a 16.6% drop in the reduction in financial depth. A similar shift from a medium- to low-intensity conflict would lead to a 14.4% drop in the reduction in financial depth. Once again, any policy measures that would reduce the intensity of conflict will enhance financial deepening in developing countries. Among the variables considered, the presence of conflict, in countries with high- and medium-intensity conflict, has the highest long-run adverse effect on financial depth. In high-intensity conflict countries, two governance indicators, government effectiveness and its regulatory burden, follow conflict in their adverse effect on financial depth. A worsening of the regulatory indicator reduces depth by 4.2% while a similar worsening in the effective indicator leads to a 4.08% reduction.

It is well known that financial development and deepening is key to achieving long-term growth (Addison, Chowdhury and Murshed, 2002). Therefore, the task of rebuilding financial institutions, and in some cases the currency, is paramount. There are three salient points in this connection. First is the task of reviving an old central banking system, or establishing a new one in failed states or new emerging states such as Bosnia-Herzegovina and East Timor. One of the banking system's earliest functions is to receive aid funds, provide clearance systems facilitating international trade and be a lender to the new government (Coats, 2007).

Secondly, the introduction of a new currency or the reform of an old one is also a priority. Very often, during war, parallel currencies circulate. For example in Afghanistan at least seven versions of the currency (Afghani) circulated during the 1990s (Addison, Chowdhury and Murshed, 2005). Even if the currency does not completely collapse due to war, sometimes a new currency is introduced as a symbol of a new beginning, for example following the Rwandan genocide of 1994. Coats (2007) offers fascinating accounts of squabbles over the design of new currencies, such as in Bosnia. The most significant factor in connection with currency reform is how it should be backed, so as to establish or re-establish confidence in it. In cases where war was protracted, the pre-war currency collapsed, and in new nation states, fiat money is not always a sensible option, particularly when there is substantial foreign aid to cover the state's fiscal obligations and development expenditures.

Two options exist at the initial stages (see Addison, Chowdhury and Murshed, 2005; Coats, 2007). The first is the adoption of a foreign currency, something that is known as 'dollarization' (as in Bosnia, Kosovo, East Timor). This makes domestic monetary policy redundant, which may not be such a bad thing following the collapse of state and economic institutions. It also introduces stringent anti-inflationary discipline: real or supply shocks cannot be responded to by accommodative monetary policy or currency devaluation; there is no scope for generating seigniorage revenue. The economy needs to be flexible, and prices and real wages have to adjust accordingly. Secondly, there is a 'currency board' system, where domestic currency issue needs to be backed by foreign exchange reserves. As Coats (2007) points out, this choice gives all the anti-inflationary discipline of 'dollarization', but provides the new or revived state a unique currency as a symbol of its renewal. Both dollarization and currency boards have their drawbacks; chief among which are the absence of the option to devalue the currency or accommodate adverse shocks. Their adoption is best suited to situations where new states have emerged, or there has been hyper-inflation destroying confidence in a previous currency. Even in these scenarios, their adoption should only take place in countries in receipt of substantial external assistance, with large stocks of foreign exchange reserves in the case of currency boards; otherwise their adoption can leave the economy excessively exposed to the adverse effects of short-term macroeconomic shocks, which can in turn re-ignite conflict.

Thirdly, the reform or introduction of commercial banking and other forms of financial intermediation is important if finance is to facilitate economic recovery. As pointed out by Coats (2007), two issues are salient in this regard. The first is to do with supervision of commercial banks. Financial crises are notoriously costly, and adequate prudential regulation has to be ensured in any economy; this includes issues such as reserve ratios, capital requirements and more direct monitoring. These tasks are all the more difficult in a frayed institutional setting, the rebuilding of which has to be a donor priority. Secondly, there is the matter of the ownership of banks. In conflict and pre-conflict societies, banks' balance sheets are riddled with politically motivated bad debt, as well as dangers of bank failure. In many countries commercial banks were within the public sector, which made them vulnerable to unenlightened political control. But simple privatization is also not an answer, as unscrupulous entrepreneurs may wish to asset strip these institutions. Domestic and foreign partnership may be the best way of restoring confidence.

6.3.3 Sectoral Priorities

The previous section began by outlining a variety of growth paths that may characterize post-conflict economic recovery and growth. Some of these are more broad based and inclusive, but the most broad based recovery path may take a longer time, particularly if economic activities associated with such a trajectory relate more to the productive (rather than service) sectors, which take a longer time to recover following the destructiveness of conflict. Donors and domestic policy makers are, therefore, confronted with a trade-off regarding which sectors to focus on, as economic growth is rarely balanced between different sectors of the economy.

Another policy dilemma concerns the exigencies of simultaneously maintaining macroeconomic stability and political stability, as pointed out by Boyce (2007), and Boyce and O'Donnell (2007). Macroeconomic stability was the cornerstone of the, until recently, preponderant Washington Consensus (Rodrik, 2006). This involved the control of inflation, maintaining sustainable fiscal deficits,[4] external debt servicing levels, as well as the goal of moving towards balance of trade (payments) equilibrium. These achievements, it is argued, provide the stable background for growth in the economy, which is undoubtedly the case in the long run.[5] Not only that, it was felt that these objectives were the first priority in achieving the transition from command to market based economies in the former Soviet bloc, and in many of the structural adjustment programmes designed by the Washington based international institutions for developing countries. Does the primacy of achieving these targets apply equally to post-conflict economies? In this connection it has to be pointed out that the simplest versions of the Washington consensus views fell into disrepute following the 1997 financial crises in Asia and elsewhere (Rodrik, 2006), and, as discussed in Chapter 2, these views about the supremacy of the market have been currently replaced, to a large extent, by faith in the ability of good quality institutions to deliver the necessary. Furthermore, post-accord societies are not truly post-conflict because of the regularity with which civil war re-emerges following peace treaties (Chapter 4).

As Boyce (2007) and Boyce and O'Donnell (2007) indicate, there might be a genuine trade-off between political stability and macroeconomic balance (price stability in their terms). This situation is more likely to arise when the immediate post-accord considerations do not allow the state to aim immediately for the goals of inflation, fiscal, balance of trade and debt servicing sustainability. This may be because the state has to rely on discredited trade taxes and inflationary seigniorage revenues to finance its reconstruction objectives, and achieve a lasting political settlement. Of course, policies that aid economic recovery (including macroeconomic stability), and the devising of stable political mechanisms that achieve peace (as discussed in Chapter 5) go hand in hand. So, in the long run there is no

---

[4]   A sustainable fiscal deficit is usually defined as the public sector deficit (or non-revenue financed government expenditure) as a proportion of GDP not exceeding the growth rate of the economy. Other definitions are more ad hoc; the Maastricht criterion for European Monetary Union sets this figure at 3% of GDP, with the total stock of national debt not exceeding 60% of GDP.
[5]   There is, for example, no long run inflation–output trade-off.

trade-off between these two twin objectives that guarantee a meaningful peace. In the short run, however, there may be a trade-off if the spending priorities of the post-war social contract do not allow for a target date for macroeconomic stability to be immediately set.

In this connection (the short-run trade-off between macroeconomic and political stability) two issues are crucial. First, external assistance can play a pivotal role in easing the trade-off by providing resources that ease the government's budget constraint. In this regard aid[6] aimed at reconstructing infrastructure, providing humanitarian assistance, facilitating disarmament, as well as technical assistance that rebuilds institutional capacity (reorganizing the police force, legal system, armed forces as well as fiscal and monetary institutions) is important. As discussed earlier in this chapter, aid aimed at economic growth per se is best targeted at later stages when the economy's absorptive capacity recovers. Aid, however, is notoriously fungible in its use. The money provided by aid or debt relief can be diverted to military expenditure, as analysed by Addison and Murshed (2003). Collier and Hoeffler (2006) point out that a high level of military expenditure does not reduce the risk of conflict re-igniting; rather limited spending on the military may act as a commitment device by the state to the stipulations of the peace treaty, and send out a credible signal to this effect. It is difficult for donors to realize their objectives for giving aid, because the recipient can always feign compliance with conditionality and then renege (see Murshed, 2009, for a theoretical analysis in this connection). It is also difficult for donors to suspend aid to badly behaved recipients, because of a phenomenon known as the 'Samaritans' dilemma.[7]

Boyce (2007) argues that one way of ensuring that aid is spent in the right way is to insist that the government comes up with matching funds for the activities or sectors that donors wish to focus on. Another problem with aid is that it detracts from the re-establishment of a legitimate state, or a state which is able to bridge the de jure and de facto sovereignty gap (Ghani and Lockhart, 2008; see also Chapter 5). Ghani and Lockhart (2008) argue that a functioning state must, at least, be able to meet current government expenditures from domestic revenues and resources. Aid may even discourage the development of domestic resource mobilization, if aid is substantial. Table 6.1 suggests that countries with a greater degree of strategic importance to the West – as with Egypt during the early 1990s,

---

[6] Not necessarily explicit budgetary support but also project aid and technical assistance.

[7] This means it is difficult to withhold aid to the unfortunate, even if they are not well behaved.

and more recently Pakistan and Ethiopia – are likely to receive greater support. Aid is not always given to the poorest parts of the world; there are strategic (non-humanitarian) considerations behind aid. Aid to the developing world is also dwarfed in per capita terms by assistance to economically disadvantaged and politically sensitive regions within developed countries (Murshed, 2009). Boyce (2007) argues that a long donor presence in post-conflict nations can lead to the development of a dual public sector mentality, involving both donor agencies and the state. This is, clearly, undesirable in the long term, but in the short run dual (but equal) control over the public purse may be a desirable way of achieving fiscal capacity (as with the ARTF or Afghanistan Reconstruction Trust Fund).

Secondly, and more importantly, is the issue about who gets to spend the aid money and who benefits from reconstruction. Aid can be a significant source of corruption, and has been so historically. I have argued that reconstruction needs to be broad based if the horizontal inequalities and poverty that cause conflict are to be avoided. In this regard spatial (regional) and other ethnic dimensions of the effects of reconstruction need to be measured. In many societies collecting data on horizontal-type inequalities is eschewed due to their potential political sensitivity. But in countries that have had conflict, information on horizontal inequalities is sorely needed, and transparent information and measurement in this regard will be an integral part of a viable post-conflict social contract. How the reconstruction funds are spent depends a great deal on the objectives and incentives faced by the post-conflict leadership, and this is what I now turn to.

6.4 POLITICAL ECONOMY OF RECONSTRUCTION AND WINDFALLS

Managing reconstruction funds (aid surges following a peace agreement) is akin to managing resource rent windfalls[8] after the discovery of a natural resource such as oil or a spike in oil prices. It has both (1) an economic policy dimension covering taxing and auctioning natural resource rights, whether or not to smooth consumption after a windfall, or invest in sovereign wealth funds (SWFs); and (2) a political economy dimension about spending priorities, especially so because optimal policies can never

---

[8] A windfall is an unexpected source of income, which can arise either because of a surge in external assistance, a sudden increase in the price of existing natural resources such as oil or gas, or the discovery of natural resources.

be implemented unless they conform to the incentives faced by decision makers. I will now proceed to consider both aspects in turn.

6.4.1 Windfalls and Economic Policy

Both surges in external aid and booms in natural resource revenues provide additional sources of finance. In this sub-section I will be concerned with their optimal management under ideal circumstances, where the policy maker acts in the national interest.[9] A number of issues arise in this context, including the assignment and taxation of natural resource exploitation rights and revenues respectively, as well as decisions about spending (or saving) windfall natural resource revenues. As will become apparent, most of the issues discussed in this sub-section concern resource rents, but they also have implications for managing other large inflows such as aid and foreign remittances from nationals abroad.

On the surface, taxing oil and gas revenues seems not to alter producer behaviour, as these revenues are presumed to remain on stream irrespective of the rate at which they are taxed. But, as Boadway and Keen (2008) point out, the fear that the sovereign owner of these revenues might impose punitive taxes on these flows may actually discourage investment in the development and extraction of these resources; potential investors would therefore need to be assured that future tax burdens will not be excessive. Optimality in non-renewable resource extraction requires that both present and the discounted value of future benefits and costs are included in decision making. Tax revenues from resources can be substantial, but there are considerable uncertainties about the future prices of these commodities, and hence also about the rent or profit from resource revenues. Designing tax rules are also made difficult by their international nature, because of the fact that there are many tax jurisdictions that have to be taken into account.

In assigning the right to explore, extract or transport oil and gas rents there may be asymmetrical bargaining power between weak states that are in conflict, or have just emerged from conflict, on the one hand and large multinational extractive firms on the other. Additionally, there may be asymmetrical information; the host country government may not know enough about the presence and extent of mineral wealth compared to

---

[9]   In traditional economic theory this often meant maximizing the welfare of a representative individual; alternatively in political economy terms it meant the interests of the median voter, representing the majority of the population in a democracy. Distributional aspects such as the welfare of impoverished or other minority groups are often ignored in this type of analysis.

companies that prospect for them. For these reasons, instead of assigning rights by open negotiation it might be better to auction the rights to exploration, extraction and transportation (pipelines) for oil and gas wealth. This is because auctions force companies to reveal information that they may not do in simple negotiations or tendering (also known as beauty contests). A succinct summary of issues related to auctioning rights to oil and gas for developing countries is to be found in Cramton (2007). He argues that often there are several issues to be auctioned related to exploration, extraction and pipelines, which can be described as 'blocks'. Sometimes different companies bidding for these may share a common valuation of their profitability, and on occasion the values may be additive (or separable) in their profit reckoning. He also discusses the advantages of sealed over open bid auctions. The former reveals more information about bidders, and the latter has a greater ability to prevent collusion among bidders.

Cramton (2007) favours simultaneous ascending price auctions or English auctions in general when bidders have additive values and the competition between them is weak. When competition is stronger, a simultaneous clock auction may be desirable; bidders react with quantities at prices set by the auctioneer. Of course, all of this analysis presumes actions in an ideal situation, where auctioneers or their political masters cannot be corrupted by bidders.

With regard to the macroeconomic response to temporary and unanticipated windfall revenues, van der Ploeg and Venables (2008) demonstrate that the standard permanent income hypothesis suggests that countries should increase consumption permanently at a constant (smooth) rate, which may imply some present borrowing against future rents, which are later partially invested in sovereign wealth funds (SWFs). It is these SWFs that provide future income, enabling consumption smoothing. But many low-income developing countries, particularly those emerging from conflict, might be too poor, capital constrained and riven with international debt to follow such a strategy. In these circumstances they should enhance present consumption, investment in domestic infrastructure and the economy, and repay some international debt. Once again, in an unpropitious political economy setting optimal policies may not be enacted upon. Aizenman and Glick (2008) discuss the operation of SWFs that do exist, distinguishing between those operated by countries with oil surpluses, and those with current account surpluses such as China. A SWF might maximize the (risk neutral) expected utility of a certain type of citizen by investing in higher-yielding riskier assets, compared to central bank behaviour which might go for investment in safer assets, thereby catering to more risk averse citizens. Many countries holding SWFs have strong domestic governance indicators, but many of these oil-rich nations (and countries with surpluses such as China) are weaker on the democracy front.

6.4.2 The Political Economy of Reconstruction

In this sub-section I will be concerned with the political economy of the allocation of expenditure, where the question is who gets what and why. There are three issues in this connection: distributional issues, matters related to the relationships between external and domestic decision makers, and minimizing the unenlightened raiding of these funds by individuals and groups who do not act in the national interest.

To take distributional matters first, Ross (2007) points out that it is important to bear in mind the vertical and horizontal inequality[10] consequences of a surge in resource rents, and we can extend those arguments to external assistance following conflict as well. Although the link between vertical inequality and conflict is not clear cut, no society, especially a country recovering from civil war, can completely ignore the inequality aspects of economic policies. The point is to minimize the risk of conflict re-igniting. A sudden availability of aid or resource rents causes a switch in output towards services and non-traded goods, the short-term activities illustrated in Figure 6.1. This may worsen inequality, if these sectors employ the more educated. Anecdotal evidence suggests that aid donors often employ workers who are paid considerably higher wages than in the civil service. These developments may increase resentment in post-war societies. More significantly, it is important to prevent horizontal inequalities worsening or re-emerging, as it adds to conflict risk. Many peace treaties emphasize a post-conflict revenue sharing fiscal contract, and in Chapter 5 I have considered how revenue sharing fiscal decentralization could abate conflictual tendencies in a post-war situation, particularly when resource rents are localized. Other policies need to be adopted so that the aggrieved regions in an earlier war of secession are not further disadvantaged. This includes investment in the region, and as Ross (2007) argues there may be a temporary case for restricting migration into these regions, so that employment prospects of local residents are not jeopardized. Also, it is important to manage post-conflict aspirations and to ensure that a wide gap does not appear between what people expect and what they have. Otherwise, relative deprivation sets in once more, and along with it the risk of conflict. One way forward in this regard is to give each adult citizen or household an income supplement, particularly if per capita aid is high or resource rents are substantial.

---

[10] See Chapter 3 on the differences between horizontal and vertical inequality.

Secondly, there are issues related to the relationships between governments in post-conflict and mineral-rich societies and external actors (multinational firms or aid donors). Karl (2007) points out that very often governments in oil-rich developing nations are more concerned with their interactions with multinational firms, who often corrupt them, rather than with their own citizenry. The same argument can be applied to other situations, particularly after conflict, when the economy has collapsed and the country is heavily dependent on aid (see some of the figures on aid as a proportion of GDP in Table 6.1 for Afghanistan, Burundi, Eritrea and Mozambique, for example). Revenues from natural resources (or substantial external aid) retard democratic development and the culture of accountability, because taxation does not finance government expenditure (Tilly, 1992; Ross, 2001). It also exacerbates a failing or failed state's legitimacy gap with its own people, as the people are not consulted on important issues. For these reasons, Karl (2007) and other analysts advocate a transparent fiscal contract involving developing country states, developed country donors (who also regulate multinational extractive firms), multinational extractive firms, multilateral donors and civil society NGOs.[11] The latter group, in particular, favours international mechanisms for furthering transparency in resource fund use and the payments made by multinational firms.

Finally, mechanisms that prevent aid funds or resource rents from being looted by incumbent politicians depend greatly on the incentive structures that rulers face (see Chapter 2). Inappropriate uses of these funds amount to expenditure that is narrowly focused, and not broad based, increasing conflict risk, enhancing poverty and horizontal inequality. There is sometimes a trade-off between development and repression, a trade-off that is absent only for the most visionary leaders who see broad based expenditure on development as key to their long-term survival (see Chapter 2). In factional states dominated by 'clientist' politics, broad based expenditures are deliberately eschewed, and spending is focused on political support groups, as well as personal kleptocratic interests.

In Chapter 4, I indicated that concern for the future is lower in poorer countries, where poverty is endemic. There is a broad consensus that in low-income developing countries the discount rate for the future is higher, implying short time horizons in situations of endemic poverty. This makes the present-day raiding of natural resource rents or fungible aid money to

---

[11]   Interestingly, Karl (2007) points out that traditionally developed country governments gave free rein to their oil and gas companies as long as a steady supply of these vital sources of energy were ensured. These companies often adopted tactics that corrupted actors in developing producer nations, sometimes leading to conflict.

finance personal gain and the interests of a narrow political faction all the more attractive. Very often this form of behaviour, spending on 'us' rather than 'them' is encouraged not just because of short time horizons, but also on account of the fear that if the opposition gets into power they too will be excluding in their spending and allocation decisions. This fear of exclusion makes policies of spending on 'ourselves' while in power almost imperative.

Robinson and Torvik (2005) point out that the expenditure allocations that do take place in these circumstances will be economically inefficient from the national perspective. Investments in (future) loss making 'white elephant' projects act like a commitment device that binds incumbent politicians with their particular support groups and vote banks, ensuring that they will back the political party in power in the future, because the loss making projects are only of benefit to members of that narrow support group. This explains why so much of aid and natural rents are squandered on projects that yield negative returns, damaging long-term growth prospects. This is often the case, even when official 'investment' data ostensibly shows substantial gross capital formation, as some of this investment will yield negative returns in the future. Also, spending decisions in these circumstances may actually exacerbate horizontal inequalities.

As a result, proposals for nationally owned funds, particularly for natural resource rents, have been proposed, following the example of Norway. The problem with such proposals is that these funds can only work well in countries with well-developed political institutions, as in Norway. Otherwise, as Humphreys and Sandbu (2007) argue, there is no guarantee that these state funds will not be raided to serve transient kleptocratic and factional ends. A resource fund may be economically optimal from a national perspective, but its optimal use may be time inconsistent (or incentive incompatible) to those currently in power, particularly if they discount the future heavily and operate within a factionalized polity. To prevent this, power sharing mechanisms need to be developed. Dixit (2003) demonstrates that sharing or non-exclusion is more likely the greater the weight given to the future. Ultimately, mechanism design in this regard requires the emergence of tacit coordination between decision makers across the political spectrum. This, by generating the fear of future retaliation, may moderate excessive expenditures on narrow interest groups by any faction in power (Humphreys and Sandbu, 2007). The formal mechanisms that achieve tacit agreements not to overspend while in power are the various constraints on the executive discussed in Chapter 5. These, however, are difficult to achieve in developing countries, given the constitution altering proclivities of the ruling elite.

6.5 SYNTHESIS

Economic reconstruction following war must be concerned with rebuilding damaged institutions through which economic policy is conducted. These include fiscal and monetary institutions. This is as important as repairing damaged infrastructure and rehabilitating ex-combatants. In addition to addressing humanitarian concerns immediately after the war, attention must also be paid to fostering economic recovery and growth. Here two factors are salient. First, the growth that takes place must be broad based such that the poverty and horizontal inequality that initially contributed to the outbreak of conflict is not present. Secondly, with these aims in mind, the long-term policy objective must be to allow the traded and more dynamic sectors of the economy to grow faster as they provide a more sustainable basis for growth. Post-war economic recovery, like growth, is rarely balanced between the various sectors of the economy. Foreign aid can play a crucial part in post-conflict situations, initially by easing the government's budget constraints, and later by enabling growth, although the latter role is subject to some controversy. Thus, international engagement in post-conflict situations is necessary, but then the question arises: for how long? Some argue in favour of long-term engagement; others are quick to spot the deleterious effects of aid on state formation, and domestic resource mobilization.

Based on their cross-country statistical analysis, Collier, Hoeffler and Söderbom (2008) argue that attention should not be solely focused on devising post-war political arrangements for lasting peace, as discussed in the previous chapter. Rather, priority should be given to an external military presence buttressing the peace agreement, including UN peacekeeping activities, and active external policies assisting economic recovery. The latter, in particular, guarantees peace in the long run, but at a slow pace. They argue that expenditure on reducing post-conflict risks should be inversely related to the recipient's per capita income, as lower income implies greater conflict risk. Apart from the fact that policy generalizations based on cross-country econometric analyses in conflict have serious limitations, the trouble with this view is that it regards the maintenance of peace in distant lands to be a global public good for Western donors. If that were the case, then much more would be done to achieve peace in Africa and elsewhere. I have challenged this view in Chapter 4, arguing that the Western taxpayers' utility from financing credible peace in distant lands is limited, and certainly not sustainable over a long period of decades as advocated by more 'interventionist' analysts. Consequently, donor commitment to lasting peace and economic reconstruction is, at best, partial and dictated by other interests such as the recipient's geopolitical salience and proximity to the West.

Chand and Coffman (2008) have argued that donor presence in post-conflict societies should be much longer than the seven years currently envisaged by the World Bank. Given their estimates of governments being able to generate sufficient revenue from domestic sources to meet their expenditure needs, which they believe to be the cornerstone of donor objectives in post-conflict societies, this process can take as many as 21 years for East Timor and 15 years for Liberia. They too, therefore, favour long-term donor peacekeeping engagements in post-conflict societies. They advocate compacts between the post-conflict state and the club of donors with clearly defined objectives, and by implication a timetable for donor exit. Such agreements presume that both sides symmetrically have full information about each other's objectives. Both donors and recipient governments have hidden agendas, which go beyond peace, reconstruction and poverty reduction, in which case there are information rents (Laffont, 2005) that can be extracted by both sides in an optimal, incentive compatible, contract. Mechanism design to achieve post-conflict economic reconstruction and steady budgetary support conditional on the recipient's maximizing effort to generate own revenue raising capacity would be truly challenging.

The motivations underlying aid are complex, as pointed out by Murshed (2009). Ostensibly, aid is altruistic and meant to help, particularly the poor, in developing countries. This may be true of the development assistance granted by the Netherlands and Nordic countries, for example. But aid can be, and almost always is, motivated by a number of other factors. These include strategic considerations, as well as commercial interests. Especially during the cold war, much of the USA's aid took the form of explicit military assistance. More generally, a substantial quantity of bilateral and even multilateral foreign aid amounted to a side payment or bribe, mainly to the ruling elite in developing countries, aimed at cementing their dependency on powerful donors, or at least offering an inducement not to embrace alternative ideologies and patrons. Such objectives are clearly not aimed at fostering pro-poor growth and can encourage corruption, as in Mobutu's Zaire and Marcos's Philippines, or in present-day Afghanistan or Iraq. Although the cold war is long over, new security considerations behind aid allocations have emerged. Commercial interests associated with aid are also important, particularly when it involves the sale of military equipment (British aid to Tanzania and Indonesia in the 1990s). The very existence of bilateral aid proves that aid is not just about poverty reduction; otherwise it would be optimal to have a single global agency managing a common pool of funds financing an international public good: the elimination of poverty (Kanbur, Sandler and Morrison, 1999).[12]

Finally, the fact that aid dependence discourages the development of domestic resource mobilization efforts does need reiterating. In a sense, donor presence acts like moral hazard, reducing optimal efforts towards domestic resource mobilization. Aid can even act like Dutch disease, crowding out the traded sector of the economy, including the development of a capacity to export manufactured goods and sustain long-term growth. As alluded to several times earlier, long-term aid dependence does not always help to re-establish the legitimate authority of the state, particularly given the presence of uncoordinated donor efforts and the diverse practices of both donor agencies and development NGOs, which if present for a long time undermine the authority of the state. Donors and NGOs on the one hand, and a legitimate state on the other, can either cooperate to meet people's needs, or they can evolve into competing authorities. In the latter case, it will certainly retard legitimate state formation. Donors, whether official (bilateral or multilateral) or in the form of charitable NGOs, are not accountable to the people in the lands which they assist. Therefore, there is little prospect of closing the accountability and sovereignty gaps (alluded to in Chapter 5) with the reconstructed state after conflict when external powers continue financing the budget. Consequently, aid dependence needs to be reduced and self-reliance achieved; the sooner the better.

---

[12] For example, the Marshall Plan aid to Western Europe was administered by a single agency, the OECD.

APPENDIX: A TWO-SECTOR OPEN ECONOMY MACROECONOMIC MODEL

Imagine a macroeconomy comprising two broad sectors: N and M, both of which are consumed domestically and exported. N is unprocessed natural resources and subsistence (private and public) consumption, and M is a combination of processed natural resources or some related manufactured export. One may also think of an increase in M as an increase in product variety, as in the new trade theory (Krugman, 1979); these could include industries that process domestically available natural resource based commodities. In the very short run, after the cessation of hostilities, it may be more important to kick start subsistence consumption. A greater expansion of the M sector relative to N would, however, be better from the standpoint of long-term growth, as well as broad based reconstruction that is both more pro-poor and potentially vertical inequality reducing.

National income, $Y = A + PM + N - \tau$, where τ is a specific tax that augments the exportable supply of M. We can conceive it as public expenditure on skills or technical education, or investment in infrastructure in war-torn economies. Thus, it will impact on the exportable segment of the manufacturing sector, M. This is in line with product cycle models; newer variants of manufactured goods in the developing world are at first exported, before being domestically consumed. The parameter A represents fungible foreign aid. As far as market clearing mechanisms are concerned we postulate that excess demand for M is reflected by a rise in P_M, the price of manufactures. This mechanism is in accordance with the monopolistically competitive models in the new trade theory. At first newer varieties of goods are supplied at a higher price, until free entry of firms drives down excess profits. In the N sector, however, excess demand leads to increases in the quantity supplied; this may occur at a greater price also. The postulated model bears resemblance to 'structuralist' paradigms which postulate different closure rules across sectors (for example Taylor, 1983; Murshed, 1992). Let $P = P_M/P_N$ be the domestic terms of trade, with P_N as the numeraire.

The tax that finances public expenditure on manufacturing export sector development also has the effect of diminishing the available disposable domestic income that can be devoted to consumption. It is important to have fiscal capacity to raise revenues from this tax. Domestic demand depends positively on disposable income for both goods. The relative price effect on demand is only modelled for the M sector because N is a basic good whose demand is price inelastic. Let us also assume that exports of N, X_N are exogenously given by world demand (oil, copper, cashew nuts, soybeans etc.), but recall that exports of manufactures, X_M depends positively on the publicly financed expenditure on M sector development. Additionally, natural resource booms (exogenous increases in X_N demand) may crowd out exports of manufactures. This effect usually occurs through Dutch disease–type channels, as discussed in Chapter 2. An exogenously given boom in the prices (and exports) of resource based commodities can crowd out other exports because of a relative price effect and/or nominal exchange rate appreciation.[1]

We may now formulate the fundamental excess demand equations for M and N where the markets clear in P and N respectively, in other words excess demand leads to a rise in prices in the M sector, whereas increases or decreases in net demand cause quantity adjustments in the N sector. Observe that the domestic demand for both types of goods rise with disposable income (Y).

$$D_M(Y - \tau; P) + X_M(\tau; X_N) - PM = 0$$
$$or, D_M(A + PM + N - \tau; P) + X_M(\tau; X_N) - PM = 0 \qquad (6.1)$$
$$where \cdots Y = A + PM + N \cdots D_{M1}, X_{M1} > 0; D_{M2} < 0, X_{M2} < 0$$

The partial derivative of manufactured export demand with respect to a rise in natural resource is postulated to be negative, $X_{M2} < 0$, because of Dutch disease effects. In other words, a natural resource boom will crowd out manufactured exports for the usual reasons.

$$D_N(Y - \tau) + X_N - N = 0$$
$$or, D_N(A + PM + N - \tau) + X_N - N = 0 \cdots where \cdots D_{N1} > 0 \qquad (6.2)$$

Totally differentiating 6.1 and 6.2 and writing the differentials in matrix form, where initial $\tau = 0$, but $d\tau \neq 0$:

$$\begin{bmatrix} (D_{M1} - 1)M + D_{M2} & D_{M1} \\ D_{N1}M & D_{N1} - 1 \end{bmatrix} \begin{bmatrix} dP \\ dN \end{bmatrix}$$

$$= \begin{bmatrix} D_{M1} - X_{M1} & - X_{M2} & - D_{M1} \\ D_{N1} & - 1 & - D_{N1} \end{bmatrix} \begin{bmatrix} d\tau \\ dX_N \\ dA \end{bmatrix} \qquad (6.3)$$

The trace of the Jacobian in 6.3 is negative, and the determinant is:

$$\Delta = (D_{M2} - M)(D_{N1} - 1) - D_{M1}M \qquad (6.4)$$

---

[1]   To keep the analysis simple I do not specify a balance of payments equation; the reader is referred to Murshed (1997, chapters 5 and 6) on this.

If $|D_{N1} - 1| > |D_{M1}|$, $\Delta > 0$, the model is stable. (6.5)

The implication of the stability condition is that the marginal propensity to spend national income on N sector goods (D_{N1}) is small, and by implication the same propensity for M sector (D_{M1}) is large. Assuming stability holds, we can proceed to examine changes in the exogenous parameters (τ, X_N and A), utilizing Cramer's rule to solve for multiplier effects in 6.3.

$$\frac{dP}{d\tau} = \frac{(1 - D_{N1})X_{M1}}{\Delta} \quad D_{M1}$$
(6.6)

The effect of an increase in publicly financed infrastructure or education expenditure (which requires the state to have some fiscal capacity) is to raise the supply of the manufactured M sector output. But it also diminishes disposable income, reducing domestic demand for both goods. Yet export demand for the expanded M sector, or its newer varieties rises. Using the stability conditions in 6.5, and if $X_{M1} \to 1$, the above expression is positive. Note that, even if the new equilibrium P declines, the level of exports will rise.

$$\frac{dN}{d\tau} = \frac{(D_{M2} - M)D_{N1} + X_{M1}D_{N1}M}{\Delta} < 0 \text{ if } X_{M1} < 1$$
(6.7)

There should be a switch in the composition of output towards more dynamic sectors, and the N sector ought to contract. But, as indicated above, the first term on the numerator is negative, while the second term is positive. The reason for the sign of the second term is the positive demand spill over from the manufacturing sector. As long as $X_{M1} < 1$, equilibrium N output will decline. Note that this is a sufficient, and not a necessary, condition. Furthermore, we would expect the efficiency of this type of public expenditure (the magnitude of X_{M1}) to depend upon institutional quality. In some countries poor institutional arrangements may lower this parameter value as expenditure on public infrastructure and education is less effective; in some low-income countries it may be unfeasible to finance this kind of public expenditure via taxes on the population given the history of conflict, low income levels and endemic poverty.

We now turn to exogenous driven resource booms that raise demand of resource sector exports:

$$\frac{dP}{dX_N} = \frac{(1 - D_{N1})X_{M2} + D_{M1}}{\Delta}$$
(6.8)

The first term on the numerator of 6.8 is negative, whereas the second term is positive. The former reflects the crowding out effect on manufactured exports of a resource boom, and the latter indicates positive N sector demand for M sector goods as the former expands, or what is known as the 'spending' effect of resource booms. We would expect the first effect to dominate. Turning to the resource sector:

$$\frac{dN}{dX_N} = \frac{M(1 - D_{M1}) - D_{M2} + D_{N1}MX_{M2}}{\Delta}$$

$$> 0 \cdots if \, |1 - D_{M1}| > |D_{N1}X_{M2}| \qquad (6.9)$$

As manufactured sector exports decline after the resource boom, there is less demand for N from the M sector; hence the negative effect of the last term in the numerator of 6.9.

Finally, we turn to the effects of aid:

$$\frac{dP}{dA} = \frac{D_{M1}}{\Delta} > 0 \qquad (6.10)$$

and

$$\frac{dN}{dA} = \frac{D_{N1}M(1 - \Omega)}{\Delta} > 0 \, where \, \Omega = D_{M2}/M \qquad (6.11)$$

In the short term, humanitarian aid may have the objective of raising subsistence N sector consumption in impoverished conflict economies, especially if the war has taken a heavy toll on subsistence livelihoods. According to 6.11, this is greater the higher the price elasticity of demand (Ω) for non-subsistence consumption (D_{M2}), whose relative price has risen (6.10). If subsistence aid is not allowed to augment the disposable income of the poor, aid will need to be categorically targeted towards this group via price subsidies or income transfers. Expansion in the tradable M sector is, however, central to long-term prosperity, poverty reduction and the lowering of vertical inequality. This is more likely when the marginal propensity to spend is greater in the M sector (a high D_{M1}) in 6.10. Note that this requires the economy to have substantial absorptive capacity.

7. The liberal peace and globalization

7.1 BACKGROUND

One factor that remains to be considered as a contributor to violent internal conflict is economic globalization. This relates mainly to the recent expansion in international trade and financial flows, and the various controversial policies adopted to facilitate these in developing countries, such as trade liberalization, deregulation, privatization and an increased market orientation. As has been indicated in Chapter 1, civil war has nowadays become the dominant form of conflict, but there are also other forms of organized violent protest as described by Gurr (1970) related to relative deprivation, and routine violence (Tadjoeddin and Murshed, 2007), where globalization and policies promoting it may play an important role.

In contemporary political science the term liberal peace is employed to explain the absence of fatal conflict between democratic nations that are also economically interdependent.[2] Leaders of states that share common values, or are mutually interdependent do not choose the strategy of war to settle their differences. In particular, economic interdependence makes it rational not to choose war, because of the opportunity costs of lost trade. These views stand in sharp contrast to the purely realist school in political science, which argues that mutual dependence and overlapping values do not by themselves guarantee the absence of war in the absence of other political factors precluding the strategy of war, such as the internal political dominance of the war party over the peace party.

As long ago as 1835, the English thinker Richard Cobden declared 'commerce is the grand panacea', by which he meant the pacific and civilizing effects of international trade, along with its potential for assuaging tensions between nations. The expression, liberal peace, therefore, has an economic dimension, as well as an element based on a common polity and values. Ultimately, these two strands of the liberal peace are inseparably linked. Despite this, the literature on the liberal peace may

---

[2]   It has to be admitted that there is considerable variation in the usage and meaning of the term liberal peace.

Table 7.1   Countries with five or more international armed conflicts

Country	Number of conflicts
United Kingdom	21
France	19
USA	16
Russia (Soviet Union)	9
Australia	7
Netherlands	7
China	6
Egypt	6
Israel	6
Thailand	6
Canada	5
Jordan	5
Portugal	5
Turkey	5
Vietnam	5

Source: Human Security Report, 2005, Figure 1.3, original data, PRIO.

be dichotomized into ideal and more realist tendencies. The ideal theory is traceable to Immanuel Kant's notions of *foedus pacificum* (league of peace) in his essay on the 'Perpetual Peace' (1795) where the simultaneous adoption of a republican constitution generates a cosmopolitan peace. Its modern counterpart is to be found in the thought of the contemporary philosopher, John Rawls (1999). I elaborate on this literature in section 7.2. Realist theories of the liberal peace, in its modern form, probably originate in Montesquieu's ideas (1748) about the pacific benefits of commerce between peoples; a contemporary version can be found in Gartzke (2007), who describes it as the 'capitalist' peace. I discuss this strand of the literature in section 7.3. Section 7.4 is concerned with globalization and its consequences for internal conflict in the developing world. Finally, some policy implications are considered in section 7.5.

Before proceeding further, we should note that while it may be an empirical regularity that advanced industrialized democracies do not go to war with other democracies, this does not mean that democracies do not engage in wars. Democratic nations such as the UK, France, the USA and Israel lead the list of countries in terms of their participation in interstate wars since the Second World War; see Table 7.1. In terms of the total number of conflict years (see the Human Security Report, 2005), bearing in mind that there may be more than one civil war within a single nation state, which leads to more than one conflict in a single calendar year, democratic India occupies the second place with 156 years since the Second World War, whereas the UK with 77 years is in sixth position just behind Israel (79 years). This suggests that democracies such as India, Israel and the UK are highly conflict prone. Therefore, the notion of the liberal peace needs to be nuanced.

7.2   IDEAL THEORIES OF THE LIBERAL PEACE

As indicated above, the idea of liberal peace originates in Kant's essay, 'Perpetual Peace' (1795), where he argues that although war is the natural state of man,[3] peace can be established through deliberate design. This requires the simultaneous adoption of a republican constitution by all nations, which *inter alia* would check the war-like tendencies of both monarchs and the citizenry. The cosmopolitanism that would emerge among the comity of nations would preclude war, implying a confederation among such nation states (*foedus pacificum*).

Kant's (1795) essay on the 'Perpetual Peace' provides us with information about the nature of the republican constitution.[4] First, observe the usage of the expression 'perpetual', implying permanence as opposed to a transient truce. In contemporary parlance, such agreements or contracts would be described as renegotiation proof or self-enforcing, so that there are no incentives to violate the stipulations of the league of peace (unlike the transient peace treaties considered in Chapter 4, which Kant describes as *pactum pacis*). Secondly, and most crucially, Kant refers to the separation of powers[5] between the executive and legislature, which I have alluded to in chapters 2 and 5. Put simply, this concept implies good government that holds the domestic social contract (as discussed in Chapter 5) together. Our contemporary understanding of good governance can include a host of other factors beyond the separation of powers, such as decentralized decision making powers. Thirdly, the stability of the peace depends upon the source of sovereignty or legitimate power within the nation. Although not enamoured of rabble-led democracy, Kant nevertheless points out that good governance provided by a dictator or an absolute monarch is

---

[3]   Similar to Thomas Hobbes's concept of the non-contractual 'state of nature'.

[4]   Although Kant speaks about a perpetual peace between nations, we can extend his argument to groups within a nation state.

[5]   Despotism is when there is no separation of powers; those who administer laws are one and the same as those who decree them. Despotism is not simply confined to absolute monarchy or dictatorship, but can also be a feature of flawed democracies that are endemic currently in the developing world.

inherently unstable as he or his successors face temptations to deviate from good government. The assurance of good governance is more forthcoming in a system of power that is accountable to, and representative of the people. Central to the Kantian republican constitution is a system of checks and balances or a separation of powers which are largely absent from the fledgling democracies that permeate developing countries.

Interestingly, Kant (1795) argued that this cosmopolitan peace between nations might exclude distant lands, and aggressive wars, such as those associated with colonialism, might be waged against peoples deemed to be outside the pale of civilization. He refers to these as the 'inhospitable actions of the civilized', directed by European countries against peoples in what we now refer to as developing countries.[6] A similar point has recently been made by Gartzke (2007) in a different context where development and common goals preclude wars between countries at a similar level of development, but make wars with (or in) distant countries (Iraq, Afghanistan) at a lower level of development more likely.

Mirroring Kant's thoughts is the contemporary philosopher, John Rawls's (1999) notion of peace between liberal societies, which he refers to as peoples and not states. Rawls's Law of Peoples is inspired by Kant's *foedus pacificum* and is termed a 'realistic utopia' by Rawls. The notion of a realistic utopia follows Rousseau's social contract, referring to men both as they are and how they should be. There is an appeal to both natural law and the possible implementation of an ideal morality. An ideal state is reasonable, even if in an imperfect world it may be rational to deviate from such optima. In many ways, Rawls's Law of Peoples, which is an understanding between peoples or nations, is an extension of his notions of fairness and justice in the domestic realm (see Rawls, 1971). He speaks of well ordered peoples, a term he borrows from Jean Bodin.[7] These are mainly constitutional liberal democracies, which arrive at such a polity based on notions of public reason. Public reason encompasses the realm of the political, and is not necessarily part of any comprehensive doctrine that individuals may believe in (for example religions such as Judaism, Christianity or Islam or secular beliefs such as Marxism), although some of these comprehensive beliefs may be compatible with a publicly reasoned

---

[6] Referring to the colonizing actions of the British East India Company in 18th-century South Asia, Kant says: 'In East India (Hindustan), under the pretence of economic undertakings, they brought in foreign soldiers and used them to oppress the natives, excited widespread wars among the various states, spread famine, rebellion, perfidy, and the whole litany of evils which afflict mankind' (1795); see http://www.mtholyoke.edu/acad/intrel/kant/kant1.htm, p. 7.

[7] Jean Bodin employs the expression '*République bien ordonée*', in his *Les Six Livres de la République* (1576).

well-ordered society. In a well-ordered society based on public reason, human rights are respected, and the distribution of primary goods (a decent living standard, dignity, respect and the ability to participate) for each citizen's functioning are acceptably arranged.[8] Above all, the principle of reciprocity characterizes the determination and functioning of public reason and its workings as a constitutional liberal democracy. This implies both tolerance of difference and respect for all other citizens.

It is worthwhile elaborating on Rawls's idea of well-ordered peoples because the Law of Peoples extends the domestic social contract based on the criterion outlined above to a relation between peoples who reside in different nations. First, there are the liberal peoples described above. Secondly, there are decent peoples who have consultative hierarchies and associational organizations. Presumably, these are more conservative and less 'democratic' societies. Rawls gives an example of a hypothetical Muslim state labelled 'Kazanistan'. Here there is no separation of church and state, but it respects human rights, tolerates other religions (as was historically the case in Islamic empires and states), has consultative associative bodies and a reasonably equitable distribution of primary goods, making them well-ordered peoples.[9] Thirdly, there are benevolent absolutisms; they respect human rights, but because they lack decent consultative structures they cannot be considered well ordered. Fourthly, there are those societies that are burdened by unfavourable conditions that prevent the realization of a well-ordered decent outcome with human rights for all. Clearly, much of the developing world falls into this category. Finally, there is what Rawls describes as outlaw states. These countries (such as contemporary Mynamar) deliberately violate human rights. Furthermore, they may behave aggressively towards others; even coveting their resources. Rawls appears to ignore the fact that it is possible for some societies, such as Israel or apartheid-era South Africa, to be well ordered and decent across a certain favoured group within the state, but not to others.

The consequence of being a liberal people possibly explains the empirically observed fact that 'true' democracies do not fight each other. Rawls stresses that the interaction is between peoples and not states, in the sense of citizens and not subjects cooperating with other peoples. He distances himself from the 'Westphalian' sovereign state, which had the right to make war in pursuit of its rational interests, and speaks instead of peoples,

---

[8] The private ownership of property, and by implication economic inequality, is acceptable on the grounds of efficiency. Only those with proprietorial rights will care for and sustainably nurture the assets (capital) that they own; these are ultimately society's assets.

[9] Rawls appears to be unacquainted with the Islamic concept of a social contract (*aqd*) between the ruler and the ruled (Abou El Fadl, 2004), which arguably pre-dates European thought on the social contract.

the decent varieties among whom are just. It is also possible that a law of peoples, replicating a perpetual (sustainable) peace, exists between the first two categories of liberal and decent peoples, and might even extend to benevolent absolutisms. These peoples may also engage in associational ventures (confederations), as in a more representative and reciprocative version of the United Nations. To the peoples who are burdened by unfavourable circumstances, others have a duty of assistance, according to Rawls, but not one that results in outcomes completely eliminating international inequality. When outlaw states behave aggressively towards others, a just war with them is justifiable, provided that the universally accepted code of conduct for wars (the Geneva Convention, for example) is respected.

Economic interdependence between peoples has little to do with his analysis. Rawls argues that liberal societies do not go to war with each other because their needs are satisfied, they are non-acquisitive in the sense of not wishing to grow beyond an achieved steady state level of (presumably high) income, and they are tolerant of differences. They will only fight in self-defence, and invade to prevent gross human rights abuses such as genocide in other countries. Democracies may, however, be driven by greed and the lust for power to wage war against other smaller non-democracies, as during the colonial period, the cold war era and even during the present-day war on terror.[10]

As far as the implications for developing countries are concerned, first the duty of assistance could extend to the principle of military intervention in countries burdened by unfavourable circumstances. For example, there is an increasing tendency favouring Western military intervention to end certain long-standing civil wars, which is justified on developmental grounds and security considerations. Is this always justified? Secondly, developing countries facing economic stagnation, as discussed in Chapter 2, may find themselves on a downward spiral that takes them from being liberal or decent peoples to becoming outlaw states (see Chapter 5 on the failure of a once functioning social contract). Is there a special duty of assistance in this regard? Finally, economic decline may give rise to illiberal tendencies towards certain groups within a country, even in less affluent democracies such as India (caste related oppression and violence towards Muslims) and in Eastern Europe (discriminatory practices against the Roma or Turkish minorities). The nation may become characterized by

---

[10] Even if the war on terror is justified, its conduct by the 'coalition of the willing' is often unjust, as exemplified in contemporary Iraq and especially Afghanistan with the multitude of civilian casualties in Afghanistan and Pakistan despite the so-called 'smart' weapons of our era.

factions that do not extend the principle of reciprocity towards others, thus encouraging the outbreak of violent conflict. I believe that the best antidote against all of these tendencies is economic development, which not only leads to institutional improvement, but also eventually creates the pre-conditions for a more meaningful and inclusive democracy.

7.3 REALIST THEORIES OF THE LIBERAL PEACE

Nation states have long been regarded as existing in a state of non-contractual anarchy vis-à-vis each other, making the exercise of power or the gathering of power by going to war an opportunistic act based on perceptions of self-interest.[11] Yet there are beliefs that a common set of values, and/or inter-state commerce will moderate or eliminate these war-like tendencies (see Doyle, 1986, and Oneal and Russett, 1997, for example).

The liberal view that trade between nations directly contributes to peace may be traced back to the Baron de Montesquieu's *De l'Esprit des Lois* (The Spirit of the Laws, 1748), where he states that commerce tends to promote peace between nations; mutual self-interest precludes war and trade softens attitudes of peoples towards each other. The fact that commerce promotes peace was also pointed out by Tom Paine (1791, 1792). Similar views were aired more strongly by Richard Cobden (1835). Sir Norman Angell-Lane (1910) asserted that nations could never enrich themselves through war, and even a victorious nation would always come off economically worse from a war. Schumpeter (1951) argued that advanced capitalism would produce rationalism among the new influential classes that would discourage war. These views may be regarded as semi-idealistic, as they point to the inevitability of peace induced by increased economic interdependence; the recognition of economic interdependence would induce leaders to eschew acts that disrupt gains from economic interdependence, such as war. Angell-Lanes's (1910) view about the irrationality of war between the Great Powers of Europe in 1910 was based on a universal notion of rationality; bounded or limited rationality would not rule out wars, especially in the presence of misperceptions such as an exaggerated view of the probability of victory.

It has to be remembered that trade is just one (peaceful) means of economically benefiting from the endowments of another country. The other

---

[11] The 19th-century British statesman and prime minister, Lord Palmerston, had famously declared that nations have no permanent friends or allies, they only have permanent interests, see http://thinkexist.com/quotation/nations-have-no-permanent-friends-or-allies-they/771609.html.

means is war, which represents the forceful acquisition of another country's resources – the mercantilist wars of the 17th century and the various colonial wars of conquest from the 16th to the 19th centuries offer copious examples of these. Similarly, war between two nation states does disrupt their bilateral and multilateral economic interdependence, but the damage done to the enemy may be greater, prompting the economically more powerful nation to go to war.

Polachek (1997) made the strongest case for the pure form of the economic liberal peace, arguing that a common polity (democracy) is largely immaterial. He presents empirical evidence to suggest that advanced democracies cooperate, not because of their similar political systems, but due to their vast and multiple layered economic interdependence. Indeed, democracies might act aggressively against other non-democracies. The analogy of these views with contemporary neoclassical economic theory is that trade reproduces the integrated economy. Free and unfettered trade in a neoclassical economic framework leads to product and factor price equalization, hence producing economic integration, even if nation states continue to be politically separated. War disrupts these networks, and is therefore against the interests of the nation states who are thus connected.

The trouble with the pacific interpretation of international trade is that during the two world wars of the 20th century highly interdependent economies went to total war with each other; especially during the First World War. Consequently, the economic interdependence argument for peace needs re-examination. Barbieri (1996) demonstrated that the liberal peace based upon the pacific effects of economic interdependence may be a chimera. Oneal and Russett (1999) show that trade and peace are highly correlated. While all analysts agree that war impedes trade, the realist view is that the mere existence of economic interdependence does not preclude war in the absence of pro-war 'politics'. Indeed, countries may choose to disrupt their potential enemy's gains from trade by ceasing trade with them, even if this means hostilities. There are also instances of nations trading even when they are at war, as was the case during the Napoleonic Wars. Barbieri and Levy (1999), using an interrupted time series framework found little impact of war on trading relationships for seven dyads from 1870. They argue that any disruption to bilateral trade caused by war is, in many instances, remedied after peace emerges. Both trade and war produce winners and losers. Even if there are losses to the aggregate economy from war or diminished trade, some groups may gain, and these groups may be the more politically influential. Kim and Rousseau (2005) emphasize the reverse causality running between economic interdependence and conflict; correcting (instrumenting) for this difficulty on data for 1960–88 they find that conflict diminishes economic interdependence, but not the other way around (economic dependence does not necessarily prevent war), providing only partial support for the opportunity cost of trade liberal peace theory. Other factors, besides trade, must be at work.

Hegre (2000) argued that economic interdependence reinforces peace, but mainly between more developed economies. Russett and Oneal (2001) argue that it is the economic dependence on trade of the least dependent on the other member of a group of nations that will determine the pacific effect of trade. In short, only advanced and highly economically interdependent democracies would be at peace with one another, which precludes most developing countries because of their widespread absolute poverty, even in democracies like India.

Among the updates proposed for the liberal peace theory based on economic interdependence is the 'capitalist' peace notion of Gartzke (2007), which goes beyond trade dependence. He argues that the intensity of trade is the least important feature in the peace engendered by capitalism. The nature of advanced capitalism makes territorial disputes, which are mainly contests over resources, less likely as the market mechanism allows easier access to resources. The nature of production makes the output of more sophisticated goods and services increasingly reliant on ideas or blueprints that are research and development oriented rather than resource intensive, and skilled personnel can be acquired through more open global labour markets. We might also add the fragmented nature of production with components produced in different international locations. Much of world trade is trade in components between the same multinational firms across national borders. Moreover, the disruption to integrated financial markets makes war less likely between countries caught up in that web of interdependence. We are all acutely aware of how disruptive are financial crises and the resultant contagion that spreads all over the world.[12] Gartzke (2007) argues that common foreign policy goals reflected in the membership of international treaty organizations (NATO, the European Union etc.) also produce peace between member states.

Dorussen and Ward (2009) rehabilitate the role of trade in engendering peace. They argue that trade has important indirect effects over and above the interdependence induced by bilateral trade. Increased trade generally, may do little to mollify war-like tendencies between a pair of countries, but if each of these countries interacts considerably with third countries, it will

---

[12] For example, the Wall Street Crash of October 1929 heralded the worldwide Great Depression of the 1930s; the Asian financial crisis of 1997 resulted in a massive recession in the region; more recently, the effects of the flawed regulation of US sub-prime lending markets have produced global fallout.

be not in their interests to go to war with each other, as it disrupts other links and networks. In other words, any two countries are unlikely to go to war with each other if each nation's trade with the rest of the world is substantial even when their bilateral trade interdependence is low. Dorussen and Ward (2009) label this phenomenon as mutual dependence.

Murshed and Mamoon (2010) find evidence of this in their study of the effects of trade and democracy on the India–Pakistan conflict. India and Pakistan are not only hostile towards each other, but their bilateral trade is very low compared to what might be predicted from their close proximity. Trade with other countries in the world (globalization) has the greatest conflict reducing effect between these two nations, along with expenditure on growth enhancing sectors such as education. The limited bilateral trade between these two countries, as well as their high levels of military expenditure, reflect their mutual hostility. But the reverse is also true; limited trade and high levels of spending on the military also produce conflict. The important point is that as they grow to be more dependent on the rest of the world for their prosperity, their mutual hostilities may become less militarized. This is true, despite the fact that hostilities between India and Pakistan are more damaging to Pakistan's trade with the rest of the world compared to the disruption to India's multilateral trade.[13]

This modern view of the economic version of the liberal peace may be summarized as asserting that similar, contiguous democracies at a high level of economic development will not fight each other (Gartzke, 2007). Gartzke argues that: 'Democracy cohabitates with peace. It does not, by itself, lead nations to be less conflict prone, not even toward other democracies', (2007, p. 170). Democracies may go to war with other democracies that are distantly located, culturally disparate and considerably poorer. Indeed, Robst, Polachek and Chang (2007) present some evidence to suggest that more democratic nations could exhibit some degree of belligerence to less democratic countries. Democracies or liberal societies that become poor, or fall behind other affluent nations because of the lack of growth or systemic changes such as the collapse of socialism may become aggressive (see Milanovic and Wenar, 2007). What is also required for peace in a pair-wise dyadic sense between nations is not just democracy and economic interdependence, but also high levels of development (see Hegre, 2000), as high-income nations have most to lose from war with one another. Gelpi and Grieco (2003) make the argument that more democratic

---

[13]   A realist interpretation of this result would suggest that the knowledge of this fact might encourage the pro-war party in India to lobby for an escalation of hostilities with Pakistan, damaging its economy and forcing it to make unilateral concessions on its disputes with India, as with the status of Kashmir.

nations have a greater stake in growth (autocracies fearing that growth may enhance the power of the potential opposition), and trade openness facilitates growth, hence democracies that are more open may be more pacific. But there are plenty of examples of dictatorships fostering growth (Indonesia under Suharto, Singapore). Equally, many dictatorships favour open or outwardly oriented economic policies, and many democracies are protectionist because free trade is against the interests of the majority.

While the arguments described above mainly pertain to the issue of war between nation states, inferences about violent internal conflict can also be made. Economic stagnation, as in Africa for the past three decades, or economic development that is very unevenly distributed can cause the tolerant niceties of an existing domestic social contract to become frayed. Those left behind and the underprivileged may revolt if coherently organized. Equally, the relatively rich may choose to prey on the less fortunate, if they are no longer prepared to subsidize or support these groups. So-called democracies are not immune from these tendencies; they are not the ideal polities as conceived by Kant or Rawls, and may therefore behave violently towards segments of their societies. Indeed, as has been argued before, post-1991 developing countries are mostly characterized by imperfect democracies or anocracies; they may contain elements of democracy (multiparty electoral competition) along with some of the more invidious traits of autocracy (no effective checks on the executive, for example). Ultimately, growth and increased economic interaction through globalization as well as rising democratization are likely to promote peace between and within developing countries, mirroring Lipset's (1960) modernization hypothesis that democracy (and peace) inevitably follows economic growth. The path to modernization is, however, fraught with the danger of different forms of conflict, and this is what I now turn to.

7.4   GLOBALIZATION AND INTERNAL CONFLICT

7.4.1   The Gains from Trade

It is worth revisiting the gains from trade. The static gain from trade, in the Ricardian model of international trade is that international trade allows the 'representative' consumer a superior consumption bundle at better relative prices. This is mainly because imported goods are cheaper compared to those produced under autarky. There is very little in the pure Ricardian theory about the distributional effects of increased international trade. In connection with this, the Heckscher–Ohlin–Samuelson (HOS) model is more informative. This theory tells us that after an expansion of trade, the factors of production engaged more intensively in the exportable sector will witness a rise in their remuneration. This is because the exportable sectors of the economy expand, and the import competing sectors contract, after increased international trade. If there are factors of production, say certain types of workers, specific to the contracting sectors, many of these individuals will become part of the unemployed, unless they can re-equip themselves into newer occupations. It is immediately apparent that globalization produces winners and losers, and in many instances the losers from increased trade or globalization demand protection, failing which they might violently protest.

In the 1990s we witnessed the growth of a new form of the old 'pauper' labour argument: that trade with the global South (developing countries) served to disadvantage unskilled workers in the global North. The changing pattern of the international division of labour reflects the shift of competitive advantage in labour intensive manufacturing production from the richer OECD countries (North) to the poorer developing countries (South), mainly in Asia, and attracted a good deal of attention from commentators in developed countries during the closing decades of the 20th century. These commentators include politicians, such as the American presidential candidate Ross Perot, and the former president of the European Commission Jacques Delors, journalists, trade unionists and even church groups. This was motivated by the decline in employment in the North's traditional manufacturing sector (see Wood, 1994), and has been accompanied by rising unemployment and/or a fall in the wages of the unskilled group of the North's manufacturing labour force, the blue-collar worker. This phenomenon of declining employment/wages of the less privileged in the North's labour force is said to have sparked off major social unrest, as well as promoting increased inequality in income, wealth and opportunity. More often than not, protection, from the insidious sources of the competition driving these processes, is demanded. The culprit is usually identified to be the relatively poorer countries in the developing world (mainly Asia), where it is stressed that low wages and generally exploitable conditions have led to the wholesale movement of certain manufacturing activities. Most studies nowadays attribute this phenomenon to technical progress that encourages the substitution of unskilled workers in the North with machines or ultimately the export of their jobs.

More recently, with the end of the multifibre agreement that governed and restricted the import of garments from developing countries into OECD nations in 2005, the remaining European Union producers (in countries such as Portugal) were hurt by Chinese goods, so they successfully lobbied for and obtained a reimposition of import controls. Society can compensate those workers who lose their jobs through generous redundancy and retraining packages. The next question is whether or not society is in a position or prepared to compensate the losers from increased trade. If there is economic growth following globalization the gainers' gain is greater than the loss of the losers; there is a potential for compensating the losers, provided enough political will exists to effect the redistribution.

In developing countries (mainly in Asia) that have experienced an increase in their export of unskilled labour intensive goods (mainly garments) one would expect a rise in the remuneration of the unskilled relative to the skilled. The Stolper–Samuelson version of the Heckscher–Ohlin theory of international trade predicts that factors of production in the expanding export sector should witness an increase in their compensation. But this has rarely happened, and the workers in labour intensive export industries have not seen a substantial rise in their real wages relative to skilled workers. The skilled–unskilled worker wage differential has on average increased. This could be because of the shortage of skilled personnel (less public education expenditure) and the huge numbers of unskilled workers coming from the hinterland in densely populated Asian countries (see Mamoon and Murshed, 2008).

So, we have an additional question: does increased international trade foster economic growth? In Chapter 2 I have outlined the case that the so-called arguments that greater openness promotes more growth can actually disguise other factors such as better institutional quality and other good policies rather than openness per se. This, however, still leaves open the fact that a deliberate policy move towards increased globalization can act as a commitment device towards superior policies, including better regulation and governance (the gradual dismantling of loss making state owned enterprises and the simplification of regulations, for example).

Furthermore, increased trade is not always the handmaiden of economic growth in the dynamic sense, although it has played an important part in historical economic development of the world's present-day affluent OECD economies. Trade may even hamper growth, if the trade is of an unequal nature. If there are increasing returns to scale or economies of scale,[14] freer trade may damage the growth prospects of smaller countries less able to take advantage of economies of scale. Krugman (1981) has shown that it can even cause laggard countries' manufacturing sectors to vanish when faced with the competition engendered by freer or increased trade. Under more restricted international trade, the manufacturing sectors of smaller nations can survive, but when opened up to freer trade it is not just the survival of the fittest, but the survival of the largest, as the larger economy

---

[14]   This means that if inputs are doubled, output is more than doubled, implying falling unit or average costs of production.

is more able to reap the lower costs permitted by economies of scale. Historically, early exporters of manufactured-type goods such as China and India were unable to compete with Britain's cotton textiles after the implementation or imposition of free trade by Britain in the 19th century, and their manufacturing evaporated, bringing about more than a century of stagnating growth. It is not that Indian and Chinese manufactures were inherently uncompetitive, they simply could not compete when increasing returns to scale elsewhere gradually raised their per unit (relative) costs.

The new economic geography literature (Krugman, 1991, for example) suggests the importance of agglomeration effects. Increased economic integration may cause greater clustering, particularly of manufacturing production, in certain regions (such as China or India), causing it to move away from certain existing areas that become peripheral. Obviously, growth in these peripheries is adversely affected, even if the nations pursue the right regulatory and open trade policies.

We also need to distinguish between policies that aim to promote freer trade and financial flows, and their success in terms of actual outcomes achieving greater international economic integration. Simply dismantling restrictions on international trade, such as import and export taxes, and permitting international financial transactions does not mean that a country embarking on this path will achieve a greater value of trade or succeed in obtaining more foreign capital. For example, most countries in sub-Saharan Africa are caught in a staple trap, and export a few commodities – minerals or fuels for countries which have these, or coffee and cocoa. For them, policies that liberalized external trade (the structural adjustment programmes of the 1980s and 1990s) have left them very open economies in terms of their policy stance, but they have not witnessed an expansion in their share of world exports compared to countries such as China or India, who have been much more wary about liberalizing their international trade and financial policy regimes. Murshed (2002b) points to three inimical factors that have contributed to the failure of globalization as far as the less successful or marginalized developing countries are concerned. They are: the negative effects of structural adjustment programmes in the 1980s, the debt crises of the 1980s and early 21st century and the endemic protectionism in the North towards the South's exports, mainly (but not exclusively) in agriculture.

Secondly, countries such as India and China get a great deal of foreign direct investment flows despite not entirely liberalizing their financial markets. They also managed to escape the financial contagion that followed the Asian financial crisis of 1997. As Murshed (2002b) points out, most poor low-income developing countries receive little foreign direct investment (FDI) except in extractive sectors despite having policies in place that encourage these.[15] They are more likely to experience capital flight once restrictions on financial movements are relaxed. Thirdly, policies that promote international integration, if they are to pay off, must encourage greater economic diversification in the long run; Murshed (2004) shows that in the 1970 to 2000 period it is those developing countries that export manufactured goods (as opposed to primary commodities) that have done best in terms of growth and democratization.

Finally, globalization increases inequality both between nations (Milanovic, 2005, discussed in Chapter 2), and within countries (Mamoon and Murshed, 2008). This is because of the differential effects of globalization, both across nations and between different economic occupations. I have already shown how globalization can adversely impact on the unskilled in both the global North and South. As far as inequalities between nations are concerned, one approximation is the gap in average or per capita incomes between the richest and poorest countries in the world. UNDP (1999) reproduces figures to show that this gap was only 3:1 during the dawn of the Industrial Revolution in 1820, rising to 11:1 by the end of the first episode of globalization in 1913. More recently, it grew to 35:1 in 1950, rising slightly to 44:1 by 1973. After the commencement of the present round of globalization in the 1980s, this figure has acquired a staggering magnitude of 72:1. Accompanying this widening gap is the grave human cost in terms of malnutrition, morbidity and mortality. This is the most conclusive evidence of the marginalization of some nations and groups from the process of globalization, and must also contain the seeds of conflict.

7.4.2 Globalization and Conflict

Policies aimed at greater economic integration or globalization have the potential for increasing internal conflict because they produce winners and losers, particularly if such policies are a limited success or a failure in countries that have experienced stagnation and growth failure as in sub-Saharan Africa, parts of the erstwhile Soviet Union (Central Asian republics without oil or gas) and even Latin America. Chua (2002) argued that exporting free market democracy (the so-called neocon agenda) would lead to greater internal conflict and revive old ethnic hatreds. On the other hand, the economic variant of the liberal peace argues that societies that have achieved greater degrees of openness to international trade and finance are more peaceful (see, for example Hegre, Gleditsch

---

[15] China, Mexico and Brazil account for about 50% of total developed country FDI flows into developing nations.

and Gissinger, 2003). How are we to reconcile these two contradictory predictions?

Bussman and Schneider (2007) argue that policies aimed at greater globalization lead to a conflict risk increasing outcome, but highly open economies cannot sustain high levels of international trade and foreign direct investment inflows if they remain in conflict. Indeed, they find some empirical evidence to support these findings in a cross-sectional econometric investigation of conflict risk. This is particularly true if countries pursuing liberalization are at lower stages of economic development and have been unsuccessful in promoting economic growth (in Africa, for example). Interestingly, foreign direct investment flows lower conflict risk in their model, although the authors do not directly recognize it. This is mainly because FDI flows go mainly to a handful of 'emerging' developing country economies (Murshed, 2002b). Democratic transitions also raise the probability of conflict. They do not find that countries with a more unequal distribution of income are more prone to conflict. This, however, pertains to vertical inequality, and still leaves a substantial role for (intergroup) horizontal inequality.

Table 7.2 shows the recent degree of openness, defined as the ratio of international trade (comprising the sum of exports plus imports) over national income or GDP for conflict affected countries. First of all, many conflict affected nations are highly open. Secondly, if we run a simple correlation between the months of conflict (essentially a proxy for the duration or intensity of conflict) and the degree of openness, we only find it weakly correlated (-0.17). So, open economies can experience conflict, and their globalization aspirations may only be weakly impeded by violent internal conflict. This only applies to international trade; investment flows may be discouraged more by conflict. The analytical model in the appendix to this chapter depicts conflict between a state and a discontented segment of the population. Increased globalization and democracy may create situations that enable the state to make concessions towards its adversaries if it is so minded, but not for potential rebels if they are disaffected by globalization. The net effect of globalization on internal conflict is therefore, ambiguous.

Throughout this book, I have argued that the rational choice approach to analysing civil war has a consensual view that the lack of economic development, particularly endemic poverty, enhances conflict risk. What about other forms of conflict, those that are not necessarily directly aimed at overthrowing the state; routine violence as in Tadjoeddin and Murshed (2007)? Secondly, in the more successful developing countries (as in East or South Asia), can increased prosperity breed more violence even if it is not directly aimed against the state?

Table 7.2   Trade openness of conflict countries

Region	Country	Trade (% of GDP)	Conflict months 1960–2005
Americas &	Argentina	43.933	59
Caribbean	Bolivia	75.095	7
	Chile	76.281	1
	Colombia	47.286	461
	Cuba	34.660	1
	Dominican Republic	73.516	1
	El Salvador	74.040	148
	Guatemala	46.228	468
	Haiti	57.273	13
	Mexico	65.102	4
	Nicaragua	92.132	113
	Panama	144.503	1
	Paraguay	115.224	774
	Peru	48.471	213
	Surinam	76.270	28
	Trinidad and Tobago	107.976	1
	Uruguay	60.162	12
	Venezuela	57.601	11
East Asia &	Cambodia (Kampuchea)	144.587	219
Pacific	Indonesia	56.943	393
	Laos	78.234	85
	Malaysia	216.980	85
	Myanmar (Burma)	..	2139
	Papua New Guinea	134.769	85
	Philippines	94.015	774
	Thailand	143.531	88
	Vietnam, Republic of	150.259	60
Middle East &	Algeria	71.434	157
North Africa	Djibouti	97.198	50
	Egypt	61.519	70
	Iran	75.221	359
	Iraq	–	490
	Israel	88.360	540
	Lebanon	63.635	186
	Morocco	71.431	179
	Oman	99.224	48
	Saudi Arabia	92.930	1
	Syria	74.976	34
	Tunisia	108.672	1
	Yemen	79.438	120

Table 7.2 (continued)

Region	Country	Trade (% of GDP)	Conflict months 1960–2005
South Asia	Afghanistan	68.083	320
	Bangladesh	44.218	204
	India	48.779	1547
	Nepal	45.289	125
	Pakistan	38.605	74
	Sri Lanka (Ceylon)	74.784	141
Sub-Saharan Africa	Angola	111.696	392
	Burkina Faso	35.842	1
	Burundi	58.704	159
	Cameroon	52.691	1
	Central African Republic	35.547	18
	Chad	97.252	419
	Comoros	47.267	2
	Congo	136.966	42
	Congo, DRC	70.414	156
	Equatorial Guinea	144.666	1
	Eritrea	58.057	32
	Ethiopia	57.475	915
	Gabon	89.100	1
	Gambia	110.202	1
	Ghana	103.025	19
	Guinea	67.404	17
	Guinea-Bissau	95.415	11
	Ivory Coast	92.262	28
	Kenya	62.175	1
	Lesotho	149.014	1
	Liberia	99.645	113
	Madagascar	70.681	5
	Mali	72.343	19
	Mozambique	88.919	190
	Niger	38.945	52
	Nigeria	91.079	36
	Rwanda	43.178	142
	Senegal	69.815	163
	Sierra Leone	59.427	116
	South Africa	63.060	364
	Sudan	42.756	385
	Togo	83.853	2
	Uganda	44.370	348
	Zimbabwe	129.781	95

Table 7.2   (continued)

Region	Country	Trade (% of GDP)	Conflict months 1960–2005
Europe & Central Asia	Azerbaijan	111.263	33
	Bosnia-Herzegovina	72.304	84
	Croatia	104.635	48
	Cyprus	87.838	–
	Georgia	89.921	49
	Macedonia FYR	118.273	8
	Moldova	139.152	5
	Romania	78.463	1
	Russia	55.069	–
	Spain	58.415	60
	Tajikistan	80.706	78
	Turkey	64.089	261
	United Kingdom	61.574	253
	Uzbekistan	63.377	12
	Yugoslavia (Serbia)	73.398	25

Source: World Bank 2005/2006 indicators, own calculations based on Uppsala-PRIO data.

Historical accounts suggest that in early stages of development violence and increasing prosperity initially go hand in hand, but decline thereafter (Bates, 2001). Traditional societies may have rules and norms that manage violent behaviour; even making peaceful dispute settlement self-enforcing. An increase in prosperity may encourage predatory behaviour in the form of private violence by the less fortunate, or group violence if the collective action problem is resolved. Once growth progresses further, violence has to decline to sustain the security of investment, and the state has to perform regulatory functions. This includes the near (Weberian) monopoly of violence by the state, and its role in keeping the peace and punishing perpetrators of crime, something that now becomes a transgression against society at large. Increasing violence may be symptomatic of the return of privatized social violence, precipitated by economic decline and the frustration spawned by greater awareness in the midst of the lack of commensurate progress. This is emphasized by Gurr (1970) through his notion of relative deprivation. When people perceive that they have less than what they regard as their just deserts they will revolt. This is more likely to occur when the general or average level of prosperity is increasing, but some groups are left behind – as is often the case following globalization. Furthermore, the long shadow cast by political transition and the demise of traditional means of conflict resolution can produce the return of 'private' violence. Economic recovery may not initially reduce violence, until that recovery is sustained enough to reduce societal frustrations, and the accumulation of human capital is accompanied by institutional developments towards peaceful and public conflict resolution.

Mansfield and Snyder (2005) have argued that the road to democracy for countries at an early stage in this process may contribute to the risk of conflict. This is because national sentiments may rise to the fore in the presence of weak institutions.

Tadjoeddin and Murshed (2007) study the causes behind the incidence of routine violence in Java, Indonesia. Routine violence is partly political, but not purely so, and is not entirely criminal either. They refer to group brawls, protests and witch hunts, for instance. Notably, these forms of violence peaked following the Asian financial crisis of 1997, which gravely affected the Indonesian economy. Overall, however, achieving higher growth and combating poverty has a significant and substantial violence reducing effect because the violence increasing impact of rising income is offset by a larger violence reducing effect of growth. The relationships between violence and the levels of education and income are, however, non-linear, in the form of inverted U-shape curves. The reason for this is as follows: starting from low levels of average income and educational attainment, when these rise slightly there is much to compete over and quarrel about; this tendency declines with further increments in income and education, as there is much more to lose from violence. Overall, human development index (HDI) increases have a significant violence reducing result. Since the impact of income and education on violence is non-linear in this way, these results suggest that in order to achieve a violence reducing outcome from income and education their levels need to continue rising. Stagnating levels of income and education below critical turning points may result in persistent violence. These results suggest that other forms of violence, besides outright civil war, may be encouraged by a greater globalization, even in the economically more successful parts of the third world.

What about the policies that might mitigate the conflict enhancing effects of globalization? Rodrik (1998) pointed out that in general more open economies tended to have bigger governments. The larger size of government (relative to national income) is predicated by the need for the state to provide a form of insurance or social safety net against the temporary adverse economic shocks that tend to strike at more open economies with greater frequency. More open and globalized economies are more susceptible to external shocks, caused by the vagaries of the international economic system.

In a similar vein, Rodrik (1999) argued that one of the reasons for the decline in growth in many parts of the developing world was due to a decline in social cohesion. A more equitable and less conflict prone society is better able to withstand shocks and recover, as was shown by South Korea, for example, following the Asian financial crisis of 1997. This is related to my arguments about a working social contract in Chapter 5; countries with viable mechanisms of dispute settlement can avoid violent open conflict, but these mechanisms require consensus and must be broad based and sufficiently inclusive, along with mechanisms for cushioning the economically most vulnerable.

It is important to bear in mind that the destiny of nations depends on the type of leadership they have historically had. Until recently, most developing countries were autocracies. But some leaders had a greater incentive, or simply chose to engage in more development relative to repression. Recall from Chapter 2 that Auty and Gelb (2001) provide us with a typology of states, where some pursue policies of competitive broad based industrialization compared to others with strategies that are more repressive. The former group of countries were more successful, managed globalization better, grew faster and even democratized to an extent. Repression and economic stagnation characterized the latter group. Presumably they are the world's more conflict prone countries.

7.5   POLICY IMPLICATIONS

The argument that democratic countries that are highly economically interdependent never go to war with each other is only partially true. The nature of economic interdependence needs to be examined carefully, and does not depend solely on trade. Democratic nations have, and still can, prey on distant less developed countries. An important dimension of the liberal peace is whether increased globalization promotes greater internal peace in developing countries. In some ways it can, but only once a high living standard similar to Lipset's (1960) modernization thesis has been achieved. But the policies that promote globalization may cause greater conflict, either because they fail to produce economic benefits for society as a whole, or due to the fact that some groups do not share in any increased prosperity. Both these reasons may apply in stagnating countries that have experienced little or no development for a long period.

As far as the policy implications for the management of globalization and conflict management are concerned, first laggard developing countries (mainly in Africa) have not really obtained major benefits from their open policies. These countries urgently need to pursue more broad based development, an effort in which the more affluent countries owe a duty of assistance as suggested by Rawls (1999). Secondly, when globalization is only partially successful as in parts of the Middle East, rulers face the temptation to engage in more repressive policies relative to policies that encourage development, as this is often a quick fix to the reaction when globalization disadvantages certain groups in society. Even in the more successful developing countries, globalization and growth may encourage more routine violence until a higher steady state average income is achieved. Thus the agenda emphasizing broad based growth with an equitable distribution is back on the table, if we are to manage the discontent that globalization breeds. Otherwise the seeds of conflict will be indelibly sown.

The ideal version of the liberal peace, as enunciated by Kant (1795) or Rawls (1999) is not irrelevant for developing countries. The democratic transition is fraught with danger, and managing both globalization and democratic maturity in developing countries requires the placement of effective checks and balances on executive power, such as an independent judiciary. Only, in this way can we restrain the executive's repressive proclivities. Sadly strategic interests still dominate donor thinking, and this goal is often ignored by powerful aid donors when developing country leaders seem to act in conformity with the great powers' geopolitical strategic vision, even when they repress their own people.

APPENDIX: COSTLY CONCESSIONS

The model below is similar to the models employed in the appendices to chapters 3 and 5, and is related to the model in Murshed and Mamoon (2010). There are two groups: the government and rebels, indexed by subscripts G and H respectively. Imagine two states of nature, denoted by superscripts; one more peaceful or dovish (D), and the other associated with greater hawkishness (H). Their probabilities are defined to be π and $1 - \pi$, respectively. The probability of either state is in turn affected by actions and efforts; (a) for the government and (e) for the rebels. These are also the strategic variables employed by the two sides. The probability of the peaceful state π rises with the input of action and effort by the two sides, but at diminishing rates. One can imagine a range of activities by one or both sides if they wish to promote peace, including a greater willingness to compromise, reduce military expenditure and more resources directed towards peaceful economic development (by the government) and so on.

Actions and efforts to seek peace entail costs for each party. The costs of actions to promote peace can take a variety of forms, but, above all, there is the loss of face to either party's own hawkish political constituencies. Increased globalization may, however, augment the stock of rhetoric available to leaders who wish to push their 'peace' agenda through the political process. Secondly, and in a more palpable sense, increased international trade and the growth it brings may provide the additional resources to buy off domestic 'war' lobbies for the government. A more democratic government, following military rule, may similarly use its mandate from the people to justify greater peace and reduced military expenditure.

The expected utility of the government is given by

$$U_G = \pi(a, e) U_G^D(E_G^D + S_G^D) + (1 - \pi)(a, e) U_G^H(E_G^H + S_G^H) - Z(a(T, P)) \tag{7.1}$$

Where U_G^D and U_G^H denote utilities or pay-offs in dovish and hawkish states respectively, weighted by the probabilities of the two states. $E_G^D + S_G^D$, $E_G^H + S_G^H$ indicate the exogenous pair of pay-offs from consumption and security expenditure respectively in the less belligerent and more belligerent states respectively. The difference is that in the dovish state security spending is lower and private consumption higher than in the hawkish state. Most importantly, the dovish state of nature will imply greater poverty reduction. Z is the cost function of undertaking the action a. Action a increases the probability of peace, π, however, undertaking it entails a cost, as described above. T indicates greater globalization (more trade with the rest of the world), and this is postulated to reduce the cost of making peace via the cost function (Z) as discussed above, $Z_{al} < 0$, but so does a hybrid concept called increased democratization (P) for the government ($Z_{a2} < 0$), as more democratic governments are clearly mandated to make peace. Also, $\pi_a > 0$, but $\pi_{aa} < 0$; there are diminishing returns to these actions. Both $Z_a > 0$ and $Z_{aa} > 0$.

Turning to the rebels, we symmetrically have

$$U_R = \pi(a, e) U_R^D(E_R^D + S_R^D) + (1 - \pi)(a, e) U_R^H(E_R^H + S_R^H) - L(e(T))$$
(7.2)

L is the cost of effort, e, which increases the probability of peace, π. As with the government, greater globalization may lower the marginal cost of making peaceful concessions, but it may harden grievances if globalization impoverishes the rebels; therefore, $L_{el} < ?$. Also, $\pi_e > 0$, but $\pi_{ee} < 0$, $L_e > 0$ and $L_{ee} > 0$.

In the non-cooperative Cournot–Nash game each side maximizes its own utility function with respect to its own choice variable a and e:

$$\pi_a \lfloor U_G^D(\cdot) - U_G^H(\cdot) \rfloor = Z_a$$
(7.3)

and

$$\pi_e \lfloor U_R^D(\cdot) - U_{PR}^H(\cdot) \rfloor = L_e$$
(7.4)

Greater globalization changes the marginal cost of peaceful behaviour (Z_{al}, L_{el}). Analytically this means a change in the first-order conditions for both sides to:

$$\pi_a \lfloor U_G^D(\cdot) - U_G^H(\cdot) \rfloor = Z_{al}dT$$
(7.5)

$$\pi_e \lfloor U_R^D(\cdot) - U_R^H(\cdot) \rfloor = L_{el}dT$$
(7.6)

This pertains to the trade effects of the liberal peace. For the government side, the cost of making peace declines on the right-hand side of 7.5 as $Z_{al} < 0$. But if the rebels are economically hurt by globalization, the costs could rise in 7.6 and $L_{el} > 0$. There could be greater conflict, unless globalization is broad based enough to advantage the rebels also. The costs of peaceful actions may also be easier to bear if the government becomes more democratic, corresponding to the Kantian peace, causing the first-order condition for the government to become ($Z_{a2} < 0$):

$$\pi_a \lfloor U_G^D(\cdot) - U_G^H(\cdot) \rfloor = Z_{a2}dP$$
(7.7)

8. Conclusions

Thrasymachus: I declare that justice is nothing else than that which is advantageous to the stronger.

Plato, *The Republic*, translated by A. D. Lindsay, 1937, p. 14

This cynical statement regarding the 'convenient' nature of justice made in the early part of Plato's historic work is gradually debunked as we delve deeper into his *Republic*. Justice, along with its moral, political and economic dimensions, lies at the very heart of a stable and peaceful society. This concept of justice must be genuine, not simply self-serving for the stronger. Plato, along with his student and disciple Aristotle, attributed tendencies towards internal conflict in the Athens of antiquity to three factors (see Jacoby, 2008, p. 10) that still resonate with our modern reality more than two millennia later. They consist of the inequalities within Athenian society, which is nowadays reflected in the horizontal inequalities, polarization and relative deprivation discussed in Chapter 3; the incompetence of the Athenian leadership, whose contemporary form lies partially in poor institutional quality, particularly the lack of constraints on the executive; and the avariciousness in elements of Athenian society, whose modern counterparts are the opportunistic greed theories outlined in Chapter 3. Thus, greed and grievance can, and do, exist simultaneously, particularly after the dynamics of conflict are set in motion. Greed can never be the sole cause of conflict; its large-scale violent expression necessitates institutional failure; this message also runs through the recent work of influential greed theorists such as Paul Collier (Collier and Hoeffler, 2007). The risk of large-scale violent conflict can be minimized in settings of well-ordered societies with functioning social contracts built upon the bedrock of genuine justice and fairness, where dispute settlement mechanisms prevent either greed or grievance manifesting itself in mass violence.

As seen in Chapter 2, economic growth and material progress cannot occur in the longer term without sound institutional quality.[1] This introduces the inseparability of politics and economics. In this connection it is important to bear in mind that the presence of capturable natural resource

---

[1] The mainstream literature's current emphasis on the salience of institutions mirrors an earlier faith in the omnipotence of free markets.

rents in developed countries with weak institutions creates incentives for rulers further to undermine restraints on unbridled executive power, such as an independent judiciary and other institutional constraints. These leaders have been aptly described by Easterly (2006) as gangsters. Such developments not only lower growth prospects (Chapter 2), but they sow the seeds of conflict based on greed and grievances (Chapter 3). Greedy gangsters may also opportunistically revert back to war, after externally sponsored peace treaties are forced on them by the great powers or influential aid donors as analysed in Chapter 4.

Growth is ultimately the best antidote to conflict risk, because it lays the foundations for poverty reduction, as well as the mitigation of group inequalities that foment mass violence. Generalized poverty creates ripe conditions for individual participation in violence and civil wars. Economic growth may lower conflict risk, as groups in more affluent settings have more to lose from violent actions, but the strategies adopted to foster economic growth, such as greater economic openness, produce, at least in the short term, winners and losers. The latter group may revolt and resort to violence, even if it does not manifest itself in the shape of civil war. Thus, growth must be inclusive before it actually reduces conflict risk. In this connection it has to be remembered that the growing inequality between rich and poor states (Milanovic, 2005) does not make for a contented world, and those left behind may wish to react against those they regard as responsible, including their own governments. Economic justice, therefore, not only requires the diminution of domestic inequalities, but also a greater degree of international distributive justice that can only come about through the narrowing of the gap between rich and poor nations.

In chapters 3 and 5 I argued that a functioning set of institutions (or the social contract) may prevent large-scale violence from erupting. Its reconstruction and refashioning, along with inequality and poverty reducing growth, is essential for post-conflict reconstruction. Here, what sustains peace agreements may not just lie in the power sharing formulas that peacemakers seem so preoccupied with, but also in a greater degree of the separation of powers between various contending factions. These may require constructions that are federal, signalling a more robust commitment to peace, including mechanisms such as fiscal federalism that preempt secessionism (by richer regions). In many post-war societies of the contemporary developing world reconstruction involves rebuilding shattered state capacity, as well as the economic institutions through which economic policy is conducted, all of which are systematically undermined by conflict entrepreneurs. Broad based and sustainable economic recovery is more likely to proceed from unbalanced growth in the traded sector of the economy.

Then there is the role of aid, and donor presence in institution and state building in post-war countries. Economic aid and a donor presence in rebuilding institutional capacity and enforcing the peace can play a positive role but only in partnership with state. In Chapter 4 I have demonstrated the potential harmful effects of half-hearted sanctions-cum-aid packages in post-conflict societies; these can actually increase incentives among some groups to revert to war. Aid dependence in the long term retards the development of state capacity and domestic resource mobilization; the former because donor agencies (including NGOs) replace state functions, the latter because aid can act as Dutch disease and prevent the growth of the traded sector along with the revenues that flow from it. Thus, there is debate regarding the merits of both the duration and scope of donor presence in post-conflict societies.

Easterly (2006), in his magisterial analysis of contemporary development assistance, makes us realize that the contemporary rationale for intervention in developing countries has grown out of (or is an extension of), the older colonial justification for imperialism, based on the broad concept of the 'white man's burden', and the need for the West to civilize the 'rest'. He points out that both types of interventions were (and can be) quite harmful. For example, he demonstrates that self-reliant (hence less aid dependent) states have grown considerably faster, as have nations whose boundaries were not too rigidly defined by colonial intervention. Secondly, he argues that although markets, democracy and good institutions are all important to development, attempts at foisting them that are not (at least partially) sui generis are doomed to failure. Finally, there is a creeping danger of a post-modern imperialism, which can be labelled neo-trusteeship, underpinning and justifying interventions by the great powers and donors. This is the new guise of colonialism, and we would do well to note that 19th-century colonialism mainly caused economic stagnation, negating much of any avowed 'liberal' purpose.

It is worth distinguishing between the notions of negative and positive peace, as originally developed by Johan Galtung (1964). The absence of war describes the negative peace; its achievement is very much the subject matter of contemporary rational choice approaches to civil war, as well as the realist school in political science and international relations. The goal is to seek mechanisms for avoiding conflict, reducing its risk and managing its ferocity; much of the present book is in this tradition. The concept of negative peace could also embrace the three pillars upon which the liberal peace rests: economic interdependence, common democratic values and joint membership of international associations. The positive peace requires the 'integration of human society' leading to pax omnium cum omnibus (universal peace towards all; Galtung, 1964, p. 2). Thus, the positive peace would require nations to be well ordered and tolerant in the sense of John Rawls, allowing society to be at peace with itself and others. It would also encompass Kant's notion of the foedus pacificum; the global confederation of like-minded societies with republican constitutions. Both these ideas have been analysed in Chapter 7. Such ideal states cannot be achieved without justice; and at least a partial degree of fairness or justice (or the absence of flagrant injustice) must also characterize the negative peace. Even a prominent realist theorist of international relations such as Morgenthau (1946) suggested that a moral dimension complements mankind's insatiable lust for power. In the quest for power, human actions require a rational basis, as well as ethical justification. Thus, power politics also requires a moral foundation.

The establishment of a positive and lasting peace requires healing at both the individual and national levels. This may be facilitated by processes of truth and reconciliation, whose origins may be traced back to the work of Lederach (2003). Like Galtung, he advocates the pursuit of 'conflict transformation', as opposed to 'conflict resolution' or 'conflict management'. Conflict resolution implies that conflict is harmful – hence it is something that should be ended. It also assumes that it is a short-term phenomenon that can be resolved permanently through mediation or other interventions. Conflict management presumes conflicts to be long-term processes that often cannot be quickly resolved, but the notion of 'management' suggests that people can be directed or controlled. Conflict transformation involves altering negative forces in a positive direction for constructive change.

Reconciliation is, therefore, part and parcel of conflict transformation. It is a long-term process, which needs to be broad and inclusive of individuals and communities if success is to be achieved, and its path can be associated with ups and downs instead of following a linear progression (see van der Mark, 2007). Central to reconciliation is the achievement of peace through justice, with truth as an important ingredient. Another important input is reparation. Truth and reconciliation commissions are, therefore, a mechanism for achieving justice and reconciliation. They are becoming a part of facilitating the reconciliation process following civil war or other forms of conflict in many parts of Africa, most famously in South Africa, but also in Rwanda, Sierra Leone and elsewhere. It is part of a process known as transitional justice. There is the issue of whether truth commissions should be combined with other processes such as war crimes trials; if so, whether that should be at the national or international level.

If there is healing, it can help achieve national reconciliation, which lays the foundations for power sharing and long-term democratization discussed in chapters 4 and 5. It requires achieving a common national position regarding the events of the past, where all sides assume responsibility for errors and crimes. It has to be remembered that often the perpetrator of crimes in violent conflict is a victim at some other level, as is most graphically illustrated in the case of child soldiers. Healing, or reconciliation for that matter, cannot be achieved without justice, which in turn requires some punishment (or at least the acknowledgement of crimes in the case of amnesties) and restitution. The latter has an important economic dimension – the livelihoods of both perpetrators and victims need to be guaranteed. This requires broad based economic reconstruction following the cessation of hostilities, and not a recovery path that is skewed towards short-term economic activities for the few, as discussed in Chapter 6. Also, apologies for egregious actions during the colonial era, which often have direct causal links to present-day conflicts in the Middle East, South Asia and Africa (such as the post-First World War carving up of the Middle East,[2] the hurried partition of India in 1947, the artificial boundaries of many African states) would greatly assist reconciliation processes.

The idea of international trials and tribunals for war crimes dates back to the Nuremberg and Tokyo War Crimes Tribunals to try the perpetrators of war crimes in Nazi Germany and wartime Japan. Despite the truly stupendous crimes committed by Nazi Germany and Imperial Japan during the Second World War, there was more than a hint of victor's justice in these two proceedings. This would not be the case, however, if war crimes were routinely tried as a matter of course.

Attempts by the UN General Assembly and an International Law Commission to set up a permanent war crimes court were thwarted by cold war politics (see Dempsey, 1998). After the end of the cold war, two ad hoc tribunals were established to try war crimes in the former Yugoslavia at The Hague in the Netherlands, and for the Rwandan genocide in Arusha, Tanzania. In 2002 the International Criminal Court (ICC) was set up at The Hague to try war-related crimes. It emerged out of a UN General Assembly conference in Rome in 1998, where the USA and Israel voted against its creation. At present it has some 106 full member states, but in addition to the USA, China and India have still not joined, making its functioning and jurisdiction rather weak. The court cannot exercise jurisdiction unless the accused is a national of a fully fledged member state, and it is meant to complement existing national systems of justice in handling war crimes. To date, the court's activities have been exclusively focused

---

[2] The novelist Arthur Koestler described the Balfour Declaration permitting a Jewish nation in Palestine even before the British controlled Palestine as an act where 'one nation solemnly promised to a second nation the country of a third'.

on Africa: Uganda, the Democratic Republic of the Congo (DRC), the Central African Republic (CAR) and the Sudan.

The retributive demands for justice have to be balanced against the concessions necessary for a peace accord. Since we are concerned mainly with civil wars, the best systems of justice dealing with crimes associated with civil war are national judicial institutions, because it provides for a home grown solution to a domestic problem that is not externally imposed by the great powers. The presence of weak domestic institutional capacity may justify some external assistance in carrying out these judicial processes at home or abroad, but the absence of national ownership could make the system of transitional justice only in the interests of the stronger.

Civil war incidence may be on the wane. This is occurring in the backdrop of a contemporary Roman-style *pax* (Galtung, 1981), which may be described as *pax Americana*, with democracy and capitalism as its cornerstones. Despite this, the imposition of an imperfect democracy may result in increased future vulnerability to conflict in many countries. We may also characterize the peace in our time as a mutation of 19th-century liberal imperialism, where the ostensible benefits are meant to be universally distributed. Our present political and economic dispensation is, however, far from being universally perceived as just, with injustices perhaps most acutely felt in Muslim countries (examples of which are the situations in Palestine and Kashmir). This may explain why the share of civil wars in Muslim countries is rising (Gleditsch, 2008). These rebellions are mainly directed against Western backed undemocratic rulers in the Muslim world.

Both truth and justice have their convenient and true sides. I would like to conclude with a plea for the independent search for truth. Analysts of conflict must not allow themselves to be captured by the interests of the powerful, whose aim is the maintenance of the global status quo. This means eschewing the convenient institutional truths and fashions that serve the interests of the mighty (as stated by Thrasymachus in Plato's *Republic*), and which perennially afflict scientific research, particularly in the social sciences. Challenging the institutional truth is unlikely to win us many plaudits and prizes, but can, however, be a source of inner satisfaction. As John Kenneth Galbraith famously stated: 'To the adherents of the institutional truth there is nothing more inconvenient, nothing that so contributes to discomfort, than open, persistent articulate assertion of what is real'.[3]

---

[3]   J.K. Galbraith, Commencement address to Smith College, Massachusetts, in *Guardian*, 28 July 1989.

References

Abou El Fadl, Khaled (2004). *Islam and the Challenge of Democracy*, Princeton, NJ: Princeton University Press.

Acemoglu, Daron and James A. Robinson (2006). 'Economic Backwardness in Political Perspective', *American Political Science Review* 100(1): 115–31.

Acemoglu, Daron, Simon Johnson and James A. Robinson (2001). 'The Colonial Origins of Comparative Development: An Empirical Investigation', *American Economic Review* 91(5): 1369–401.

Acemoglu, Daron, Simon Johnson, and James A. Robinson (2005). 'Institutions as the Fundamental Cause of Long-Run Growth', in Philippe Aghion and Steven Durlauf (eds), *Handbook of Economic Growth* 1(1), Amsterdam: Elsevier: 385–472.

Adam, Christopher, Paul Collier and Victor Davis (2008). 'Postconflict Monetary Reconstruction', *World Bank Economic Review* 22(1): 87–112.

Addison, Tony and S. Mansoob Murshed (2001). 'From Conflict to Reconstruction: Reviving the Social Contract', UNU/WIDER Discussion Paper 48, Helsinki, UNU/WIDER, www.wider.unu.edu/publications/publications.htm.

Addison, Tony and S. Mansoob Murshed (2002). 'Credibility and Reputation in Peacemaking', *Journal of Peace Research* 39(4): 487–501.

Addison, Tony and S. Mansoob Murshed (2003). 'Debt Relief and Civil War', *Journal of Peace Research* 40(2): 159–76.

Addison, Tony and S. Mansoob Murshed (2005). 'Post-Conflict Reconstruction in Africa: Some Analytical Issues', in Paul Collier and Augustin Fosu (eds), *Post Conflict Reconstruction in Africa*, London: Palgrave: 3-17.

Addison, Tony and S. Mansoob Murshed (2006). 'The Social Contract and Violent Conflict', in Helen Yanacopoulos and Joseph Hanlon (eds), *Civil War, Civil Peace*, Oxford: Currey: 137–63.

Addison, Tony, Abdur Rahman Chowdhury and S. Mansoob Murshed (2002). 'By How Much Does Conflict Reduce Financial Development?' WIDER, Discussion Paper 2002/48.

Addison, Tony, Abdur Rahman Chowdhury and S. Mansoob Murshed (2003). 'Raising Tax Revenues: Why Conflict and Governance Matter', mimeo, WIDER.

Addison, Tony, Abdur Rahman Chowdhury and S. Mansoob Murshed (2004). 'The Fiscal Dimensions of Conflict and Reconstruction', in Tony Addison and Alan Roe (eds), *Fiscal Policy for Development: Poverty, Growth, and Reconstruction*, London: Palgrave: 260–73.

Addison, Tony, Abdur Rahman Chowdhury and S. Mansoob Murshed (2005). 'Financing Reconstruction', in Gerd Junne and Willemijn Verkoren (eds), *Post-Conflict Development: Meeting New Challenges*, Boulder, CO: Lynne Rienner: 211–23.

Addison, Tony, Philippe Le Billon and S. Mansoob Murshed (2002). 'Conflict in Africa: The Cost of Peaceful Behaviour', *Journal of African Economies* 11(3): 365–86.

Aizenman, Joshua and Reuven Glick (2008). 'Sovereign Wealth Funds: Stylized Facts about their Determinants and Governance', National Bureau of Economic Research Working Paper 14562, www.nber.org/papers, Cambridge, Mass.

Akerlof, George and Rachel E. Kranton (2000). 'Economics and Identity', *Quarterly Journal of Economics* 115(3): 715–53.

Alemán, Eduardo and Daniel Treisman (2005) 'Fiscal Politics in "Ethnically Mined", Developing Federal States: Central Strategies and Secessionist Violence', in Philip G. Roeder and Donald Rothchild (eds), *Sustainable Peace. Power and Democracy after Civil Wars*, London: Cornell University Press: 173–216.

Anderson, Jørgen Juel and Silje S. Aslaksen (2006). 'Constitutions and the Resource Curse', Department of Economics Working Paper Series 11/2006, Trondheim, Norwegian University of Science and Technology.

Angell-Lane, Ralph Norman (1910). *The Great Illusion: A Study of the Relation of Military Power in Nations to Their Economic and Social Advantage*, London: Heinemann.

Aoun, Marie-Claire (2006). 'The Oil Rent Effects on the Economic Performance of Oil Exporting Countries', mimeo, Paris, CGEMP, Dauphine University.

Armstrong, Karen (2003). *Muhammad: A Biography of the Prophet*, London: Phoenix Press.

Atkinson, Giles and Kirk Hamilton (2003). 'Savings, Growth and the Resource Curse Hypothesis', *World Development* 31(11): 1793–807.

Auty, Richard (1997). 'Natural Resources, the State and Development Strategy', *Journal of International Development* 9(4): 651–63.

Auty, Richard M. and Alan G. Gelb (2001). 'Political Economy of Resource Abundant States', in Richard M. Auty (ed.), *Resource Abundance and Economic Development*, Oxford: Oxford University Press: 126–44.

Azam, Jean-Paul (1995). 'How to Pay for the Peace? A Theoretical

Framework with References to African Countries', *Public Choice* 83(1/2): 173–84.

Baldwin, Robert E. (1956). 'Patterns of Development in Newly Settled Regions', *Manchester School of Social and Economic Studies* 24(2): 161–79.

Barbieri, Katherine (1996). 'Economic Interdependence: A Path to Peace or a Source of Interstate Conflict?', *Journal of Peace Research* 33(1): 29–49.

Barbieri, Katherine and Jack Levy (1999). 'Sleeping with the Enemy: The Impact of War on Trade', *Journal of Peace Research* 36(4): 463–79.

Barro, Robert and David Gordon (1983). 'Rules, Discretion and Reputation in a Model of Monetary Policy', *Journal of Monetary Economics* 12(1): 101–21.

Bates, Robert H. (2001). *Prosperity and Violence*, New York: Norton.

Besançon, Marie (2005). 'Relative Resources: Inequality in Ethnic Wars, Revolutions and Genocides', *Journal of Peace Research* 42(4): 393–415.

Birdsall, Nancy, Thomas Pinckney and Richard Sabot (2001). 'Natural Resources, Human Capital and Growth', in Richard M. Auty (ed.), *Resource Abundance and Economic Development*, Oxford: Oxford University Press: 57–75.

Boadway, Robin and Michael Keen (2008). 'Theoretical Perspectives on Resource Tax Design', mimeo, IMF.

Bodin, Jean (1576). *Les Six Livres de la République*, translation by M.J. Tooley, printed in 1955, Oxford: Blackwell.

Bourguignon, François and Thierry Verdier (2000). 'Oligarchy, Democracy, Inequality and Growth', *Journal of Development Economics* 62(2): 285–313.

Boyce, James (2007). 'Public Finance, Aid and Post-Conflict Recovery', Working Paper 2007-09, University of Massachusetts-Amherst.

Boyce, James and Madalene O'Donnell (2007). 'Policy Implications: The Economics of Postwar Statebuilding', in James Boyce and Madalene O'Donnell (eds), *Peace and the Public Purse*, London: Lynne Rienner: 271–99.

Brams, Steven J. (2006). 'Fair Division', in Barry R. Weingast and Donald Wittman (eds), *Oxford Handbook of Political Economy*, New York: Oxford University Press: 425–37.

Brams, Steven J. and Marc D. Kilgour (2007a). 'The Instability of Power Sharing', MPRA Paper 5769, http://mpra.ub.uni-muenchen.de/5769/.

Brams, Steven J. and Marc D. Kilgour (2007b). 'Stabilizing Power Sharing', MPRA Paper 5771, http://mpra.ub.uni-muenchen.de/5771/.

Brancati, Dawn (2006). 'Decentralization: Fueling the Fire or Dampening the Flames of Ethnic Conflict and Secessionism?', *International Organization* 60(3): 651–85.

Brown, Graham (2005). 'Horizontal Inequalities, Ethnic Separatism, and Violent Conflict: The Case of Aceh, Indonesia', background paper for Human Development Report 2005, UNDP.

Brunnschweiler, Christa N. and Erwin H. Bulte (2008a). 'Natural Resources and Violent Conflict: Resource Abundance, Dependence and the Onset of Civil Wars', Economics Working Paper 08/78, ETH Zurich.

Brunnschweiler, Christa N. and Erwin H. Bulte (2008b). 'The Resource Curse Revisited and Revised: A Tale of Paradoxes and Red Herrings', *Journal of Environmental Economics and Management* 55(3): 248–64.

Bussman, Margit and Gerald Schneider (2007). 'When Globalization Discontent Turns Violent: Foreign Economic Liberalization and Internal War', *International Studies Quarterly* 51(1): 79–97.

Campos, Neantro F. and Jeffrey B. Nugent (1999). 'Development Performance and the Institutions of Governance: Evidence from East Asia and Latin America', *World Development* 27(3): 439–52.

Caselli, Francesco and Tom Cunningham (2007). 'Political Decision Making in Resource Abundant Countries', paper presented at the Oxcarre Conference, Oxford University, 13–14 December.

Chand, Satish and Ruth Coffman (2008). 'How Soon Can Donors Exit From Post-Conflict States', Working Paper 141, Center for Global Development.

Chua, Amy (2002). *World on Fire: How Exporting Free Market Democracy Breeds Ethnic Hatred and Global Instability*, New York: Doubleday.

Clarida, Richard H. and Ronald Findlay (1992). 'Government, Trade and Comparative Advantage', *American Economic Review* 82(2): 122–7.

Coats, Warren (2007). 'Currency and Sovereignty: Why Monetary Policy is Critical', in James Boyce and Madalene O'Donnell (eds), *Peace and the Public Purse*, London: Lynne Rienner: 213–44.

Cobden, Richard (1835). 'Commerce is the Grand Panacea' , reprinted in E.K. Bramsted and K.J. Melhish (eds), *Western Liberalism: A History in Documents from Locke to Croce*, London: Longman, 1978: 354–7.

Collier, Paul (1999). 'On the Economic Consequence of Civil War', *Oxford Economic Papers* 51(1): 168–83.

Collier, Paul (2004) 'Reducing the Global Incidence of Civil War: A Discussion of the Available Policy Instruments', http://www.inwent.org/ef-texte/military/collier.htm.

Collier, Paul (2007). *The Bottom Billion: Why the Poorest Countries are Failing and What Can Be Done About It,* Oxford: Oxford University Press.

Collier, Paul and Benedikt Goderis (2007). 'Commodity Prices, Growth, and the Natural Resource Curse: Reconciling a Conundrum', CSAE Working Paper 2007-15, Oxford University.

Collier, Paul and Anke Hoeffler (1998). 'On Economic Causes of Civil War', *Oxford Economic Papers* 50(4): 563–73.

Collier, Paul and Anke Hoeffler (2002). 'On the Incidence of Civil War in Africa', *Journal of Conflict Resolution* 46(1): 13–28.

Collier, Paul and Anke Hoeffler (2004a). 'Aid, Policy and Growth in Post-Conflict Societies', *European Economic Review* 48(5): 1125–45.

Collier, Paul and Anke Hoeffler (2004b). 'Greed and Grievance in Civil Wars', *Oxford Economic Papers* 56(4): 563–95.

Collier, Paul and Anke Hoeffler (2006). 'Military Expenditure in Post-Conflict Societies', *Economics of Governance* 7(1): 89–107.

Collier, Paul and Anke Hoeffler (2007). 'Testing the Neo-Con Agenda: Democracy in Resource-Rich Societies', mimeo, Department of Economics, University of Oxford.

Collier, Paul, Anke Hoeffler and Dominic Rohner (2007). 'Beyond Greed and Grievance: Feasibility and Civil War', CSAE Working Paper 2006-10, University of Oxford.

Collier, Paul, Anke Hoeffler and Måns Söderbom (2004). 'On the Duration of Civil War', *Journal of Peace Research* 41(3): 253–73.

Collier, Paul, Anke Hoeffler and Måns Söderbom (2008). 'Post-Conflict Risks', *Journal of Peace Research* 45(4): 461–78.

Collier, Paul, Lani Elliot, Håvard Hegre, Anke Hoeffler, Marta Reynal-Querol and Nicholas Sambanis (2003). *Breaking the Conflict Trap: Civil War and Development Policy*, World Bank, Oxford: Oxford University Press.

Cornes, Richard and Todd Sandler (1996). *The Theory of Externalities, Public Goods, and Club Goods*, 2nd edition, Cambridge: Cambridge University Press.

Cramer, Chris (2002). 'Homo Economicus Goes to War: Methodological Individualism, Rational Choice and the Political Economy of War', *World Development* 30(11): 1845–65.

Cramton, Peter (2007). 'How Best to Auction Oil Rights', in Macartan Humphreys, Jeffrey Sachs and Joseph Stiglitz (eds), *Escaping the Resource Curse*, New York: Columbia University Press: 114–51.

Cuesta José (2004). 'From Economicist to Culturalist Development Theories: How Strong is the Relation between Cultural Aspects and Economic Development', *ISS Working Paper* 400, www.iss.nl, the Hague, the Netherlands.

Cuesta José and S. Mansoob Murshed (2008). 'The Micro-foundations of Social Contracts, Civil Conflicts and International Peace-Making', MICROCON Working Paper 8, www.microcon.eu.

Cukierman, Alex (2000). 'Establishing a Reputation for Dependability by Means of Inflation Targets', *Economics of Governance* 1(1): 53–76.

Demekas, Dmitri, Jimmy McHugh and Theodora Kosma (2002). 'The Economics of Post Conflict Aid', IMF Working Paper 02/198, IMF.

Dempsey, Gary T. (1998). 'Reasonable Doubt: The Case Against the Proposed International Criminal Court', Cato Institute, http://www.cato.org/pubs/pas/pa-311es.html.

de Soysa, Indra (2002). 'Paradise is a Bazaar? Testing the Effects of Greed, Creed, Grievance and Governance on Civil War, 1989–1999', *Journal of Peace Research* 39(4): 395–416.

de Soysa, Indra and Eric Neumayer (2007). 'Resource Wealth and the Risk of Civil War Onset: Results from a New Dataset on Natural Resource Rents, 1970–99', *Conflict Management and Peace Science* 24(3): 201–18.

Deutsch, Morton (1971). 'Conflict and its Resolution', in C. G. Smith (ed.), *Conflict Resolution: Contributions of the Behavioural Sciences*, Notre Dame: University of Notre Dame Press.

Dixit, Avinash K. (2003). 'Some Lessons from Transaction-Cost Politics for Less-Developed Countries', *Economics and Politics* 15(2): 107–33.

Djankov, Simeon and Martha Reynal-Querol (2007). 'The Colonial Origins of Civil War', World Bank.

Dorussen, Han and Hugh Ward (2009). 'Trade Networks and the Kantian Peace', *Journal of Peace Research*, forthcoming.

Doyle, Michael W. (1986). 'Liberalism and World Politics', *American Political Science Review* 80(4): 1151–69.

Duclos, Jean-Yves, Joan-Maria Esteban and Debraj Ray (2004). 'Polarization: Concepts, Measurement, Estimation', *Econometrica*, 72(6): 1737–72.

Dunning, Thad (2005). 'Resource Dependence, Economic Performance, and Political Stability', *Journal of Conflict Resolution* 49(4): 451–82.

Easterly, William (2006). *The White Man's Burden: Why the West's Efforts to Aid the Rest Have Done so Much Ill and so Little Good*, London: Penguin.

Easterly, William (2007). 'Inequality Does Cause Underdevelopment', *Journal of Development Economics* 84(2): 755–76.

Easterly, William and Ross Levine (2003). 'Tropics, Germs and Crops: How Endowments Influence Economic Development', *Journal of Monetary Economics* 50(1): 3–39.

Edgeworth, Francis Y. (1881). *Mathematical Psychics*, London: C. Kegan Paul.

Eifert, Benn, Alan Gelb and Nils Borje Talroth (2002). 'The Political

Economy of Fiscal Policy and Economic Management in Oil Exporting Countries', Policy Research Working Paper 2899, World Bank.

Elbadawi, Ibrahim, Linda Kaltani and Klaus Schmidt-Hebbel (2008). 'Foreign Aid, the Real Exchange Rate, and Economic Growth in the Aftermath of Civil Wars', *World Bank Economic Review* 22(1): 113–40.

Esteban, Joan-Maria and Debraj Ray (1994). 'On the Measurement of Polarization', *Econometrica* 62(4): 819–51.

Esteban, Joan-Maria and Debraj Ray (2008). 'Polarization, Fractionalization and Conflict', *Journal of Peace Research* 45(2): 163–82.

Esteban, Joan-Maria and Gerald Schneider (2008). 'Polarization and Conflict: Theoretical and Empirical Issues', *Journal of Peace Research* 45(2): 131–41.

Fearon, James (2004). 'Why Do Some Civil Wars Last so Much Longer Than Others', *Journal of Peace Research* 41(3): 379–414.

Fearon, James (2005). 'Primary Commodity Exports and Civil War', *Journal of Conflict Resolution* 49(4): 483–507.

Fearon, James and David Laitin (2003). 'Ethnicity, Insurgency and Civil War', *American Political Science Review* 97(1): 75–90.

The Federalist Papers (1787–8). Edited by Jacob E. Cooke, 1961, Middletown, CT: Wesleyan University Press.

Findlay, Ronald and Mats Lundahl (1994). 'Natural Resources, "Vent for-Surplus" and the Staples Theory', in Gerald M. Meir (ed.), *From Classical Economics to Development Economics*, New York: St Martin's Press: 68–93.

Gallup, John L., Jeffrey D. Sachs and Andrew D. Mellinger (1998). 'Geography and Economic Development', NBER Working Paper 6849.

Galtung, Johan (1964). 'An Editorial', *Journal of Peace Research* 1(1): 1–4.

Galtung, Johan (1981). 'Social Cosmology and the Concept of Peace', *Journal of Peace Research* 22(2): 183–99.

Gartzke, Erik (2007). 'The Capitalist Peace', *American Journal of Political Science* 51(1): 166–91.

Gelpi, Christopher and Joseph Grieco (2003). 'Economic Interdependence, the Democratic State, and the Liberal Peace', in Edward Mansfield and Brian Pollins (eds), *Economic Interdependence and International Conflict*, Ann Arbor: University of Michigan Press: 44–59.

Ghani, Ashraf and Clare Lockhart (2008). *Fixing Failed States*, Oxford: Oxford University Press.

Glaeser, Edward, L., Raphael La Porta, Florencio Lopez-de-Silanes and Andrei Shleifer (2004). 'Do Institutions Cause Growth?', *Journal of Economic Growth* 9(3): 271–303.

Gleditsch, Nils Petter (2008). 'The Liberal Moment Fifteen Years On', *International Studies Quarterly* 15(4): 691–712.

Grossman, Herschel I. (1991). 'A General Equilibrium Model of Insurrections', *American Economic Review* 81(4): 912–21.

Gupta, Sanjeev (2008). 'Enhancing Effective Utilization of Aid in Fragile States', WIDER Research Paper 2008/07.

Gurr, Ted R. (1970). *Why Men Rebel*, Princeton, NJ: Princeton University Press.

Gurr, Ted R. (2000). *Peoples versus States: Minorities at Risk in the New Century*, Washington, DC: Unites States Institute for Peace Press.

Gyalfason, Thorvaldur (2001a) 'Natural Resources and Economic Growth: What is the Connection?', CESifo Working Paper 530, mimeo.

Gyalfason, Thorvaldur (2001b). 'Natural Resources, Education and Economic Development', *European Economic Review* 45(4/6): 847–59.

Harbom, Lotta, Erik Melander and Peter Wallensteen (2008). 'Dyadic Dimensions of Armed Conflict', *Journal of Peace Research* 45(5): 697–710.

Hegre, Håvard (2000). 'Development and the Liberal Peace: What Does It Take to Be a Trading State', *Journal of Peace Research* 37(1): 5–30.

Hegre, Håvard (2004). 'The Duration and Termination of Civil War', *Journal of Peace Research* 41(3): 243–52.

Hegre, Håvard, Nils Petter Gleditsch and Ranveig Gissinger (2003). 'Globalization and Conflict: Welfare, Distribution and Political Unrest', in G. Schneider, K. Barbieri and N. P. Gleditsch (eds), *Globalization and Armed Conflict*, Lanham, MD: Rowman and Littlefield, pp. 25–76.

Hegre, Håvard, Tanja Ellingsen, Scott Gates and Nils Petter Gleditsch (2001). 'Towards a Democratic Civil Peace? Democracy, Civil Change, and Civil War 1816–1992', *American Political Science Review* 95(1): 17–33.

Heldt, Birger and Peter Wallensteen (2006). *Peace-Keeping Operations: Global Patterns of Intervention and Success*, 2nd edition, Sandöverken: Folke Bernadotte Academy Publications.

Hibbs, Douglas A. (1973). *Mass Political Violence: A Cross-National Causal Analysis*, London: Wiley.

Hirschman, Albert O. (1958). *The Strategy of Economic Development*, New Haven, CT: Yale University Press.

Hirshleifer, Jack (1995). 'Anarchy and its Breakdown', *Journal of Political Economy* 103(1): 26–52.

Hobbes, Thomas (1651). *Leviathan*, reprinted 1998, Oxford: World Classics.

Hoddie, Matthew and Caroline Hartzell (2005). 'Power Sharing in Peace

Settlements: Initiating the Transition from Civil War', in Philip Roeder and Donald Rothchild (eds), *Sustainable Peace: Power and Democracy After Civil Wars*, London: Cornell University Press: 83–106.

Human Security Report (2005). University of British Columbia, http://www.humansecurityreport.info/.

Humphreys, Macartan (2005). 'Natural Resources, Conflict, and Conflict Resolution. Uncovering the Mechanisms', *Journal of Conflict Resolution* 49(4): 508–37.

Humphreys, Macartan and Martin Sandbu (2007). 'The Political Economy of Natural Resource Funds', in Macartan Humphreys, Jeffrey Sachs and Joseph Stiglitz (eds), *Escaping the Resource Curse*, New York: Columbia University Press: 194–233.

Humphreys, Macartan and Jeremy Weinstein (2007). 'Demobilization and Reintegration', *Journal of Conflict Resolution* 51(4): 531–67.

ICG (2006). 'Fuelling the Niger Delta Crisis', Africa Report 118, Brussels, International Crisis Group.

IMF (2005). *World Economic Outlook*, September 2005, Washington, DC: International Monetary Fund.

Isham, Jonathan, Lant Pritchett, Michael Woolcock and Gwen Busby (2005). 'The Varieties of Resource Experience: Natural Resource Export Structures and the Political Economy of Economic Growth', *World Bank Economic Review* 19(2): 141–74.

Jacoby, Tim (2008). *Understanding Conflict and Violence. Theoretical and Interdisciplinary Approaches*, Oxford: Routledge.

Jarstad, Anna (2006). 'The Logic of Power Sharing After Civil War', paper presented at the PRIO workshop on Power-Sharing and Democratic Governance, Oslo, 21–22 August 2006, www.prio.no.

Jarstad, Anna and Desirée Nilsson (2008). 'From Words to Deeds: The Implementation of Power-Sharing Pacts in Peace Accords', *Conflict Management and Peace Science* 25(3): 206–23.

Kakwani, Nanak and Edward Pernia (2000). 'What is Pro-Poor Growth', *Asian Development Review* 16(1): 1–16.

Kanbur, Ravi, Todd Sandler with Kevin Morrison (1999). 'The Future of Development Assistance: Common Pools and International Public Goods', Overseas Development Council (ODC) Policy Essay 25, Washington, DC, ODC.

Kant, Immanuel (1795). *Perpetual Peace and Other Essays on Politics, History and Morals*, reprinted 1983, Indianapolis: Hackett Publishing.

Karl, Terry Lynn (1999). 'The Perils of the Petro-State: Reflections on the Paradox of Plenty', *Journal of International Affairs* 53(1): 31–52.

Karl, Terry Lynn (2007).'Ensuring Fairness: The Case for a Transparent Fiscal Social Contract', in Macartan Humphreys, Jeffrey Sachs and

Joseph Stiglitz (eds), *Escaping the Resource Curse*, New York: Columbia University Press: 256–85.

Kaufmann, Daniel, Aart Kraay and Massimo Mastruzzi (2006). 'Governance Matters V, Aggregate and Individual Governance Indicators for 1996–2005, World Bank, www.worldbank.org.

Kim, Hyung Min and David Rousseau (2005). 'The Classical Liberals Were Half Right (or Half Wrong): New Tests of the "Liberal Peace", 1960–88', *Journal of Peace Research* 42(5): 523–43.

Klingebiel, Stephan (2005). 'Africa's New Peace and Security Architecture and the Role of External Support', *European Journal of Development Research* 17(3): 437–48.

Koubi, Vally (2005). 'War and Economic Performance', *Journal of Peace Research* 42(1): 67–82.

Krugman, Paul (1979). 'Increasing Returns, Monopolistic Competition, and International Trade', *Journal of International Economics* 9(4): 469–79.

Krugman, Paul (1981). 'Trade, Accumulation and Uneven Development', *Journal of Development Economics* 8: 149–61.

Krugman, Paul (1987). 'The Narrow Moving Band, the Dutch Disease and the Competitive Consequences of Mrs Thatcher: Notes on Trade in the Presence of Dynamic Scale Economies', *Journal of Development Economics* 27(1/2): 41–55.

Krugman, Paul (1991). *Geography and Trade*, Cambridge, MA: MIT Press.

Kuran, Timur (2004). 'Why the Middle East is Economically Underdeveloped: Historical Mechanisms of Institutional Stagnation', *Journal of Economic Perspectives* 18(3): 71–90.

Laffont, Jean-Jacques (2005). *Regulation and Development*, Cambridge: Cambridge University Press.

Lane, Philip and Aaron Tornell (1996). 'Power, Growth and the Voracity Effect', *Journal of Economic Growth* 1(2): 213–41.

Lederach, John Paul (2003). *The Little Book of Conflict Transformation*, Intercourse, PA: Good Books.

Lijphardt, Arend (1977). *Democracy in Plural Societies*, London: Yale University Press.

Lijphardt, Arend (1999). *Patterns of Democracy. Government Forms and Performances in Thirty-Six Countries*, London: Yale University Press.

Lipset, Seymour (1960). *Political Man: The Social Bases of Politics,* New York: Doubleday.

Lujala, Päivi, Nils Petter Gleditsch and Elisabeth Gilmore (2005). 'A Diamond Curse? Civil War and a Lootable Resource', *Journal of Conflict Resolution* 49(4): 538–62.

Lujala, Päivi, Jan Ketil Rød and Nadja Thieme (2007). 'Fighting over Oil: Introducing a New Dataset', *Conflict Management and Peace Science* 24(3): 239–56.

Maddison, Angus (2001). *The World Economy: A Millennial Perspective*, Paris: OECD.

Mahani, Zainal Abidin (2001). 'Competitive Industrialization with Natural Resource Abundance: Malaysia', in Richard M. Auty (ed.), *Resource Abundance and Economic Development*, Oxford: Oxford University Press: 147–64.

Mamoon, Dawood and S. Mansoob Murshed (2008). 'Unequal Skill Premiums and Trade Liberalization: Is Education the Missing Link?', *Economics Letters* 100(2): 262–66.

Mancini, Luca (2008). 'Horizontal Inequality and Communal Violence: Evidence from Indonesian Districts', in Frances Stewart (ed.), *Horizontal Inequalities and Conflict*, Basingstoke: Palgrave Macmillan: 106–35.

Mansfield, Edward and Jack Snyder (2005). *Electing to Fight: Why Emerging Democracies Go to War,* Cambridge, MA: MIT Press.

van der Mark, Iris (2007). *Reconciliation: Bridging Theory to Practice. A Framework for Practitioners*, The Hague: Albani Drukkers for the Centre for Justice and Reconciliation (CJR).

Matsen, Egil and Ragnar Torvik (2005). 'Optimal Dutch Disease', *Journal of Development Economics* 78(2): 494–515.

Matsuyama, Kiminori (1992). 'Agricultural Productivity, Comparative Advantage and Economic Growth', *Journal of Economic Theory*, 58(2): 317–34.

Mavrotas, George, S. Mansoob Murshed and Sebastian Torres (2007). 'Natural Resource Endowment and Recent Economic Performance', mimeo, ISS, the Hague, the Netherlands.

Mehlum, Halvor, Karl Moene and Ragnar Torvik (2006). 'Institutions and the Resource Curse', *Economic Journal* 116(508): 1–20.

Menocal, Alina Rocha, Timothy Othieno with Alison Evans (2008). 'The World Bank in Fragile Situations: An Issues Paper', paper prepared for the Dutch Ministry of Foreign Affairs and the World Bank conference on an Eye on the Future: The World Bank Group in a Changing World, Amsterdam, 12–13 July 2008.

Metcalfe, Robert (2007). 'The Natural Resource Curse: An Unequivocal Hypothesis', mimeo, London: Imperial College.

Miguel, Edward, Shanker Satyanath and Ernest Sergenti (2004). 'Economic Shocks and Civil Conflict: An Instrumental Variables Approach', *Journal of Political Economy* 112(4): 725–53.

Milanovic, Branko (2005). *World Apart: Measuring International and Global Inequality*, Princeton: Princeton University Press.

Milanovic, Branko and Leif Wenar (2007). 'Are Liberal Peoples Peaceful?', mimeo, World Bank, Washington DC.

Mill, John Stuart (1848). *Principles of Political Economy*, reprinted 1998, Oxford: Oxford Classics.

Mill, John Stuart (1861). *Considerations on Representative Government*, reprinted 1962, Chicago: Henry Regnery.

Montalvo, Jose G. and Marta Reynal-Querol (2005). 'Ethnic Polarization, Potential Conflict, and Civil Wars', *American Economic Review* 95(3): 796–816.

Montalvo, Jose G. and Marta Reynal-Querol (2007). 'Ethnic Polarization and the Duration of Civil Wars', *World Bank Policy Research Working Paper* 4192, Washington, DC: World Bank.

Montesquieu, Charles-Louis de (1748). *De l'Esprit des Lois*, reprinted 1979, Paris: Flammarion.

Morgenthau, Hans (1946). *Scientific Man vs. Power Politics*, Chicago: University of Chicago Press.

Murdoch, James C. and Todd Sandler (2004). 'Civil Wars and Economic Growth: Spatial Dispersion', *American Journal of Political Science* 48(1): 138–51.

Murphy, Kevin, Andrei Shleifer and Robert Vishny (1989). 'Industrialization and the Big Push', *Journal of Political Economy* 97(5): 1003–26.

Murphy, Kevin, Andrei Shleifer and Robert Vishny (1991). 'The Allocation of Talent: Implications for Growth', *Quarterly Journal of Economics*, 106(2): 503–30.

Murshed, S. Mansoob (1992). *Economic Aspects of North–South Interaction: Analytical Macroeconomic Issues*, London: Academic Press.

Murshed, S. Mansoob (1997). *Macroeconomics for Open Economies*, London: Dryden Press.

Murshed, S. Mansoob (2001). 'Short-Run Models of Natural Resource Endowment', in Richard M. Auty (ed.), *Resource Abundance and Economic Development*, Oxford: Oxford University Press: 113–25.

Murshed, S. Mansoob (2002a). 'Civil War, Conflict and Underdevelopment', *Journal of Peace Research* 39(4): 387–93.

Murshed, S. Mansoob (2002b). 'Perspectives on Two Phases of Globalization', in S. M. Murshed (ed.), *Globalization, Marginalization and Development*, London: Routledge: 1–19.

Murshed, S. Mansoob (2004). 'When Does Natural Resource Abundance Lead to a Resource Curse', IIED-EEP Working Paper 04-01, www.iied.org.

Murshed, S. Mansoob (2006). 'Turning Swords into Ploughshares and Little Acorns to Tall Trees: The Conflict Growth Nexus and the Poverty of Nations', background paper for the United Nations Department for

Economic and Social Affairs's World Economic Survey, 2006, http://www.un.org/esa/policy/wess/.

Murshed, S. Mansoob (2009). 'On the Non-Contractual Nature of Donor-Recipient Interaction in Development Assistance', *Review of Development Economics*, 13(3): 416–28.

Murshed, S. Mansoob and Scott Gates (2005). 'Spatial-Horizontal Inequality and the Maoist Conflict in Nepal', *Review of Development Economics* 9(1): 121–34.

Murshed, S. Mansoob and Dawood Mamoon (2010). 'Not Loving Thy Neighbour as Thyself: The Trade, Democracy and Military Expenditure Explanations Underlying India–Pakistan Rivalry', *Journal of Peace Research*, forthcoming.

Murshed, S. Mansoob and Somnath Sen (1995). 'Aid Conditionality and Military Expenditure Reduction in Developing Countries: Models of Asymmetric Information', *Economic Journal* 105(429): 498–509.

Neary, J. Peter and Sweder van Wijnbergen (1984). 'Can an Oil Discovery Lead to a Recession? A Comment on Eastwood and Venables', *Economic Journal* 94(394): 390–5.

Neary, J. Peter and Sweder van Wijnbergen (1986). 'Natural Resources and the Macroeconomy: A Theoretical Framework', in J. Peter Neary and Sweder van Wijnbergen (eds), *Natural Resources and the Macroeconomy*, Oxford: Blackwell: 13–45.

Nilsson, Desirée (2008). 'Partial Peace: Rebel Groups Inside and Outside of Civil War Settlements', *Journal of Peace Research* 45(4): 479–95.

North, Douglass C. (1990). *Institutions, Institutional Change and Economic Performance*, Cambridge: Cambridge University Press.

OECD Statistical Website, www.oecd.org

Olson, Mancur (1965). *The Logic of Collective Action*, Cambridge, MA: Harvard University Press.

Olson, Mancur (1996). 'Big Bills Left on the Sidewalk: Why Some Nations are Rich, and Others Poor', *Journal of Economic Perspectives* 10(1): 3–24.

Oneal, John, and Bruce Russett (1997). 'The Classical Liberals Were Right: Democracy, Interdependence, and Conflict, 1950–1985', *International Studies Quarterly* 41(2): 267–93.

Oneal, John and Bruce Russett (1999). 'Assessing the Liberal Peace with Alternative Specifications: Trade Still Reduces Conflict', *Journal of Peace Research* 36(4): 423–32.

Organski, A. F. K. and Jacek Kugler (1977). 'The Costs of Major War: The Phoenix Factor', *American Political Science Review* 71(4): 1347–66.

Østby, Gudrun (2006). 'Horizontal Inequalities, Political Environment and Civil Conflict', *CRISE Working Paper* 26, Queen Elizabeth House, University of Oxford.

Østby, Gudrun (2008). 'Polarization, Horizontal Inequalities and Civil Conflict', *Journal of Peace Research* 45(2): 143–62.

Paine, Thomas (1791, 1792). *The Rights of Man*, reprinted in 1995 as *Rights of Man, Common Sense and Other Political Writings*, edited by Mark Philip, Oxford: Oxford Classics.

Perälä, Maiju (2000). 'Explaining Growth Failures: Natural Resource Type and Growth', UNU/WIDER and University of Notre Dame.

Plato (1937). *The Republic*, translated by A.D. Lindsay, London: Everyman Books.

van der Ploeg, Frederick and Anthony Venables (2008). 'Harnessing Windfall Revenues in Developing Economies: Sovereign Wealth Funds and Optimal Tradeoffs Between Citizen Dividends, Public Infrastructure and Debt Reduction', OxCarre Research Paper 2008–09.

Polachek, Solomon W. (1997). 'Why Democracies Cooperate More and Fight Less: The Relationship Between International Trade and Cooperation', *Review of International Economics* 5(3): 295–309.

Polity IV Project, Center for International Development and Conflict Management, http://www.cidcm.umd.edu/polity.

Prebisch, Raul (1950). *The Economic Development of Latin America and its Principal Problems*, New York: United Nations.

Przeworski, Adam and Fernando Limongi (1993). 'Political Regimes and Economic Growth', *Journal of Economic Perspectives* 7(3): 51–69.

Ramsey, Frank (1928), 'A Mathematical Theory of Saving', *Economic Journal*, 38(152): 543–59.

Rawls, John (1971). *A Theory of Justice*, Cambridge, MA: Harvard University Press.

Rawls, John (1999). *The Law of Peoples*, Cambridge, MA: Harvard University Press.

Reynal-Querol, Marta (2002). 'Ethnicity, Political Systems, and Civil Wars', *Journal of Conflict Resolution* 46(1): 29–54.

Robinson, James A. and Ragnar Torvik (2005). 'White Elephants', *Journal of Public Economics* 89(2/3): 197–210.

Robinson, James A., Thierry Verdier and Ragnar Torvik (2006). 'Political Foundations of the Resource Curse', *Journal of Development Economics* 79(2): 447–68.

Robst, John, Solomon Polachek and Yuan-Ching Chang (2007). 'Geographic Proximity, Trade and International Conflict/Cooperation', *Conflict Management and Peace Science* 24(1): 1–24.

Rodriguez, Francisco and Rodrik, Dani (2000). 'Trade Policy and Economic Growth: A Skeptic's Guide to the Cross-National Evidence', in Ben Bernanke and Kenneth Rogoff (eds), *Macroeconomics Annual 2000*, Cambridge, MA, MIT Press for NBER.

Rodrik, Dani (1998). 'Why Do More Open Countries Have Bigger Government', *Journal of Political Economy*, 106(5): 997–1032.

Rodrik, Dani (1999). 'Where Did All the Growth Go? External Shocks, Social Conflict, and Growth Collapses', *Journal of Economic Growth* 4(4): 385–412.

Rodrik, Dani (2006). 'Goodbye Washington Consensus, Hello Washington Confusion', *Journal of Economic Literature* 44(4): 973–89.

Rodrik, Dani, Arvind Subramanian and Francesco Trebbi (2004). 'Institutions Rule: The Primacy of Institutions Over Geography and Integration in Economic Development,' *Journal of Economic Growth* 9(2): 131–65.

Roeder, Philip (2005). 'Power Dividing as an Alternative to Ethnic Power Sharing', in Philip G. Roeder and Donald Rothchild (eds), *Sustainable Peace. Power and Democracy after Civil Wars*, London: Cornell University Press: 51–82.

Ross, Michael L. (2001). 'Does Oil Hinder Democracy', *World Politics* 53(3): 325–61.

Ross, Michael L. (2003). 'Oil, Drugs and Diamonds: The Varying Role of Natural Resources in Civil Wars', in Karen Ballentine and Jake Sherman (eds), *The Political Economy of Armed Conflict: Beyond Greed and Grievance*, Boulder, CO: Lynne Rienner: 47–70.

Ross, Michael L. (2004a). 'Does Taxation Lead to Representation?', *British Journal of Political Science* 34(2): 229–49.

Ross, Michael L. (2004b). 'What Do We Know About Natural Resources and Civil Wars', *Journal of Peace Research* 41(3): 337–56.

Ross, Michael L. (2006). 'A Closer Look at Oil, Diamonds and Civil War', *Annual Review of Political Science* 9: 265–300.

Ross, Michael L. (2007). 'How Mineral-Rich States can Reduce Inequality', in Macartan Humphreys, Jeffrey Sachs and Joseph Stiglitz (eds), *Escaping the Resource Curse*, New York: Columbia University Press: 237–55.

Rothchild, Donald (2005). 'Reassuring Weaker Parties After Civil Wars: The Benefits and Costs of Executive Power-Sharing Systems in Africa', *Ethnopolitics* 4(3): 247–67.

Rothchild, Donald (2008). 'Africa's Power Sharing Institutions as a Response to Insecurity: Assurance Without Deterrence', in Stephen M. Saideman and Marie-Joelle J. Zahar (eds), *Intra-State Conflict, Governments and Security: Dilemmas of Deterrence and Assurance*, London: Routledge: 138–60.

Rothchild, Donald and Philip G. Roeder (2005). 'Dilemmas of State-Building in Divided Societies', in Philip Roeder and Donald Rothchild (eds), *Sustainable Peace. Power and Democracy After Civil Wars*, London: Cornell University Press: 1–25.

Russett, Bruce M. (1964). 'Inequality and Instability: The Relation of Land Tenure to Politics', *World Politics* 16(3): 442–54.

Russett, Bruce and John Oneal (2001). *Triangulating Peace: Democracy Interdependence and International Organizations*, New York: Norton.

Sabine, George H. (1961). *A History of Political Theory*, 3rd edition, New York: Holt, Rinehart and Winston.

Sachs, Jeffrey (1999). 'Resource Endowments and the Real Exchange Rate: A Comparison of Latin America and East Asia', in Takatoshi Ito and Anne Krueger (eds), *Changes in Exchange Rates in Rapidly Developing Countries: Theory, Practice and Policy Issues*, Chicago: Chicago University Press: 133–53.

Sachs, Jeffrey and Andrew Warner (1995). 'Economic Reform and Process of Global Integration', *Brookings Papers on Economic Activity* 1: 1–118.

Sachs, Jeffrey and Andrew Warner (1999a). 'The Big Push, Natural Resource Booms and Growth', *Journal of Development Economics* 59(1): 43–76.

Sachs, Jeffrey and Andrew Warner (1999b). 'Natural Resource Intensity and Economic Growth', in Jörg Mayer, Brian Chambers and Ayisha Farooq (eds), *Development Policies in Natural Resource Economies*, Cheltenham, UK and Northampton, USA: Edward Elgar: 13–38.

Sachs, Jeffrey and Andrew Warner (2001). 'The Curse of Natural Resources', *European Economic Review* 45(4/6): 827–38.

Schumpeter, Joseph (1951). *Imperialism and Social Classes*, New York: Augustus M. Kelley.

Shell, Karl (1966). 'Towards a Theory of Inventive Activity and Capital Accumulation', *American Economic Review* 56(2): 62–8.

Singer, Hans (1950). 'The Distribution of Gains Between Borrowing and Investing Nations', *American Economic Review* 40(2): 473–85.

Sisk, Timothy D. (1996). *Power Sharing and International Mediation in Ethnic Conflicts*, Washington, DC: US Institute of Peace Press.

Skaperdas, Stergios (1992). 'Cooperation, Conflict and Power in the Absence of Property Rights', *American Economic Review* 82(5): 720–39.

Skaperdas, Stergios (2002). 'Warlord Competition', *Journal of Peace Research* 39(4): 435–46.

Smith, Benjamin (2004). 'Oil Wealth and Regime Survival in the Developing World, 1960–1999', *American Journal of Political Science* 48(2): 232–46.

Snyder, Richard and Ravi Bhavnani (2005). 'Diamonds, Blood and Taxes. A Revenue-Centered Framework for Explaining Political Order', *Journal of Conflict Resolution* 49(4): 563–97.

Sokoloff, Kenneth L. and Stanley L. Engerman (2000). 'Institutions, Factor Endowments, and Paths of Development in the New World', *Journal of Economic Perspectives* 14(3): 217–32.

Starr, Martha A. (2005). 'Violent Conflict and Economic Growth: Re-Examining the Evidence', mimeo, Washington, DC: American University.

Stepan, Alfred (1999). 'Federalism and Democracy: Beyond the U.S. Model', *Journal of Democracy* 10(4): 19–34.

Stewart, Frances (2000). 'Crisis Prevention: Tackling Horizontal Inequalities', *Oxford Development Studies* 28(3): 245–62.

Stewart, Frances, Graham Brown and Luca Mancini (2005). 'Why Horizontal Inequalities Matter: Some Implications for Measurement', CRISE Working Paper 19, Queen Elizabeth House, University of Oxford.

Stijns, Jean-Philippe (2006). 'Natural Resource Abundance and Human Capital Accumulation', *World Development* 34(6): 1060–83.

Suhrke, Astri, Espen Villanger and Susan Woodward (2005). 'Economic Aid to Post-Conflict Countries: A Methodological Critique of Collier and Hoeffler, *Conflict, Security and Development* 5(3): 329–61.

Tadjoeddin, Mohammad Zulfan (2003). 'Communal Conflicts and Horizontal Inequalities in Indonesia: Dynamics and Consequences', paper presented at the IPSK-CNRS group meeting on conflict, LIPI Jakarta, 15 January.

Tadjoeddin, Mohammad Zulfan (2007). 'A Future Resource Curse in Indonesia: The Political Economy of Natural Resources, Conflict and Development', *CRISE Working Paper* 35, Queen Elizabeth House, University of Oxford.

Tadjoeddin, Mohammad Zulfan and S. Mansoob Murshed (2007). 'Socioeconomic Determinants of Everyday Violence in Indonesia: An Empirical Investigation of Javanese Districts, 1994–2003', *Journal of Peace Research* 44(6): 689–707.

Tadjoeddin, Mohammad Zulfan, Widjajanti I. Suharyo and Satish Mishra (2003). 'Aspiration to Inequality: Regional Disparity and Centre-Regional Conflicts in Indonesia', paper presented at the UNU/WIDER conference on Spatial Inequality in Asia, Tokyo, Japan, 28–9 March.

Tavares, José and Romain Wacziarg (2001). 'How Democracy Affects Growth', *European Economic Review* 45(8): 1341–78.

Taylor, Lance (1983). *Structuralist Macroeconomics*, New York: Basic Books.

Tilly, Charles (1978). *From Mobilization to Revolution*, Reading, MA: Addison-Wesley.

Tilly, Charles (1992). *Coercion, Capital and European States, AD 990–1992*, Cambridge, MA: Blackwell.

Tilly, Charles (1998). *Durable Inequality*, Berkeley: University of California Press.

Tobin, James (1969). 'A General Equilibrium Approach to Monetary Theory', *Journal of Money, Credit and Banking* 1: 15–29.

Torvik, Ragnar (2002). 'Natural Resources, Rent Seeking and Welfare', *Journal of Development Economics* 67(2): 455–70.

Torvik, Ragnar (2007). 'Why Do Some Resource Abundant Countries Succeed While Others Do Not?', paper presented at the Oxcarre conference, Oxford University, 13–14 December.

Tranchant, Jean-Pierre (2007). 'Decentralization and Ethnic Conflict: The Role of Empowerment', MPRA Paper 3713, http://mpra.ub.uni-muenchen.de/3713/.

Tranchant, Jean-Pierre (2008). 'Fiscal Decentralization, Institutional Quality and Ethnic Conflict: A Panel Data Analysis, 1985–2001', *Conflict Security and Development*, 8(4): 491–514.

Tullock, Gordon (1967). 'The Welfare Costs of Tariffs, Monopolies and Theft', *Western Economic Journal* 5(3): 224–32.

Tullock, Gordon (1980). 'Efficient Rent Seeking', in J. M. Buchannan, R. D. Tollison and G. Tullock (eds), *Towards a Theory of the Rent-Seeking Society*, College Station: Texas A&M University: 97–112.

UCDP (Uppsala Conflict Data Programme) (2006), www.prio.no/cwp/armedconflict.

UNDP (1999). *Human Development Report 1999*, New York: United Nations.

Walter, Barbara F. (2002). *Committing to Peace: The Successful Settlement of Civil Wars,* Princeton, NJ: Princeton University Press.

Walter, Barbara F. (2004). 'Does Conflict Beget Conflict? Explaining Recurring Civil War', *Journal of Peace Research* 41(3): 371–88.

Wick, Katharina and Erwin Bulte (2006). 'Contesting Resources – Rent Seeking, Conflict and the Natural Resource Curse', *Public Choice* 128(3/4): 457–76.

Wood, Adrian (1994). *North–South Trade, Employment and Inequality: Changing Fortunes in a Skill Driven World*, Oxford: Clarendon Press.

Wood, Elisabeth Jean (2003). 'Modelling Robust Settlements to Civil War: Indivisible Stakes and Distributional Compromises', www.prio.no.

World Bank (2001). *World Development Report, 2000/2001: Attacking Poverty*, New York: Oxford University Press.

World Bank (2006). *World Development Indicators*, Washington, DC: World Bank.

Zhang, Xiaobo and Ravi Kanbur (2001). 'What Difference Do Polarisation Measures Make? An Application to China', *Journal of Development Studies* 37(3): 85–98.

Index